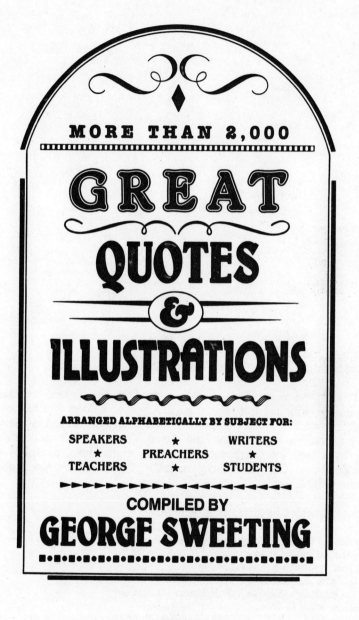

MORE THAN 2,000

GREAT

QUOTES

&

ILLUSTRATIONS

ARRANGED ALPHABETICALLY BY SUBJECT FOR:

SPEAKERS ★ WRITERS
★ PREACHERS ★
TEACHERS ★ STUDENTS

COMPILED BY

GEORGE SWEETING

WORD BOOKS
PUBLISHER
WACO, TEXAS

A DIVISION OF
WORD. INCORPORATED

Printed in the United States of America

Library of Congress Cataloging-in-Publication Data
Sweeting, George, 1924–
    Great quotes and illustrations.
    Includes indexes.
    1. Quotations, English.   2. Religion—Quotations,
maxims, etc.   I. Title.
PN6081.S84   1985   082   85–16782
ISBN 0–8499–0504–4

567898 BKC 987654321

This volume is affectionately dedicated to all who represent our Lord Jesus Christ. In particular to *James Albert Gwinn*, who has been to me a Timothy in the faith.

A word of special appreciation is offered to my son, Donald William Sweeting, for his assistance and guidance in compiling this volume.

Contents

Contents

Introduction

It is my hope that this volume will be used to encourage and expand many readers' horizons. I have drawn material from a wide source of literature and human experience. It is recommended that the reader wisely and appropriately apply the truths where they fit. In some cases a quotation may be used to stimulate a thought or encourage further exploration.

Early in my ministry I noticed the power and impact of quotations and illustrations. The eloquent Charles Haddon Spurgeon commented, "He who never quotes is never quoted."

I discovered that as windows admit light to a house, quotations and illustrations can shed clarity on a lesson, sermon, or speech. Even the most academic member of your audience will sit up and listen attentively when you use such a tool. Abraham Lincoln was a gifted user of stories: "They say I tell many stories; I reckon I do, but I have found in the course of a long experience that common people, take them as they run, are more easily informed through the medium of a broad illustration than in any other way, and as to what the hypercritical few may think, I don't care." Edmund Fuller comments, "Anecdotes are stories with points. They are tools—nail sinkers to drive home arguments firmly. They are the origin of all teaching."

It is my desire that this volume will not be a crutch but a useful device to drive home eternal truths. Those items signed "G. S." are my own contributions to the book.

Acknowledgments

Grateful acknowledgment is hereby expressed to the following who have granted permission to include copyrighted materials in this book. Any inadvertent omission of credit will be gladly corrected in future editions.

ABINGDON PRESS: Clarence E. Macartney, *Maccartney's Illustrations* © 1945.

BAKER BOOK HOUSE: *Aspects of Christian Social Ethics* by Carl F. H. Henry © 1980, and *Christian Personal Ethics* by Carl F. H. Henry © 1977.

BROADMAN PRESS: B. J. Chitwood, *A Faith That Works* (Nashville: Broadman Press, 1969). All rights reserved.

CHRISTIAN PUBLICATIONS: *Born after Midnight, The Dwelling Place of God, Of God and Men, Roots of the Righteous,* and *That Incredible Christian* by A. W. Tozer, published by Christian Publications of Camp Hill, PA; used by permission.

CITADEL PRESS: From *Quotations for the New Age.* Copyright © 1978 by M. S. Rosenberg. Published by arrangement with Citadel Press.

WILLIAM COLLINS SONS & CO: C. S. Lewis, *The Abolition of Man,* William Collins Sons & Co Ltd, London, © 1947.

DAVID C. COOK PUBLISHING CO.: Reprinted with permission from *The Last Thing We Talk About* © 1973 Joseph Bayly. David C. Cook Publishing Co., Elgin, Illinois 60120.

DOUBLEDAY & COMPANY, INC.: "Quotation," from *Abandonments to Divine Providence* by Jean-Pierre De Caussade, translated by John Beevers. Copyright © 1975 by John Beevers. Reprinted by permission of Doubleday & Company, Inc.

WILLIAM B. EERDMANS PUBLISHING CO.: *The Meaning of the City* by Jacques Ellul, © 1970, William B. Eerdmans Publishing Co.

FABER AND FABER LTD: Reprinted by permission of Faber and Faber Ltd from *Markings* by Dag Hammarskjold, translated by W. H. Auden and Leif Sjoberg.

GOOD NEWS BROADCASTING ASSOCIATION: Taken from *The Perfect Will of God* by G. Christian Weiss, © 1950, 1984 by the Good News Broadcasting Association, Inc. All rights reserved; used by permission.

HARCOURT BRACE JOVANOVICH: From *The World's Last Night,* copyright © 1960 by C. S. Lewis. Reprinted by permission of Harcourt Brace Jovanovich, Inc.

INTERVARSITY PRESS: Taken from *A Long Obedience in the Same Direction* by Eugene H. Peterson. © 1980 by Inter-Varsity Christian Fellowship of the USA and used by permission of InterVarsity Press. Taken from *Escape from Reason* by Francis A. Schaeffer. © 1968 by Inter-Varsity Fellowship, England, and used by permission of InterVarsity Press. Taken from *The God Who Is There* by Francis A. Schaeffer. © 1968 by L'Abri Fellowship, Switzerland, and used by permission of InterVarsity Press. Taken from *Your Mind Matters* by John Stott. © 1972 by Inter-Varsity Press, England, and used by permission of InterVarsity Press, Downers Grove, IL 60515.

Acknowledgments

Paul Little, *How to Give Away Your Faith* © 1966. Used by permission of Marie H. Little, Prospect Heights, Illinois.

MOODY PRESS: From *God's Will for Your Life* by S. Maxwell Coder, copyright 1946, Moody Press. From *Balancing the Christian Life* by Charles Ryrie, copyright 1969, Moody Press. From *Live Like a King* by Warren Wiersbe, copyright 1976, 1983, Moody Press. Moody Bible Institute of Chicago. Used by permission.

THOMAS NELSON PUBLISHERS: Thomas Howard, *Evangelical Is Not Enough.*

READER'S DIGEST: Mrs. Paul A. Ciulhe. Reprinted with permission from the December 1954 *Reader's Digest.*

SERVANT PUBLICATIONS: From *The Christian Mind,* © 1963 by Harry Blamires. From *Man and Woman in Christ,* © 1980 by Stephen B. Clark. Published by Servant Publications, Box 8617, Ann Arbor, Michigan 48107. Used with permission.

HAROLD SHAW PUBLISHERS: Reprinted from *Lord, Open the Heavens* by Stephen F. Olford by permission of Harold Shaw Publishers. Harold Shaw Publishers edition copyright © 1980 by Stephen F. Olford.

A. W. Tozer, *The Divine Conquest;* used by permission.

YMCA: Henry Clay, *Individual Word for Individuals.* Quoted with permission. YMCA of the USA, Chicago, IL.

YALE UNIVERSITY PRESS: *Daily Life in Ancient Rome* by Jerome Carcopino. Reprinted by permission of Yale University Press.

ZONDERVAN PUBLISHING HOUSE: Taken from *Loving God* by Charles Colson. Copyright © 1983 by Charles Colson. Taken from *Sourcebook of 500 Illustrations* by Robert G. Lee. Copyright © 1964 by Zondervan Publishing House. Taken from *Evangelical Illustrations from the Bible* by Faris D. Whitesell. Copyright © 1955, 1983 by Zondervan Publishing House. Used by permission.

He who resolves never to ransack any mind but his own will be soon reduced, from mere barrenness, to the poorest of all imitations: he will be obliged to imitate himself.

Sir Joshua Reynolds to the students of the
Royal Academy of Arts

← A →

Ability

If every man stuck to his talent, the cows would be well tended.

J. P. DE FLORIAN

I add this also, that rational ability without education has oftener raised man to glory and virtue, than education without natural ability.

CICERO

It is all one to me if a man comes from Sing Sing or Harvard. We hire a man, not his history.

HENRY FORD

Abilities are like tax deductions—we use them or we lose them.

SAM JENNINGS

When love and skill work together, expect a masterpiece.

JOHN RUSKIN

Ability and learning contrasted. Charles II once expressed his astonishment that such a learned man as Dr. Owen should go so often to hear Bunyan, the ignorant tinker preacher. "Had I the tinker's ability, please your Majesty," was the reply, "I would gladly relinquish my learning."

T. DE WITT TALMAGE

Every man who can be a first-rate something—as every man can be who is a man at all—has no right to be a fifth-rate something; for a fifth-rate something is no better than a first-rate nothing.

J. G. HOLLAND, *Plain Talks on Familiar Subjects*

The winds and waves are always on the side of the ablest navigators.

EDWARD GIBBON

Do what you can, with what you have, where you are.

THEODORE ROOSEVELT

Ability
1. Able to save rough fishermen, Peter, Andrew, James, and John: John 1:35–42, Luke 5:3–11.

2. Able to save despised tax collectors: Matthew, Luke 5:27–29; Zacchaeus, Luke 19:1–10.
3. Able to save a master in Israel, a religious teacher and highly moral man, Nicodemus: John 3.
4. Able to save a much married and religiously heretical woman: John 4:7–39.
5. Able to save a woman taken in adultery: John 8:1–11.
6. Able to save a dying thief: Luke 23:39–43.
7. Able to save a sorcerer: Acts 8:9–24.
8. Able to save the chief of sinners, the leading opponent and persecutor of Christianity, Saul of Tarsus: Acts 9:1–31; 1 Timothy 1:15.
9. Able to save a Roman military officer, Cornelius: Acts 10.
10. Able to save a business woman, Lydia: Acts 16:14–15.
11. Able to save a brutal jailer: Acts 16:30–34.
12. Able to save an innumerable multitude out of all tribes and tongues and nations whom John saw already safe in heaven: Revelation 7:9–17.

F. D. WHITESELL, *Evangelistic Illustrations*

What we do upon some great occasion will probably depend on what we already are; and what we are will be the result of previous years of self-discipline.

H. P. LIDDON

Men are often capable of greater things than they perform.—They are sent into the world with bills of credit, and seldom draw to their full extent.

HORACE WALPOLE

A genius can't be forced; nor can you make an ape an alderman.

THOMAS SOMERVILLE

Action

Eighty percent of success is showing up.

WOODY ALLEN

When Demosthenes was asked what were the three most important aspects of oratory, he answered, "Action, Action, Action."

PLUTARCH

The actions of men [are] the best interpreters of their thoughts.

JOHN LOCKE

Dwight L. Moody was a man of action. Once he mentioned a clever promotion idea to a church leader and asked, "What do you think?"

"We've been aimin' to do it for two years," the layman replied.
"Well, now," Moody retorted, "don't you think it's time to fire?"

G. S.

People should never become so indifferent, cynical, or sophisticated that they are not shocked into action.

MARGARET CHASE SMITH

Action may not always bring happiness; but there is no happiness without action.

BENJAMIN DISRAELI

The secret of getting action: What the mind attends to, it considers. What it does not attend to, it dismisses. What the mind attends to continually, it believes. And what the mind believes, it eventually does.

EARL NIGHTINGALE

In their book *In Search of Excellence,* Thomas J. Peters and Robert H. Waterman suggest eight qualities that are characteristic of excellent companies in the United States. The first is "a bias for action," which Peters and Waterman describe as a tendency to act rather than to remain passive.

The authors use phrases like, "do it," "fix it," "try it," and state that "chaotic action is preferable to orderly inaction."

Ludwig van Beethoven arose at daybreak and immediately began composing until 2 P.M. when he would have dinner. He worked in long stretches of unbroken time to allow his thoughts to unfold and flow uninterrupted. He exemplified a bias for action.

John Wesley, the founder of Methodism, traveled more than 250,000 miles on horseback, preaching often fifteen times a week for over fifty years. As an octogenarian, he complained that he found it difficult to work more than fifteen hours a day.

C. T. WINCHESTER

My hat's in the ring! The fight is on and I am stripped to the buff!

THEODORE ROOSEVELT

Thou wilt find rest from vain fancies if thou doest every act in life as though it were thy last.

MARCUS AURELIUS

We must not sit still and look for miracles; up and be doing, and the Lord will be with thee. Prayer and pains, through faith in Christ Jesus, will do anything.

JOHN ELIOT, "Apostle to the Indians"

Adversity

It is difficult to steer a parked car, so get moving.

HENRIETTA MEARS

Adversity

Fire is the test of gold; adversity of strong men.

SENECA

When I dig another out of trouble, the hole from which I lift him is the place where I bury my own.

ANONYMOUS

I'll say this for adversity: People seem to be able to stand it, and that's more than I can say for prosperity.

"KIN" HUBBARD

There are three things to remember concerning trials:
1. Trials are the common experience of all of us. No one is immune. Trials are a part of living.
2. Trials are transitory. C. B. Williams translates 1 Peter 1:6 this way: "In such a hope keep on rejoicing, although for a little while you must be sorrow-stricken with various trials." Trials, though difficult, are "for a little while."
3. Trials are lessons that shouldn't be wasted. Though not enjoyable or necessarily good in themselves, trials constitute a divine work for our ultimate good. Jesus never promised an easy journey, but He did promise a safe landing.

G. S.

No author, without a trial, can conceive of the difficulty of writing a romance about a country where there is no shadow, no antiquity, no mystery, no picturesque and gloomy wrong, not anything but a commonplace prosperity, in broad and simple daylight, as is happily the case with my dear native land. . . . Romance and poetry, ivy, lichens and wallflowers need ruin to make them grow.

NATHANIEL HAWTHORNE, Preface to *The Marble Faun*

Pressure produces! As we face the pressures and problems of life, let us seek not a *passive* patience, but rather a *positive,* enthusiastic cooperation with God's purpose for our lives.

G. S.

A young boy was sailing a small sailboat. The string that held his boat snapped, and the little boat was blown farther and farther out on the water. An older boy picked up some stones and began to throw them in the direction of the boat. That infuriated the little boy. But shortly he learned that the older boy's purpose was for his good. Each stone went just beyond the boat, and the resulting waves gently pushed it back to shore.

G. S.

Sweet are the uses of adversity;
Which, like the toad, ugly and venomous,
Wears yet a precious jewel in his head;
And this our life, exempt from public haunt,
Finds tongues in trees, books in the running brooks,
Sermons in stones, and good in every thing.

WILLIAM SHAKESPEARE, *As You Like It*

Advertising

The Devil comes along with something the natural man wants, and he paints the town red to let them know he is coming. The church comes along with something the natural man doesn't want, and thousands of pastors seem to think a mere announcement of the project from the pulpit is quite enough.

W. E. BIEDERWOLF

Very old indeed is advertising. The rainbow in the clouds, according to Scripture, was one of the early advertisements. It promised that men should not be destroyed by a flood again. In that advertisement, brilliant in color, magnified in size, Supreme Power announced the fact that that particular flood was to be the last flood.

ARTHUR BRISBANE

Advertising may be described as the science of arresting the human intelligence long enough to get money from it.

STEPHEN LEACOCK

I do not read advertisements—I would spend all my time wanting things.

ARCHBISHOP OF CANTERBURY

Advice

In his own gentle, procrastinating way, Dr. George Harris did much as president of Amherst College, but the unpleasant duties of such a post he neglected or ignored. He was not really opposed to work, but

I never heard him say much in favor of it. One autumn he rose in chapel to address the students at the first assembly of the year, but after three or four sentences he got tired and, breaking into a happy smile, said: "I intended to give you some advice, but now I remember how much is left over from last year unused." With that he took his hat and walked out.

JOHN ERSKINE, *The Memory of Certain Persons*

It takes a great man to give sound advice tactfully, but a greater to accept it graciously.

J. C. MACAULAY

A good scare is worth more to a man than good advice.

E. W. HOWE

Don't follow any advice, no matter how good, until you feel as deeply in your spirit as you think in your mind that the counsel is wise.

DAVID SEABURY

In those days he was wiser than he is now—he used frequently to take my advice.

WINSTON CHURCHILL

Advocate

There is an old ploughman in the country I sometimes talk with, and he often says, though in uncouth words, some precious things. He said to me one day, "The other day, sir, the devil was tempting me and I tried to answer him; but I found he was an old lawyer, and understood the law a great deal better than I did, so I gave over, and would not argue with him any more; so I said to him, 'What do you trouble me for?'

" 'Why,' said he, 'about your soul.'

" 'Oh!' said I, 'that is no business of mine; I have given my soul over into the hand of Christ; I have transferred everything to him; if you want an answer to your doubts and queries, you must apply to my Advocate.' "

CHARLES H. SPURGEON

The words the Lord Jesus used when He promised to send the Holy Spirit leave no room for the idea that He is merely a force or an impersonal influence. Jesus said, "I will pray the Father, and he shall give you another Comforter" (John 14:16). The word *another* in the Greek means "one the same as." The Holy Spirit is the same as Christ; He is a person. The word *comforter* is from the Greek word *paraklete,* which means "one called alongside." It is the same word translated "advocate" in 1 John 2:1. It is a word that only makes sense if it is applied to a personal being. The Holy Spirit is our Paraclete. He is one called to aid us, to instruct us, to intercede for us. He is a person.

G. S.

Is Christ thy advocate to plead thy cause?
Art thou his client? Such shall never slide.
He never lost his case. . . .
My case is bad, Lord, be my advocate.
My sin is red: I'm under God's arrest.

EDWARD TAYLOR

Affliction

Nothing can render affliction so insupportable as the load of sin. Would you then be fitted for afflictions? Be sure to get the burden of your sins laid aside, and then what affliction soever you may meet with will be very easy to you.

JOHN BUNYAN

The Lord gets his best soldiers out of the highlands of affliction.

CHARLES H. SPURGEON

Affliction is not sent in vain, young man,/From that good God, who chastens whom he loves.

ROBERT SOUTHEY

Iron till it be thoroughly heated is uncapable to be wrought; so God sees good to cast some men into the furnace of affliction, and then beats them on his anvil into what frame he pleases.

ANNE BRADSTREET

God will not permit any troubles to come upon us, unless He has a specific plan by which great blessing can come out of the difficulty.

PETER MARSHALL

Afflictions are but the shadow of God's wings.

GEORGE MacDONALD

If all the skies were sunshine
Our faces would be fain
To feel once more upon them
The cooling plash of rain.

HENRY VAN DYKE

Age

I waited patiently for the Lord; and he inclined unto me, and heard my cry.

PSALM 40:1

Hear my voice, O God, in my prayer: preserve my life from fear of the enemy.

PSALM 64:1

For thou, O God, hast proved us: thou hast tried us, as silver is tried.

PSALM 66:10

It is good for me that I have been afflicted; that I might learn thy statutes.

PSALM 119:71

Age

If a thing is old, it is a sign that it was fit to live. Old families, old customs, old styles survive because they are fit to survive. The guarantee of continuity is quality. Submerge the good in a flood of the new, and the good will come back to join the good which the new brings with it. Old-fashioned hospitality, old-fashioned politeness, old-fashioned honor in business had qualities of survival. These will come back.

ANONYMOUS

Age should not have its face lifted, but it should rather teach the world to admire wrinkles as the etchings of experience and the firm line of character.

RALPH BARTON PERRY

We are happier in many ways when we are old than when we were young. The young sow wild oats. The old grow sage.

WINSTON CHURCHILL

It's not how old you are, but how you are old.

MARIE DRESSLER

Many foxes grow gray, but few grow good.

BENJAMIN FRANKLIN

> Grow old along with me!
> The best is yet to be,
> The last of life, for which the first was made:
> Our times are in his hand
> Who saith: "A whole I planned,
> Youth shows but half; trust God: see all, nor be afraid!"

ROBERT BROWNING, Rabbi Ben Ezra

10

Preparation for old age should begin not later than one's teens. A life which is empty of purpose until 65 will not suddenly become filled on retirement.

ARTHUR MORGAN

When a man's friends begin to compliment him about looking young, he may be sure that they think he is growing old.

WASHINGTON IRVING

I married an archeologist because the older I grow, the more he appreciates me.

AGATHA CHRISTIE

Life begins at 40—but so do fallen arches, lumbago, faulty eyesight, and the tendency to tell a story to the same person three or four times.

BILL FEATHER

Lord, Thou knowest better than I know myself that I am growing older. Keep me from getting too talkative, and thinking I must say something on every subject and on every occasion. Release me from craving to straighten out everybody's affairs. Teach me the glorious lesson that occasionally it is possible that I may be mistaken. Make me thoughtful, but not moody, helpful, but not bossy; for Thou knowest, Lord, that I want a few friends at the end.

ANONYMOUS

> Ah, nothing is too late,
> Till the tired heart shall cease to palpitate.

HENRY WADSWORTH LONGFELLOW

We have no right to look for a happy old age if in our living we habitually violate physical and spiritual law. The full blessing of length of days comes to those who have known how to live, and the beauty of the years of maturity can be assured only by maintaining high standards of living.

JANET BAIRD

To me—old age is fifteen years older than I am.

BERNARD M. BARUCH

I've never known a person to live to be one hundred and be remarkable for anything else.

JOSH BILLINGS

You know you're getting old when the candles cost more than the cake.

BOB HOPE

Alcohol, Ambition

Whatever poet, orator or sage may say of it, old age is still old age.

SINCLAIR LEWIS

You've heard of the three ages of man: youth, age, and "you're looking wonderful!"

FRANCIS JOSEPH SPELLMAN

Growing old isn't so bad when you consider the alternative.

MAURICE CHEVALIER

Alcohol

Good-bye, John. You were God's worst enemy. You were Hell's best friend.

BILLY SUNDAY, Sermon on the beginning of prohibition—"John" was John Barleycorn—Norfolk, Virginia, 16 July 1920

Some of the most dreadful mischiefs that afflict mankind proceed from wine; it is the cause of disease, quarrels, sedition, idleness, aversion to labor, and every species of domestic accord.

FRANÇOIS FÉNELON

There is a devil in every berry of the grape.

The Koran

O thou invisible spirit of wine, if thou hast no name to be known by, let us call thee devil!

WILLIAM SHAKESPEARE, *Othello*

Ambition

Cromwell, I charge thee, fling away ambition:
By that sin fell the angels; how can man, then,
The image of his Maker, hope to win by it?
Love thyself last: cherish those hearts that hate thee;
Corruption wins not more than honesty.
Still in thy right hand carry gentle peace,
To silence envious tongues. Be just, fear not. . . .

WILLIAM SHAKESPEARE, *King Henry VIII*

I . . . had ambition not only to go farther than any man had ever been before, but as far as it was possible for a man to go.

CAPTAIN JAMES COOK

Keep away from people who try to belittle your ambitions. Small people always do that, but the really great make you feel that you, too, can become great.

MARK TWAIN

Keep your feet on the ground, but let your heart soar as high as it will. Refuse to be average or to surrender to the chill of your spiritual environment.

A. W. TOZER

Ambition is the germ from which all growth of nobleness proceeds.

T. D. ENGLISH

America

Haveing undertaken, for the glorie of God, and advancements of the Christian faith and honour of our king & countrie, a voyage to plant the first colonie in the Northerne parts of Virginia, doe by these presents solemnly & mutualy in the presence of God, and one of another, covenant & combine our selves togeather into a civill body politick; for our better ordering, & preservation & furtherance of the ends aforesaid; and by vertue hearof to enacte, consistute, and frame such just & equall lawes, ordinances, Act, constitutions, & offices, from time to time, as shall be thought most meete & convenient for the generall good of the Colonie: unto which we promise all due submission and obedience.

WILLIAM BRADFORD

The real democratic American idea is, not that every man shall be on a level with every other man, but that every man shall have liberty to be what God made him, without hindrance.

HENRY WARD BEECHER

> Give me your tired, your poor,
> Your huddled masses yearning to breathe free,
> The wretched refuse of your teeming shore,
> Send these, the homeless, tempest-tossed, to me:
> I lift my lamp beside the golden door.

EMMA LAZARUS, Inscription on Statue of Liberty

America—where people do not inquire of a stranger, "What is he?" but "What can he do?"

ANONYMOUS

America is a large, friendly dog in a very small room. Every time it wags its tail, it knocks over a chair.

ARNOLD TOYNBEE, News summaries, 14 July 1954

13

Double—no triple—our troubles and we'd still be better off than any other people on earth. . . . It is time that we recognized that ours was, in truth, a noble cause.

RONALD REAGAN

Many years ago, Alexis de Tocqueville, the famous French political philosopher, visited America. He came here when this nation was very young to find the secret of our greatness.

He traveled from town to town, talking with people and asking questions. He examined our young national government, our schools and centers of business, without finding the reason for our strength.

Not till he visited the churches of America and witnessed the pulpits of this land "aflame with righteousness" did he find the secret of our greatness.

Returning to France, he summarized his findings with this word of warning: "America is great because America is good, and if America ever ceases to be good, America will cease to be great."

G. S.

I am well aware of the toil, and blood, and treasure, that it will cost us to maintain this declaration, and support and defend these States. Yet through all the gloom, I can see the rays of ravishing light and glory. . . . The second day of July, 1776, will be the most memorable epoch in the history of America. I am apt to believe that it will be celebrated by succeeding generations as the great anniversary festival. It ought to be commemorated as the day of deliverance, by solemn acts of devotion to God Almighty. It ought to be solemnized with pomp and parade, with shows, games, sports, guns, bells, bonfires, and illuminations, from one end of this continent to the other, from this time forward forevermore.

JOHN ADAMS, Letter to Abigail Adams, 3 July 1776

Back of every great civilization, behind all the power and wealth, is something as powerful . . . a set of ideas, attitudes, convictions and the confidence that those ideas and convictions are viable. No nation can achieve greatness unless it believes in something—and unless that something has the moral dimensions to sustain a great civilization.

JOHN W. GARDNER, *No Easy Victors*

In the book *The Ugly American* [by William Lederer and Eugene Burdick] an Asian journalist writes, "Poor America. It took the British a hundred years to lose their prestige in Asia. America has managed to lose hers in ten years." The book in general gives the impression that we are loud, ostentatious, self-centered, and, worst of all, proud and haughty.

G. S.

Ancestors

My ancestors didn't come over on the *Mayflower,* but they were there to meet the boat.

WILL ROGERS

Every man is an omnibus in which his ancestors ride.

OLIVER WENDELL HOLMES, SR.

The kind of ancestors we have had is not as important as the kind of descendants our ancestors have.

ANONYMOUS

Whoever serves his country well has no need of ancestors.

VOLTAIRE

He who boasts of his descent, praises the deeds of another.

SENECA

Angels

Fools rush in where angels fear to tread.

ALEXANDER POPE, *Essay on Criticism*

What is the question now placed before society with the glib assurance which to me is most astonishing? That question is this: Is man an ape or an angel? I, my lord, I am on the side of the angels. I repudiate with indignation and abhorrence those newfangled theories.

BENJAMIN DISRAELI

Angels are bright still, though the brightest fell.

WILLIAM SHAKESPEARE, *Macbeth*

> Around our pillows golden ladders rise,
> And up and down the skies,
> With winged sandals shod,
> The angels come, and go, the Messengers of God!

R. H. STODDARD

Anger

> Anger is a wind
> which blows out the
> lamp of the mind.

ANONYMOUS

Anger: an acid that can do more harm to the vessel in which it is stored than to anything on which it is poured.

ANONYMOUS

Anger

When you lose your temper—you really lose something. You lose the ability to think sanely and to make balanced decisions.

G. S.

Next time you feel the surge of anger, say to yourself, "Is this really worth what it's going to do to me and others emotionally? I will make a fool of myself. I may hurt someone I love, or I might lose a friend." Practice realizing that it is not worth it to get so worked up about things, and always remember Seneca who said, "The greatest cure of anger is delay."

NORMAN VINCENT PEALE

Be not angry that you cannot make others as you wish them to be, since you cannot make yourself as you wish to be.

THOMAS A KEMPIS

A student said to me, "I lose my temper, but it's all over in a minute." I answered, "And so is the hydrogen bomb. But think of the damage it produces!"

G. S.

Legend has it that Jonathan Edwards, third president of Princeton and one of America's great preachers, had a daughter with an uncontrollable temper. As often happens, this fault was not known to many people outside the family. A young man fell in love with this daughter and asked to marry her.

"You can't have her," was the abrupt answer of Jonathan Edwards.
"But I love her," the young man replied.
"You can't have her," repeated Edwards.
"But she loves me," replied the young man.
Again Edwards said, "You can't have her."
"Why?" asked the young man.
"Because she is not worthy of you."
"But," he asked, "she is a Christian, isn't she?"
"Yes, she is a Christian. But the grace of God can live with some people with whom no one else could ever live!"

G. S.

It is the intermittent fever which bespeaks unintermittent disease within; the occasional bubble escaping to the surface which betrays some rottenness underneath; a sample of the most hidden products of the soul dropped involuntarily when off one's guard; in a word, the lightning form of a hundred hideous and unchristian sins. For a want of patience, a want of kindness, a want of generosity, a want of courtesy, a want

16

of unselfishness, are all instantaneously symbolized in one flash of Temper.

Hence it is not enough to deal with the Temper. We must go to the source, and change the inmost nature. . . . Souls are made sweet not by taking the acid fluids out, but by putting something in—a great Love, a new Spirit, the Spirit of Christ. . . . This only can eradicate what is wrong, work a chemical change, renovate . . . the inner man.

HENRY DRUMMOND, *The Greatest Thing in the World*

The words of the wicked are to lie in wait for blood: but the mouth of the upright shall deliver them.

PROVERBS 12:6

A soft answer turneth away wrath: but grievous words stir up anger.

PROVERBS 15:1

The sacrifice of the wicked is an abomination to the Lord: but the prayer of the upright is his delight.

PROVERBS 15:8

It is better to dwell in the wilderness, than with a contentious and an angry woman.

PROVERBS 21:19

Scornful men bring a city into a snare: but the righteous doth sing and rejoice.

PROVERBS 29:8

Antichrist

Our world is fast becoming a madhouse and the inmates are trying to run the asylum. It is a strange time when the patients are writing the prescriptions, the students are threatening to run the schools, the children to manage the homes, and church members—not the Holy Spirit—to direct the churches. Such lawlessness always brings a dictator and the last of the line will be the Antichrist, now in the offing awaiting his cue.

VANCE HAVNER

Antichrist is so proud as to go before Christ; so humble as to pretend to come after him; and so audacious as to say that himself is he.

JOHN BUNYAN

The world is looking for a powerful leader—an international figure to offer practical solutions to the world's problems of war, suffering, hunger, and pestilence. Weary of hollow promises, people want a tried and proven super-leader, a shining knight strong enough to guarantee peace.

In the world today, international leaders change with amazing speed. Looking back over the past ten years, we see that the roster of leaders who were in power ten years ago and still are today is incredibly short. They have been removed from power by resignation, assassination, revolution, and death, and often their power base crumbles with their passing. Those who succeed them often blur their predecessor's achievements and discredit his words; then they fall from power just as quickly.

It is into this kind of political atmosphere that the Antichrist will come. He will offer peace and prosperity, but ultimately he will threaten the very existence of civilization. His power will be so complete and evil that only Jesus Christ will be able to conquer him and free the world from his grip, thereby bringing down the curtain on the present age.

G. S.

The word *Antichrist* means "one who stands against Christ," and he will do just that. After he has deceived the world into accepting his rule, he will abuse his power and oppose and exalt himself against God, even to the point of sitting "in the temple of God, shewing himself that he is God" (2 Thessalonians 2:4).

G. S.

Antichrist's power will extend to every area of life in every part of the world. His dictatorship will be religious, political, and economic. He will have supernatural abilities, including the power to counterfeit miracles.

G. S.

Apathy (see Neglect)

The crime against life, the worst of all crimes, is not to feel. And there was never, perhaps, a civilization in which that crime, the crime of torpor, of lethargy, of apathy, the snake-like sin of coldness-at-the-heart, was commoner than in our technical civilization.

ARCHIBALD MACLEISH

In Germany they came first for the Communists, and I didn't speak up because I wasn't a Communist. Then they came for the Jews, and I didn't speak up because I wasn't a Jew. Then they came for the trade unionists, and I didn't speak up because I wasn't a trade unionist. Then they came for the Catholics, and I didn't speak up because I was a Protestant. Then they came for me, and by that time no one was left to speak up.

MARTIN NIEMOELLER

The hottest places in Hell are reserved for those who in time of great moral crises maintain their neutrality.

DANTE ALIGHIERI

Appreciation

A New York school superintendent entered the hospital for an operation. When he came out from under the anesthetic, a telegram was waiting for him. It read: "The school board voted eight to six last night to wish you a speedy recovery."

The class assignment was to write a short paper on "Things I Am Most Thankful For." One fourth-grade boy put first, "My glasses. They keep the boys from punching me and the girls from kissing me."

When I'm not thank'd at all, I'm thank'd enough,/I've done my duty, and I've done no more.

HENRY FIELDING

You can't appreciate home till you've left it, money till it's spent, your wife till she's joined a woman's club, nor Old Glory till you see it hanging on a broomstick of a consul in a foreign town.

O. HENRY

Let never day nor night unhallow'd pass,/But still remember what the Lord hath done.

WILLIAM SHAKESPEARE, *Henry VI*

Arguing

But curb thou the high spirit in thy breast,
For gentle ways are best, and keep aloof
From sharp contentions.

HOMER, *The Iliad*

I cannot argue while men die. I do not know who the man on the "Jericho Road" is. I do not know who hit him nor where or why. I only know, there he is! He may not be a member of our tribe, our group, our convention, but he needs my help, and I must help him.

OSCAR JOHNSON

Art

Silence is one of the hardest things to refute.

JOSH BILLINGS

The test of a man or woman's breeding is how they behave in a quarrel.

GEORGE BERNARD SHAW

Art

Art, like morality, consists in drawing the line somewhere.

G. K. CHESTERTON

A man paints with his brains and not with his hands.

MICHELANGELO

Abstract Art: A product of the untalented, sold by the unprincipled to the utterly bewildered.

AL CAPP

If that's art, I'm a Hottentot!

HARRY S. TRUMAN

Michelangelo was also a superb applied psychologist. At first, he was ignored and disdained by his own generation. But he had faith in his ability and decided to use some psychology on his critics. Knowing that they were fascinated by excavating in old ruins to dig up supposedly priceless works of art, he tinted one of his masterpieces and then had it buried where an excavating party would be sure to find it. The critics were enraptured. They pronounced it an antique of rare value. The Cardinal of San Giorgio was so impressed that he paid a huge sum to add it to his art collection. Then Michelangelo deftly let the cat out of the bag. The art critics . . . were so far out on a limb that they had to admit that he was an artistic genius. After that, Michelangelo was commissioned to do important work.

GEORGE CRANE

The function of art is to make that understood which in the form of argument would be incomprehensible.

CONSTANTIN BRANCUSI

A doctor can bury his mistakes, but an architect can only advise his client to plant vines.

FRANK LLOYD WRIGHT

He bores me. He ought to have stuck to his flying machine.

AUGUSTE RENOIR, of Leonardo da Vinci

I hope with all my heart there will be painting in heaven.

JEAN-BAPTISTE COROT

When I am finishing a picture I hold some God-made object up to it—a rock, a flower, the branch of a tree or my hand—as a kind of final test. If the painting stands up beside a thing man cannot make, the painting is authentic. If there's a clash between the two, it is bad art.

MARC CHAGALL

Ascension

And He departed from our sight that we might return to our heart, and there find Him. For He departed, and behold, He is here.

SAINT AUGUSTINE

Soar we now where Christ has led; Alleluia!
Following our exalted Head; Alleluia!
Made like Him, like Him we rise; Alleluia!
Ours the cross, the grave, the skies. Alleluia!

CHARLES WESLEY

In the days of His earthly ministry, only those could speak to Him who came where He was. If He was in Galilee, men could not find Him in Jerusalem; if He was in Jerusalem, men could not find Him in Galilee. But His Ascension means that He is perfectly united with God; we are with Him wherever we are present to God; and this is everywhere and always.

WILLIAM TEMPLE

Atheism

How to trap an atheist: Serve him a fine meal, then ask him if he believes there is a cook.

ANONYMOUS

Atheism is rather in the lip than in the heart of man.

FRANCIS BACON, *Essays, of Atheism*

It is true, that a little philosophy inclineth man's mind to atheism, but depth in philosophy bringeth men's minds about to religion.

FRANCIS BACON, *Essays, of Atheism*

Atonement

The atheist who is moved by love is moved by the Spirit of God; an atheist who lives by love is saved by his faith in the God whose existence (under that name) he denies.

WILLIAM TEMPLE

I can see how it might be possible for a man to look down upon the earth and be an atheist, but I cannot conceive how he could look up into the heavens and say there is no God.

ABRAHAM LINCOLN

An atheist is a man who looks through a telescope and tries to explain all that he can't see.

ANONYMOUS

Atonement

Christ took our sins and the sins of the whole world as well as the Father's wrath on his shoulders, and he has drowned them both in himself so that we are thereby reconciled to God and become completely righteous.

MARTIN LUTHER

This is the mystery of the riches of divine grace for sinners; for by a wonderful exchange our sins are now not ours but Christ's, and Christ's righteousness is not Christ's but ours.

MARTIN LUTHER

The blood of Christ stands not simply for the sting of sin on God but the scourge of God on sin, not simply for God's sorrow over sin but for God's wrath on sin.

P. T. FORSYTH

I would like to examine the three Rs of the atonement—three significant benefits man receives from Christ's work for us on the cross.

The first is redemption. Redemption comes from a Greek word that is sometimes translated "ransom." It means "a payment." To a first-century Greek, the term *redemption* suggested a payment to free a slave. If a slave could obtain enough money to buy his freedom, that was called "redemption."

Did you know that Jesus' death on the cross was actually a payment of ransom? When He died for us, He paid the price to free us from the slavery of sin. Romans 6:23 says, "The wages of sin is death." Verse 7 of that same chapter says, "For he that is dead is freed from sin."

The second R of the atonement is reconciliation. When we think of reconciliation we usually think in terms of two marriage partners who have separated but are getting back together. *Reconciliation* means, "a settling of differences, a bringing together of two conflicting sides."

Man's sin built a wall of separation between him and God. God, a holy and perfectly righteous being, cannot tolerate the presence of sin. Sin is contrary to His nature. Man's decision to sin was a decision to be at enmity with God. Man had declared war.

But that did not change God's love for man. Although God in His perfect righteousness could not tolerate sin, He was not willing to stay at enmity with man. He could not simply overlook sin, so He paid for it Himself in the Person of the Lord Jesus. In that way He was able to declare man righteous without sacrificing His own righteousness.

The third R of the atonement is resurrection. Without the resurrection there is no meaning to the atonement. Paul wrote in 1 Corinthians 15:17, "If Christ be not raised, your faith is vain; ye are yet in your sins."

The resurrection is the heart of the gospel. "That he rose again the third day according to the scriptures" (1 Corinthians 15:4) was central in the apostles' preaching—and with good reason.

It is the resurrection of Christ that gives us the assurance that the atonement was accepted by God. The resurrection was the Holy Spirit's seal of approval on the work of Christ. Paul wrote to the Romans that Christ was "declared to be the son of God with power, according to the spirit of holiness, by the resurrection of the dead" (Romans 1:4).

G. S.

Attitudes

An optimist may see a light where there is none, but why must the pessimist always run to blow it out?

MICHEL DE SAINT-PIERRE

One man gets nothing but discord out of a piano; another gets harmony. No one claims the piano is at fault. Life is about the same. The discord is there, and the harmony is there. Study to play it correctly, and it will give forth the beauty; play it falsely, and it will give forth the ugliness. Life is not at fault.

ANONYMOUS

Forget your past circumstances, whether they be sorrows or joys. The one is not without remedy, the other not perfect. Both are past; why remember them? Why should you carry about parched corn when you dwell among fields white unto harvest? Why carry putrid water in the bottom of a rancid skin, when living in a land of fountains and brooks that run among the hills? Why clasp a handful of poor withered flowers, when the grass is sown with their bright eyes opening to the sunshine?

ALEXANDER MACLAREN

If you wish to travel far and fast, travel light. Take off all your envies, jealousies, unforgiveness, selfishness and fears.

GLENN CLARK

I got a simple rule about everybody. If you don't treat me right—shame on you!

LOUIS ARMSTRONG

He was always leaning forward, pushing something invisible ahead of him.

JAMES THURBER

I would rather be first in a little Iberian village than second in Rome.

JULIUS CAESAR

Any manager who can't get along with a .400 hitter is crazy.

JOE MCCARTHY, NEW YORK YANKEES

In War: Resolution. In Defeat: Defiance. In Victory: Magnanimity. In Peace: Goodwill.

WINSTON CHURCHILL

Growl all day and you'll feel dog tired at night.

ANONYMOUS

We lost because we told ourselves we lost.

LEO TOLSTOY, *War and Peace*

Don't introduce me to that man! I want to go on hating him, and I can't hate a man whom I know.

CHARLES LAMB (attributed)

An optimist is a driver who thinks that empty space at the curb won't have a hydrant beside it.

Changing Times

The basis of optimism is sheer terror.

OSCAR WILDE

A wise clergyman kept on his desk a special notebook labeled "Complaints of Members." Whenever one of his people began to criticize another's doings, he would say, "I'll just write it out so I can take it up with the board." The sight of the complaint book and the ready pen had its effect. The clergyman kept the book for 40 years, opened it hundreds of times, and never had occasion to write a line in it.

LEEWIN B. WILLIAMS, *The Master Book of Humourous Illustrations*

Life would be a perpetual flea hunt if a man were obliged to run down all the innuendoes, inveracities, insinuations and misrepresentations which are uttered against him.

HENRY WARD BEECHER

Irritation in the heart of a believer is always an invitation to the devil to stand by.

ANONYMOUS

Optimism is the cheerful frame of mind that enables a teakettle to sing, though in hot water up to its nose.

ANONYMOUS

On the back of an envelope found among his effects after his death in a plane crash, former Atomic Energy Commission Chairman, Gordon Dean, had scrawled:
1. Never lose your capacity for enthusiasm.
2. Never lose your capacity for indignation.
3. Never judge people, don't type them too quickly; but in a pinch always assume that a man is good and that at worst he is in the gray area between good and bad.
4. If you can't be generous when it's hard, you won't be when it's easy.
5. The greatest builder of confidence is the ability to do something— almost anything—well.
6. When that confidence comes, then strive for humility; you aren't as good as all that.
7. And the way to become truly useful is to seek the best that other brains have to offer. Use them to supplement your own, and give credit to them when they have helped.
8. The greatest tragedies in world and personal events stem from misunderstanding.

Gordon Dean lived by that splendid testament.

ROBERT G. LEE

I respect those who resist me, but I cannot tolerate them.

CHARLES DE GAULLE

Belief

Keep your heart right, even when it is sorely wounded.

J. C. MACAULAY

Let's not be narrow, nasty, and negative.

VERNON GROUNDS

There is little difference in people, but that little difference makes a big difference. The little difference is attitude. The big difference is whether it is positive or negative.

CLEMENT STONE

Whenever a fellow tells me he is bipartisan, I know he's going to vote against me.

HARRY S. TRUMAN

Two men looked through prison bars—One saw mud, the other stars.

ANONYMOUS

← **B** →

Belief

Being of Scotch extraction, I always greatly enjoy the broad Scotch translation of the New Testament. In that you will never find our English word, "believe," but you will find the word "lippen." For instance, John 3:16 reads, "For God sae loved the warld as to gie His Son, the only begotten Ane, that ilka ane wha lippens till Him sudna dee, but hae life for aye." What does that word mean, the word "lippen"? It just means to trust your whole weight on a thing, trust it implicitly.

A Scotch minister was visiting a poor woman who was in great distress about her soul. She just could not seem to understand. By and by he left her, and on his way back to the manse he was troubled to think he had not been able to help her. He came to a bridge over a burn in front of the house, which he started to cross, going step by step very carefully with his buckthorn cane.

An old Scotch woman called out, "Why, Doctor Man, can ye no lippen the brig?" He laughed and waved his hand and said to himself, "I have the word for my auld lady." So he went back to the cottage. She opened the door and said, "O Doctor, you've come back again?"

He said, "I have the word for you now."

"What is it, Doctor?"

"Can you no lippen to Jesus?"

"Oh, is it just to lippen to Him? Why, surely I can lippen to Him. He will never let me doon, will He?"

They bowed together, and she settled it. That is all God asks you to do. Believe the record He has given concerning Jesus; put your heart's trust in Him. You may be assured that you have life eternal for "he that hath the Son hath life; and he that hath not the Son of God hath not life. These things have I written unto you that believe on the name of the Son of God; that ye may *know*"—not merely hope, not just have a reasonable assurance, but full assurance—"that ye *have* eternal life."

H. A. IRONSIDE

It is so hard to believe because it is so hard to obey.

SÖREN KIERKEGAARD

Belief is a moral act for which the believer is to be held responsible.
H. A. HODGES, *Languages, Standpoints & Attitudes*—Riddel Lectures

If there is no God, it would be necessary to invent Him.

VOLTAIRE

Belief is a wise wager. Granted that faith cannot be proved, what harm will come to you if you gamble on its truth and it proves false? . . . If you gain, you gain all; if you lose, you lose nothing. Wager, then, without hesitation, that He exists.

BLAISE PASCAL

If we let ourselves believe that man began with divine grace, that he forfeited this by sin, and that he can be redeemed only by divine grace through the crucified Christ, then we shall find a peace of mind never granted to philosophers. He who cannot believe is cursed, for he reveals by his unbelief that God has not chosen to give him grace.

BLAISE PASCAL

When life becomes all snarled up, offer it to our Lord and let Him untie the knots.

A Book of Days for Christians

I asked a man what made his life so radiant and bright. He answered: "Looking, looking toward the Light!"

Even if I knew that tomorrow the world would go to pieces, I would still plant my apple tree.

MARTIN LUTHER

Bible

The Gateway to Christianity is not through an intricate labyrinth of dogma, but by a simple belief in the person of Christ.

WILLIAM LYON PHELPS

Belief consists in accepting the affirmations of the soul; unbelief in denying them.

RALPH WALDO EMERSON

Bible

There's no better book with which to defend the Bible than the Bible itself.

D. L. MOODY

I know the Bible is inspired because it inspires me.

10-3-93

D. L. MOODY

The Bible will keep you from sin, or sin will keep you from the Bible.

D. L. MOODY

The study of God's Word brings peace to the heart. In it, we find a light for every darkness, life in death, the promise of our Lord's return, and the assurance of everlasting glory.

D. L. MOODY

The impregnable rock of Holy Scriptures.

WILLIAM E. GLADSTONE

In all my perplexities and distresses, the Bible has never failed to give me light and strength.

ROBERT E. LEE

I must confess to you that the majesty of the Scriptures astonishes me, the holiness of the evangelists speaks to my heart and has such striking characters of truth, and is, moreover, so perfectly inimitable, that if it had been the invention of men, the inventors would be greater than the greatest heroes.

JEAN JACQUES ROUSSEAU

Those who spiritualize tell spiritual lies, because they lack spiritual eyes.

ANONYMOUS

The Bible is God's chart for you to steer by, to keep you from the bottom of the sea, and to show you where the harbor is, and how to reach it without running on rocks or bars.

HENRY WARD BEECHER

Bible

I have read many books, but the Bible reads me.

ANONYMOUS

Arguments about scripture achieve nothing but a stomachache and a headache.

TERTULLIAN

One man perverts scripture with his hand, another with his exegesis. Marcion used the knife, not the pen, massacring scripture to suit his own material. Valentinus spared the text, since he did not invent scriptures to suit his matter, but matter to suit the scriptures.

TERTULLIAN

It ain't those parts of the Bible that I can't understand that bother me, it is the parts that I do understand.

10-3-93

MARK TWAIN

> Every hour
> I read you, kills a sin,
> Or lets a virtue in
> To fight against it.

IZAAK WALTON

There is no doubt that God has often brought a certain verse to the attention of one of His children in an unusual and almost miraculous manner, for a special need, but the Word was never intended to be consulted in a superstitious manner.

S. MAXWELL CODER, *God's Will for Your Life*

Books of Old Testament—39.
Books of New Testament—27.
Total number of books—66.
Chapters in Old Testament—929.
Chapters in New Testament—260.
Total number of chapters—1,189.
Verses in Old Testament—33,214.
Verses in New Testament—7,959.
Total numbers of verses—41,173.
Words in Old Testament—593,493.
Words in New Testament—181,253.
Total number of words—774,746.
Letters in Old Testament—2,728,100.
Letters in New Testament—838,380.
Total number of letters—3,566,480.

Bible

The shortest chapter is Psalm 117.
Ezra 7:21 contains all the letters of the alphabet except "j."
Esther 8:9 is the longest verse.
John 11:35 is the shortest verse.
There is no word of more than six syllables in the Bible.

ROBERT G. LEE

God's Word is pure and sure, in spite of the devil, in spite of your fear, in spite of everything.

R. A. TORREY

On the cover of your Bible and my Bible appear the words "Holy Bible." Do you know why the Bible is called holy? Why should it be called holy when so much lust and hate and greed and war are found in it? I can tell you why. It is because the Bible tells the truth. It tells the truth about God, about man, and about the devil. The Bible teaches that we exchange the truth of God for the devil's lie about sex, for example; and drugs, and alcohol, and religious hypocrisy. Jesus Christ is the ultimate truth. Furthermore, He told the truth. Jesus said that He was the truth, and the truth would make us free.

BILLY GRAHAM

When you have read the Bible, you will know it is the word of God, because you will have found it the key to your own heart, your own happiness and your own duty.

WOODROW WILSON

The Word of God well understood and religiously obeyed is the shortest route to spiritual perfection. And we must not select a few favourite passages to the exclusion of others. Nothing less than a whole Bible can make a whole Christian.

A. W. TOZER

The book which closes the New Testament "shuts up all" "with a seven-fold chorus of hallelujahs and harping symphonies" as Milton says in his stately music, and may well represent for us, in that perpetual cloud of incense rising up fragrant to the Throne of God and of the Lamb, the unceasing love and thanksgiving which should be man's answer to Christ's love and sacrifice.

ALEXANDER MACLAREN

A readiness to believe every promise implicitly, to obey every command unhesitatingly, to stand perfect and complete in all the will of God, is the only true spirit of Bible study.

ANDREW MURRAY

No one ever graduates from Bible study until he meets its Author face to face.

EVERETT HARRIS

"But the word of God is not bound." That is the inscription on a pillar in the crypt of a church in Rome where Paul is said to have been imprisoned. The heroic apostle, bound with a chain and awaiting death, is not disheartened, discouraged, nor despairing. He has full confidence in the spread of the gospel, and in the conquest of Christ, telling Timothy at Ephesus to be true to Christ and the gospel, for which, he says, "I suffer . . . unto bonds; but the word of God is not bound" (2 Timothy 2:9). How true that statement of the apostle was—and is—is demonstrated by the simple, yet tremendous, fact that nineteen hundred years after Paul wrote from his prison in Rome, "The word of God is not bound," the words are taken as the text for a sermon on the invincible power of the Bible.

CLARENCE E. MACARTNEY

When Thomas Paine showed Benjamin Franklin the manuscript of *The Age of Reason,* Franklin advised him not to publish it, saying, "The world is bad enough *with* the Bible; what would it be without it?"

ANONYMOUS

When you read God's Word, you must constantly be saying to yourself, "It is talking to me, and about me."

SÖREN KIERKEGAARD, *For Self-Examination*

In this one book are the two most interesting personalities in the whole world—God and yourself. The Bible is the story of God and man, a love story in which you and I must write our own ending, our unfinished autobiography of the creature and the Creator.

FULTON OURSLER

England has two books, one which she has made and one which has made her: Shakespeare and the Bible.

VICTOR HUGO

To what greater inspiration and counsel can we turn than to the imperishable truth to be found in this treasure house, the Bible?

QUEEN ELIZABETH II

To me the greatest thing that has happened on this earth of ours is the rise of the human race to the vision of God. That story of the human rise to what I call the vision of God is the story which is told in the Bible.

JAN CHRISTIAN SMUTS

The worth of a book is to be measured by what you can carry away from it.

JAMES BRYCE

Unless we form the habit of going to the Bible in bright moments as well as in trouble, we cannot fully respond to its consolations because we lack equilibrium between light and darkness.

HELEN KELLER

> I am my neighbor's Bible:
>   He reads me when we meet,
> Today he reads me in my house,
>   Tomorrow in the street;
> He may be relative or friend,
>   Or slight acquaintance be;
> He may not even know my name,
>   Yet he is reading me.

ANONYMOUS

More people are troubled by what is plain in Scripture than by what is obscure.

ROY L. SMITH

Bible Endurance

Whoever is found reading the Scriptures shall forfeit his life and land.

HENRY V OF ENGLAND

In twenty-five years, the Bible will be a forgotten book.

ROBERT INGERSOLL

I have now gone through the woods with an ax, and felled trees. Here they lie. They will never grow again.

THOMAS PAINE, *The Age of Reason*

Rome also persecuted the Scriptures; but chiefly in this way: that instead of being the custodian of Scripture it became the jailor of Scripture, and for many centuries the Word of God was hidden from the people, and legends and traditions of men became the food of the human mind.

ADOLPH SAPHIR

Another century and there will not be a Bible on earth.

VOLTAIRE

Century follows century—There it stands.
Empires rise and fall and are forgotten—There it stands.
Dynasty succeeds dynasty—There it stands.
Kings are crowned and uncrowned—There it stands.
Emperors decree its extermination—There it stands.
Despised and torn to pieces—There it stands.
Storms of hate swirl about it—There it stands.
Atheists rail against it—There it stands.
Agnostics smile cynically—There it stands.
Profane prayerless punsters caricature it—There it stands.
Unbelief abandons it—There it stands.
Higher critics deny its claim to inspiration—There it stands.
Thunderbolts of wrath smite it—There it stands.
An anvil that has broken a million hammers—There it stands.
The flames are kindled about it—There it stands.
The arrows of hate are discharged against it—There it stands.
Radicalism rants and raves about it—There it stands.
Fogs of sophistry conceal it temporarily—There it stands.
The tooth of time gnaws but dents it not—There it stands.
Infidels predict its abandonment—There it stands.
Modernism tries to explain it away—There it stands.
Devotees of folly denounce it—There it stands.
It is God's highway to Paradise.
It is the light on the pathway in the darkest night.
It leads business men to integrity and uprightness.
It is the great consoler in bereavement.
It awakens men and women opiated by sin.
It answers every great question of the soul.
It solves every great problem of life.
It is a fortress often attacked but never failing.
Its wisdom is commanding and its logic convincing.
Salvation is its watchword. Eternal life its goal.
It punctures all pretense.
It is forward-looking, outward-looking, and upward-looking.
It outlives, outlifts, outloves, outreaches, outranks, outruns all other books.
Trust it, love it, obey it, and Eternal Life is yours.

A. Z. CONRAD

Bible Study

I never saw a useful Christian who was not a student of the Bible.

D. L. MOODY

Bible study is like eating peanuts. The more you eat, the more you want to eat.

PAUL LITTLE

Books and Reading

First I shake the whole [apple] tree, that the ripest might fall. Then I climb the tree and shake each limb, and then each branch and then each twig, and then I look under each leaf.

MARTIN LUTHER

The Bible is literally *God speaking to you.* It is God's instrument in salvation (Romans 10:17; 1 Peter 1:25) and God's instrument for growing mature Christians (1 Peter 2:2). It is the blueprint for the Christian.

G. S.

Prayer is the "open sesame" to the Bible. *Always* begin your Bible reading with prayer for divine guidance. All of us in reading some current book have wished the author were present to answer and explain some things, but this is rarely possible. Amazing as it seems, this *is possible* when reading the Bible.

G. S.

Commentaries are splendid; however, beware of being chained to them. Someone has humorously said, "The Bible throws a lot of light on the commentaries." Any book that takes priority over the Bible becomes a crutch which leads to weakness. To read the words of men and neglect the Word of God is to say the books of men are of greater worth.

G. S.

The very same Holy Spirit who led these men to write, longs to lead us *today* so we can understand. Without the Holy Spirit, the Bible is like an ocean which cannot be sounded, heavens which cannot be surveyed, mines which cannot be explored, and mysteries beyond unraveling. We must—we must—yield to the leadership of the Holy Spirit.

G. S.

Books and Reading

The man who does not read good books has no advantage over the man who can't read them.

MARK TWAIN

Where is human nature so weak as in the bookstore?

HENRY WARD BEECHER

Every man who knows how to read has it in his power to magnify himself, to multiply the ways in which he exists, to make his life full, significant and interesting.

ALDOUS HUXLEY

34

Boredom, Brokenness, Brotherhood

Reading is to the mind what exercise is to the body.

RICHARD STEELE

The best effect of any book is that it excites the reader to self activity.

THOMAS CARLYLE

Boredom

I spent a year in that town, one Sunday.

WARWICK DEEPING

America is said to have the highest per capita boredom of any spot on earth! We know that because we have the greatest number of artificial amusements of any country. People have become so empty that they can't even entertain themselves. They have to pay other people to amuse them, to make them laugh, to try to make them feel warm and happy and comfortable for a few minutes, to try to lose that awful, frightening, hollow feeling—that terrible, dreaded feeling of being lost and alone.

BILLY GRAHAM

The most terrible thing about materialism, even more terrible than its proneness to violence, is its boredom, from which sex, alcohol, drugs, all devices for putting out the accusing light of reason and suppressing the unrealizable aspirations of love, offer a prospect of deliverance.

MALCOLM MUGGERIDGE

Boredom is the root of all evil—the despairing refusal to be oneself.

SÖREN KIERKEGAARD

Brokenness

I have been reflecting on the inestimable value of "broken things." Broken pitchers gave ample light for victory (Judges 7:19–21); broken bread was more than enough for all the hungry (Matthew 14:19–21); broken box gave fragrance to all the world (Mark 14:3, 9); and broken body is salvation to all who believe and receive the Savior (Isaiah 53:5–6, 12; 1 Corinthians 11:24). And what cannot the Broken One do with our broken plans, projects, and hearts?

V. RAYMOND EDMAN

How else but through a broken heart/May Lord Christ enter in?

OSCAR WILDE

Brotherhood

I met a hundred men going to Delhi and everyone is my brother.

INDIAN SAYING

Brotherhood

We cannot possibly let ourselves get frozen into regarding everyone we do not know as an absolute stranger.

ALBERT SCHWEITZER, *Memories of Childhood & Youth*

You can't hold a man down without staying down with him.

BOOKER T. WASHINGTON

Respect of persons is inconsistent with God's grace. It is inconsistent with God's law. In fact, respect of persons is an act of sin. Racial discrimination and racism are an insult to God.

G. S.

To correct the evils, great and small, which spring from want of sympathy and from positive enmity among strangers, as nations or as individuals, is one of the highest functions of civilization.

ABRAHAM LINCOLN

D. L. Moody had a tremendous burden for the downtrodden and neglected. Sunday after Sunday he would travel up and down the streets of Chicago, gathering the tattered little children into the Sunday school. On one occasion Moody promised a class of thirteen boys that if they would maintain good conduct and attend Sunday school regularly through the summer and fall, he would give each of them a new suit of clothes for Christmas. Twelve of the boys earned their suits, and Moody had them photographed in their ragged clothes first, captioning it, Will It Pay? then in their new suits, labeling that, It Does Pay! About 1858, Moody opened his own Sunday school in an old saloon building. It soon became so crowded that the mayor of Chicago offered him the North Market Hall for a meeting place. As founder and director, he filled a variety of offices, from janitor to superintendent.

"Sunday was a busy day for me then," Moody wrote. "During the week I would be out of town selling boots and shoes, but I would always manage to be back by Saturday night.

"Often it was late when I got to my room, but I would have to be up by six o'clock to get the hall ready for Sunday school.

"Every Saturday night a German society had a dance there, and I had to roll out the beer kegs, sweep up the sawdust, clean up generally and arrange the chairs. This usually took most of the morning, and then I had to go out to drum up the scholars.

"By the time two o'clock came we would have the hall full, and then I had to keep order while the speaker of the day led the exercises. . . . When school was over I visited absent scholars and found out why they were not at Sunday school, called on the sick, and invited parents to attend the evening gospel service." Moody was no respecter of persons. He had a love for all men, rich and poor alike.

To this day a plaque appears at the entrance of Moody Church which reads, "Ever welcome to this house of God are the strangers and the poor."

G. S.

Imagine a large circle and in the center of it rays of light that spread out to the circumference. The light in the center is God; each of us is a ray. The closer the rays are to the center, the closer the rays are to one another. The closer we live to God, the closer we are bound to our neighbor.

FULTON J. SHEEN

Burdens

I have read in Plato & Cicero sayings that are wise and very beautiful; but I never read in either of them: "Come unto me all ye that labour and are heavy laden."

SAINT AUGUSTINE

I do not pray for a lighter load, but for a stronger back.

PHILLIPS BROOKS

God gave burdens, also shoulders.

YIDDISH PROVERB

None knowes the weight of another's burthen [sic].

GEORGE HERBERT

Business

The wayside of business is full of brilliant men who started out with a spurt and lacked the stamina to finish. Their places were taken by patient and unshowy plodders who never knew when to quit.

J. R. TODD

Business is like a wheelbarrow—it stands still until someone pushes it.

ANONYMOUS

Some see private enterprise as a predatory target to be shot, others as a cow to be milked, but few are those who see it as a sturdy horse pulling the wagon.

WINSTON CHURCHILL

A man's success in business today turns upon his power of getting people to believe he has something that they want.

GERALD STANLEY LEE

37

← C →

Capitalism

The inherent vice of capitalism is the unequal sharing of blessings; the inherent vice of socialism is the equal sharing of miseries.

WINSTON CHURCHILL

Capital as such is not evil; it is its wrong use that is evil.

MOHANDAS GANDHI

Labor is prior to, and independent of, capital. Capital is only the fruit of labor, and could never have existed if labor had not first existed. Labor is the superior of capital, and deserves much the higher consideration. Capital has its rights, which are as worthy of protection as any other rights.

ABRAHAM LINCOLN, Message to Congress, 3 December 1861

Labor in this country is independent and proud. It has not to ask the patronage of capital, but capital solicits the aid of labor.

DANIEL WEBSTER

Caring, Charity, Compassion

Care is a state in which something does matter; it is the source of human tenderness.

ROLLO MAY

It is our care for the helpless, our practice of lovingkindness that brands us in the eyes of many of our opponents. "Look!" they say, "How they love one another! Look how they are prepared to die for one another."

TERTULLIAN

> Lord, make me an instrument of Your peace.
> Where there is hatred let me sow love.
> Where there is injury, pardon.
> Where there is doubt, faith.
> Where there is despair, hope.
> Where there is darkness, light; and
> Where there is sadness, joy.

38

O Divine Master, grant that I may not so much
Seek to be consoled as to console;
To be understood as to understand;
To be loved as to love;
For it is in giving that we receive;
It is in pardoning that we are pardoned; and
It is in dying that we are born to eternal life.

SAINT FRANCIS OF ASSISI

I feel the capacity to care is the thing which gives life its deepest significance.

PABLO CASALS

The trouble is that too often charity begins and ends at home.

ANONYMOUS

In necessary things, unity; in doubtful things, liberty; in all things, charity.

RICHARD BAXTER

Biblical orthodoxy without compassion is surely the ugliest thing in the world.

FRANCIS SCHAEFFER

Perchance that I might learn what pity is,
That I might laugh at erring men no more.

MICHELANGELO

Taught by that Power that pities me,/I learn to pity them.

OLIVER GOLDSMITH

O God, show compassion on the wicked. The virtuous have already been blessed by Thee in being virtuous.

PERSIAN PRAYER

Charity gives itself rich; covetousness hoards itself poor.

PERSIAN PROVERB

Change

You cannot step twice into the same river, for other waters are continually flowing on.

HERACLITUS

Have you ever thought about the collapse of time? From the days of the Lord Jesus Christ until about 1830, man could not travel any faster than a horse. In 1960, a man went into space and traveled at a speed of 18,000 miles an hour. Look how far we have come in so short a time! Sometimes when I read the papers, I think we are trying to run the Space Age with horse-and-buggy moral and spiritual equipment. Technology, you see, has no morals; and with no moral restraints man will destroy himself ecologically, militarily, or in some other way. Only God can give a person moral restraints and spiritual strength. While our world is shaking and crumbling, we need to realize that one thing will never change, and that is God. He is the same today as He was ten million years ago, and He will be the same ten million years from today. We are like grasshoppers; we appear and hop around a bit on the earth and then we are gone.

BILLY GRAHAM

When you're through changing, you're through.

BRUCE BARTON

A truck driver told about the change Christ had made in his life, and I asked him to think of some specific way in which he was different. After a pause he said, "Well, when I find somebody tailgating my truck I no longer drive on the shoulder of the road to kick gravel on him."

BRUCE LARSON

The philosophers have only interpreted the world; the thing, however, is to change it.

KARL MARX

Character

During my eighty-seven years I have witnessed a whole succession of technological revolutions. But none of them has done away with the need for character in the individual or the ability to think.

BERNARD M. BARUCH

Integrity has no need of rules.

ALBERT CAMUS

The happiness of every country depends upon the character of its people, rather than the form of its government.

THOMAS CHANDLER HALIBURTON

When God measures man, He puts the tape around his heart—not his head.

Guideposts

Know thyself.

SOCRATES

Character is like the foundation of a house—it is below the surface.

ANONYMOUS

I am only one, but I *am* one. I can't do everything, but I *can* do something. And what I *can* do, that I ought to do. And what I *ought* to do, by the grace of God, I *shall* do.

EDWARD E. HALE

The most important thought I ever had was that of my individual responsibility to God.

DANIEL WEBSTER

I have conquered an empire but I have not been able to conquer myself.

PETER THE GREAT, A CZAR OF RUSSIA

The greatest ability is dependability.

BOB JONES, SR.

Envy is the enemy of honor.

LATIN PROVERB

If I omit practice one day, I notice it; if two days, my friends notice it; if three days, the public notices it.

ARTUR RUBINSTEIN

O Lord, thou givest us everything, at the price of an effort.

ANONYMOUS

The chains of habit are too weak to be felt until they are too strong to be broken.

SAMUEL JOHNSON

Those who can command themselves, command others.

WILLIAM HAZLITT

Nothing in excess.

IN THE TEMPLE AT DELPHI

A dear old Quaker lady, distinguished for her youthful look, was asked what she used to preserve her appearance. She replied sweetly, "I use for the lips, truth; for the voice, prayer; for the eyes, pity; for the hand, charity; for the figure, uprightness; and for the heart, love.

JERRY FLEISHMAN, *Ladies' Home Journal*

Character

Give me the boy who rouses when he is praised, who profits when he is encouraged and who cries when he is defeated. Such a boy will be fired by ambition; he will be stung by reproach, and animated by preference; never shall I apprehend any bad consequences from idleness in such a boy.

MARCUS FABIUS QUINTILIAN

People become house builders through building houses, harp players through playing the harp. We grow to be just by doing things which are just.

ARISTOTLE

Character is not made in a crisis—it is only exhibited.

ROBERT FREEMAN

Resolutions Concerning Myself

I will be joyful, that life may give me wings.
I will be courageous, that there shall be no binding fears.
I will be balanced, that neither work, nor play, nor rest, nor worship shall lose its proper share.
I will be self-reliant, that thoughts of failure shall not hold me back.
I will be self-controlled, that emotions shall not be dominant.
I will be intelligent, that straight thinking and knowledge shall direct all actions.
I will be healthy, that my body shall not fail to respond.
I will be clean in spirit, mind and action, that there shall be no shame.
I will be good-tempered, that annoyance shall not irritate.
I will be patient, that discouragement shall not seem final.
I will be persistent, that the will may carry through to completion.
I will be prepared, that emergency shall not find me in confusion.
Paul, the great apostle, who left a trail of gospel glory across the Gentile world wrote: "With the mind I *myself* serve the law of God" (Romans 7:25).
"I could wish that *myself* were accursed from Christ for my brethren, my kinsmen according to the flesh" (Romans 9:3).
"I have made *myself* servant unto all" (1 Corinthians 9:19).
"But I determined this with *myself*" (2 Corinthians 2:1).
"In all things I have kept *myself* from being burdensome unto you, and so will I keep *myself*" (2 Corinthians 11:9).

ROBERT G. LEE

Mr. Jefferson came into Congress in June, 1775, and brought with him a reputation for literature, science, and a happy talent of composition. Writings of his were handed about, remarkable for the peculiar felicity of expression. Though a silent member in Congress, he was so prompt, frank, explicit, and decisive upon committees and in conversation—not even Samuel Adams was more so—that he soon seized upon my heart.

JOHN ADAMS

How majestic is naturalness. I have never met a man whom I really considered a great man who was not always natural and simple. Affectation is inevitably the mark of one not sure of himself.

CHARLES G. DAWES

The hardest thing about any political campaign is how to win without proving that you are unworthy of winning.

ADLAI STEVENSON

Character is what you are in the dark.

D. L. MOODY

Character is always lost when a high ideal is sacrificed on the altar of conformity and popularity.

ANONYMOUS

Learn to say no; it will be of more use to you than to be able to read Latin.

CHARLES H. SPURGEON

Cheerfulness

Happiness is essentially a state of going somewhere wholeheartedly.

W. H. SHELDON

It is not fitting, when one is in God's service, to have a gloomy face or a chilling look.

SAINT FRANCIS OF ASSISI

Mirth is God's medicine. Everybody ought to bathe in it. Grim care, moroseness, anxiety—all this rust of life ought to be scoured off by the oil of mirth. It is better than emery. Every man ought to rub himself with it. A man without mirth is like a wagon without springs, in which everyone is caused disagreeably to jolt by every pebble over which it runs.

HENRY WARD BEECHER

O Holy Spirit, descend plentifully into my heart. Enlighten the dark corners of this neglected dwelling and scatter there Thy cheerful beams.

SAINT AUGUSTINE

Those who bring sunshine into the lives of others cannot keep it from themselves.

JAMES M. BARRIE

Children

Happiness adds and multiplies as we divide it with others.

A. NIELEN

Delicate humor is the crowning virtue of the saints.

EVELYN UNDERHILL

A happy family is but an earlier heaven.

JOHN BOWRING

People are always good company when they are doing what they really enjoy.

SAMUEL BUTLER

> The truest greatness lies in being kind,
> The truest wisdom in a happy mind.

ELLA WHEELER WILCOX

There is no danger of developing eyestrain from looking on the bright side of things.

ANONYMOUS

The Happiest Man

> Happy is he who by love's sweet song
> Is cheered today as he goes along.
> Happier is he who believes that tomorrow
> Will ease all pain and take away all sorrow.
> Happiest he who on earthly sod
> Has faith in himself, his friends, and God.
>
> Happiness depends, as Nature shows,
> Less on exterior things than most suppose.

WILLIAM COWPER

We have no more right to consume happiness without producing it than to consume wealth without producing it.

GEORGE BERNARD SHAW

To watch the corn grow, or the blossoms set; to draw hard breath over the ploughshare or spade; to read, to think, to love, to pray, are the things that make men happy.

JOHN RUSKIN

Children

Too many parents are not on spanking terms with their children.

ANONYMOUS

Men are generally more careful of the breed of their horses and dogs than of their children.

WILLIAM PENN

It is easiest to lead a child from five to ten years to a definite acceptance of Christ.

I rejoice in the work done by rescue missions, where we see the wrecks of manhood and womanhood changed into noble men and women. But this is not the work that produces the most satisfactory Christians. The younger we get a child to accept Christ and begin Christian training, the more beautiful the product.

The overwhelming majority in our churches today were converted before twenty-one years of age.

Whatever your church does, let it do its full duty by the children.

R. A. TORREY

> I saw tomorrow marching
> On little children's feet;
> Within their forms and faces read
> Her prophecy complete.
>
> I saw tomorrow look at me
> From little children's eyes;
> And thought how carefully we'd teach
> If we were really wise.

ANONYMOUS

If we had paid no more attention to our plants than we have to our children, we would now be living in a jungle of weeds.

LUTHER BURBANK

> Birds in their little nests agree;
> And 'tis a shameful sight,
> When children of one family
> Fall out, and chide, and fight.

ISAAC WATTS

Young people should be helped, sheltered, ignored, and clubbed if necessary.

AL CAPP

Children—The fruit of the seeds of all your finest hopes.

GLORIA GAITHER, *Rainbows Live at Easter*

It needs courage to let our children go, but we are trustees and stewards and have to hand them back to life—to God. As the old saying puts it: "What I gave I have." We have to love them and lose them.

ALFRED TORRIE

Christ

I have loved to hear my Lord spoken of, and wherever I have seen the print of His shoe in the earth, there have I coveted to put mine also.

JOHN BUNYAN

The Christian is not one who has gone all the way with Christ. None of us has. The Christian is one who has found the right road.

CHARLES L. ALLEN

When Jesus comes, the shadows depart.

INSCRIPTION

God speaks to me not through the thunder and the earthquake, nor through the ocean and the stars, but through the Son of Man, and speaks in a language adapted to my imperfect sight and hearing.

WILLIAM LYON PHELPS

Jesus, whose name is not so much written as ploughed into the history of this world.

RALPH WALDO EMERSON

The men who followed Him were unique in their generation. They turned the world upside down because their hearts had been turned right side up. The world has never been the same.

BILLY GRAHAM

The Lord has turned all our sunsets into sunrise.

CLEMENT OF ALEXANDRIA

Jesus promised His disciples three things: that they would be entirely fearless, absurdly happy, and that they would get into trouble.

W. RUSSELL MALTBY

Above all the grace and the gifts that Christ gives to his beloved is that of overcoming self.

SAINT FRANCIS OF ASSISI

The greatest thing about any civilization is the human person, and the greatest thing about this person is the possibility of his encounter with the person of Jesus Christ.

CHARLES MALIK

Association with the Lord can bring
To any life a dignity and grace,
And ever looking up to Him will give
The high, white look of Christ to any face.

GRACE NOLL CROWELL

I thank God for the honesty and virility of Jesus' religion which makes us face the facts and calls us to take a man's part in the real battle of life.

HENRY VAN DYKE

No one else holds or has held the place in the heart of the world which Jesus holds. Other gods have been as devoutly worshiped; no other man has been so devoutly loved.

JOHN KNOX

Here is the Truth in a little creed,
Enough for all the roads we go:
In Love is all the law we need,
In Christ is all the God we know.

EDWIN MARKHAM

Jesus Christ, the condescension of divinity, and the exaltation of humanity.

PHILLIPS BROOKS

We believe that the history of the world is but the history of His influence and that the center of the whole universe is the cross of Calvary.

ALEXANDER MACLAREN

In every pang that rends the heart
The Man of Sorrows has a part.

MICHAEL BRUCE

To become Christlike is the only thing in the whole world worth caring for, the thing before which every ambition of man is folly and all lower achievement vain.

HENRY DRUMMOND

By a Carpenter mankind was made, and only by that Carpenter can mankind be remade.

DESIDERIUS ERASMUS

Two thousand years ago there was One here on this earth who lived the grandest life that ever has been lived yet—a life that every thinking man, with deeper or shallower meaning, has agreed to call divine.

FREDERICK W. ROBERTSON

Christt

F

I am pretty sure that we err in treating these sayings as paradoxes. It would be nearer the truth to say that it is life itself which is paradoxical and that the sayings of Jesus are simply a recognition of that fact.

THOMAS TAYLOR

There is but one God, the Father, of whom are all things, and we in him; and one Lord Jesus Christ, by whom are all things, and we by him.

1 CORINTHIANS 8:6

F

Jesus never gained disciples under false pretenses. He never hid His scars, but rather declared, "Behold my hands and feet."

G. S.

F

Christ is the Bible's fullness, the Bible's center, the Bible's fascination. It is all about Jesus—in the Old Testament. The Old Testament conceals, infolds, promises, pictures, prophesies, localizes, symbolizes Christ. The New Testament reveals, unfolds, presents, produces, proclaims, universalizes and sacrifices Christ. Yes, the Old Testament and New Testament alike tell of Jesus, the great Fact of history, the great Force of history, the great Future of history. Of this book it can truly be said: "The Glory of God doth lighten it, and the Lamb is the Light thereof!" The name of Jesus, the Supreme Personality, the center of a world's desire, is on every page—in expression, or symbol, or prophecy, or psalm, or proverb. Take Jesus out of the Bible—and it is like taking calcium out of lime, carbon out of diamonds, truth out of history, matter out of physics, mind out of metaphysics, numbers out of mathematics, cause and effect out of philosophy. Through this book the name of Jesus, the Revealed, the Redeeming, the Risen, the Reigning, the Returning Lord, runs like a line of glimmering light. The thought of Jesus, the Desire of all nations, threads this great book like a crystal river winds it way through a continent.

ROBERT G. LEE

F

Alexander, Caesar, Charlemagne, and myself founded empires; but on what foundation did we rest the creations of our genius? Upon force. Jesus Christ founded an empire upon love; and at this hour millions of men would die for Him.

NAPOLEON BONAPARTE

Charles Lamb was once discussing the greatest literary characters of all time when the names of both William Shakespeare and Jesus Christ were mentioned. "The major difference between these two," said Charles Lamb, "is that if Shakespeare came into this room we would all stand in honor and respect. But if Jesus Christ were here, we would all humbly bow and worship Him."

F

G. S.

In his famous painting of Christ knocking at the door, artist Holman Hunt has purposely omitted from the door a knob or handle. Why? Because that is on the inside, and you, and you alone, can open the door to Jesus.

F

G. S.

Jesus is the God whom we can approach without pride and before whom we can humble ourselves without despair.

BLAISE PASCAL

F

Jesus whom I know as my Redeemer cannot be less than God!

ATHANASIUS

F

You should point to the whole man Jesus and say, "That is God."

MARTIN LUTHER

F

The most pressing question on the problem of faith is whether a man, as a civilized being . . . can believe in the divinity of the Son of God, Jesus Christ, for therein rests the whole of our faith.

FEODOR DOSTOEVSKI

F

Each eye can have its vision separately; but when we are looking at anything . . . our vision, which in itself is divided, joins up and unites in order to give itself as a whole to the object that is put before it.

JOHN CALVIN, on Christ's two natures

Christianity

[Christianity] provides a unified answer for the whole of life.

FRANCIS SCHAEFFER, *Escape from Reason*

Whatever makes men good Christians, makes them good citizens.

DANIEL WEBSTER

I have now disposed of all my property to my family. There is one thing more I wish I could give them, and that is the Christian religion.

PATRICK HENRY

Christianity, above all, has given a clear-cut answer to the demands of the human soul.

ANONYMOUS

Christianity

The test of Christian character should be that a man is a joy-bearing agent to the world.

HENRY WARD BEECHER

Most of us spend the first six days of each week sowing wild oats; then we go to church on Sunday and pray for a crop failure.

FRED ALLEN

A Christian is the combination of Christ and you.

G. S.

Salvation is an *offer,* not a demand.

G. S.

The difference between heart belief and head belief is the difference between salvation and damnation.

G. S.

God doesn't have any grandchildren.

E. STANLEY JONES

If we take the first three words of John 1:13 and the last two words, we have the phrase, "which were born . . . of God." That's a good definition. A Christian is one who is born of God.

G. S.

If Jesus Christ be God and died for me, then no sacrifice can be too great for me to make for Him.

C. T. STUDD

From history's pages we learn of a cowardly young soldier in the army of Alexander the Great. Whenever the battle grew fierce, the young soldier would yield. The general's pride was cut because this timid soldier also bore the name Alexander. One day Alexander the Great sternly addressed him and said, "Stop being a coward or drop that good name."

The call to all Christians is the same today. May we faithfully live up to all the name Christian implies. "Lord, what will You have me to do?"

G. S.

It is only when all our Christian ancestors are allowed to become our contemporaries that the real splendor of the Christian faith and the Christian life begins to dawn upon us.

LYNN HAROLD HOUGH

The Christianity which is shared is the Christianity which is convincing.
LYNN HAROLD HOUGH

Christian Living

The great difference between present-day Christianity and that of which
we read in these letters is that to us it is primarily a performance, to
them it was a real experience . . . To these men it is quite plainly
the invasion of their lives by a new quality of life altogether. They do
not hesitate to describe this as Christ "living in" them.
J. B. PHILLIPS, *Letters to Young Churches*

If you make a great deal of Christ, He will make a great deal of you;
but if you make but little of Christ, Christ will make but little of you.
R. A. TORREY

It is a bad world, Donatus, an incredibly bad world. But I have discovered in the midst of it a quiet and good people who have learned the
great secret of life. They have found a joy and wisdom which is a
thousand times better than any of the pleasures of our sinful life. They
are despised and persecuted, but they care not. They are masters of
their souls. They have overcome the world. These people, Donatus,
are Christians . . . and I am one of them.
SAINT CYPRIAN

A good example is far better than a good precept.
D. L. MOODY

The question is not "How much may I indulge in and still be saved?"
God forbid! I must rather ask, "What about Christ's will and the exam-
ple I set for my fellow Christians?"
ROBERT COOK

We are set apart unto God, in one sense of the term, the moment we
receive Christ, for we are bought with the price of His blood. Some
day we shall be set apart from sin forever, by being taken to glory
with Christ. But 1 Thessalonians 4:3 speaks of our present responsibility.
God wants us to take our stand against every form of known sin, and
to maintain that stand consistently.
S. MAXWELL CODER, *God's Will for Your Life*

A rule I have had for years is: to treat the Lord Jesus Christ as a
personal friend. His is not a creed, a mere empty doctrine, but it is
He Himself we have.
D. L. MOODY

Christian Living

Never think that Jesus commanded a trifle, nor dare to trifle with anything He has commanded.

D. L. MOODY

There are many of us that are willing to do great things for the Lord, but few of us are willing to do little things.

D. L. MOODY

Dead things cannot grow. Before there can be spiritual growth, there must be spiritual life.

G. S.

No book will make you grow like the Bible.

G. S.

Where one man reads the Bible, a hundred read you and me.

D. L. MOODY

I have had more trouble with myself than with any other man.

D. L. MOODY

A young girl was asked: "Whose preaching brought you to Christ?"
"It wasn't anybody's preaching; it was Aunt Mary's practicing," she replied. The beginning of anxiety is the end of faith, and the beginning of true faith is the end of anxiety.

GEORGE MUELLER

Periods of staleness in the life are not inevitable but they are common. He is a rare Christian who has not experienced times of spiritual dullness. Sometimes our trouble is not moral but physical. The Christian who gets tired in the work of the Lord and stays tired without relief beyond a reasonable time will go stale.
We can keep from going stale by getting proper rest, by practising complete candour in prayer, by introducing variety into our lives, by heeding God's call to move onward and by exercising quiet faith always.

A. W. TOZER

Seven Indispensable Things
1. Without shedding of blood is no remission (Hebrews 9:22).
2. Without faith it is impossible to please God (Hebrews 11:6).
3. Without works faith is dead (James 2:26).
4. Without holiness no man shall see the Lord (Hebrews 12:14).
5. Without love 1 am nothing (1 Corinthians 13:2).

6. Without chastisement ye are not sons (Hebrews 12:8).
7. Without me ye can do nothing (John 15:5).

ROBERT G. LEE

Much of our drive to build separate but equal facilities (for use by evangelicals) is the desire to forget the war we are in. We can't forget it very well with drunks stumbling over our feet, so we go to "Christian" hotels. Non-Christians upset us, not so much because they curse and carouse (we have worse sins of our own), but because they remind us of evaded responsibility. From time to time this guilt gets intolerable (down deep we do love Christ), so we mount our chrome-trimmed chargers, and like knights of old, we gallop out of our castles in search of the dragon. We usually find him in jail, or a skid-row mission or other captive audience (even a fraternity) where we can dump our gospel load and get out again with a minimum of personal involvement or time wasted. Then back to the castle we tear, mission completed. With the draw-bridge slammed shut behind us, we sing "Safe Am I" and settle down again. Often our castle is psychological, but none the less real.

JOHN GOODWIN

The Two Natures

An American Indian was giving his testimony in a gathering of Christian members of his tribe. He told of his conversion and of how in the beginning he felt as though he would never sin again; he was so happy in knowing His Saviour. But, he explained, as time went on he became conscious of an inward conflict, which he described somewhat as follows:

"It seems, my brothers, that I have two dogs fighting in my heart: one is a very good dog, a beautiful white dog, and he is always watching out for my best interests. The other is a very bad dog, a black dog, who is always trying to destroy the things that I want to see built up. These dogs give me a lot of trouble because they are alway quarreling and fighting with each other."

One of his hearers looked up and asked laconically, "Which one wins?" The other instantly replied, "Whichever one I say 'Sic 'im' to."

Surely there could not be a more apt illustration of the two natures in the believer. "If we walk in the Spirit we shall not fulfil the lusts of the flesh." But if we pander to the flesh, we will be certain to go down in defeat.

H. A. IRONSIDE

The gradual disappearance of the idea and feeling of majesty from the Church is a sign and a portent. Our God has now become our servant to wait on our will. "The Lord is *my shepherd*," we say, instead of "*The Lord* is my shepherd," and the difference is as wide as the world.

A. W. TOZER

Christianity is either relevant all the time or useless anytime. It is not just a phase of life; it is life itself.

RICHARD HALVERSON

The Christian is a person who makes it easy for others to believe in God.

ROBERT M. MCCHEYNE

Regardless of the day or the hour; whether in seeming good times or bad, the Christian lives in the world for the good of the world and for the sake of the world.

HAROLD LINDSELL, *A Christian Philosophy of Missions*

What the world requires of the Christians is that they should continue to be Christians.

ALBERT CAMUS

We need to grow because growth is *God's plan*. We must bend or be broken.

G. S.

Salvation is just the beginning of what God wants to do for you.

G. S.

Faith makes a Christian.
Life proves a Christian.
Trial confirms a Christian.
Death crowns a Christian.

ANONYMOUS

Father Abraham, whom have you in heaven? Any Episcopalians? No! Any Presbyterians? No! Any Independents or Methodist? No, no, no! Whom have you there? We don't know those names here. All who are here are Christians. . . . Oh, is this the case? Then God help us to forget party names and to become Christians in deed and truth.

GEORGE WHITEFIELD

Ivan Albright painted a picture now hanging in the Chicago Art Institute of an eight-foot door shaped like the lid of an old casket. The door is scarred and bruised, supposedly by the difficult experiences of life. A funeral wreath of wilted flowers hangs on the closed door. The colors are dull and somber. The painting is entitled, "That Which I Should Have Done I Did Not Do." What a sad thought!

G. S.

Christmas

Christmas is not a myth, not a tradition, not a dream. It is a glorious reality. It is a time of joy. Bethlehem's manger crib became the link that bound a lost world to a loving God. From that manger came a Man who not only taught us a new way of life, but brought us into a new relationship with our Creator. Christmas means that God is interested in the affairs of people; that God loves us so much that He was willing to give His Son.

BILLY GRAHAM

For to us a child is born, to us a son is given. . . . And he will be called Wonderful Counselor, Mighty God, Everlasting Father, Prince of Peace.

ISAIAH 9:6, NIV

Cold on his cradle the dew drops are shining,/Low lies his head with the beasts of the stall.

REGINALD HEBER

Merson's painting entitled "No Room" depicts a scene of deep shadows, cold stars, a lonely street, and howling dogs, as a hard-hearted innkeeper closes the door and turns Mary away, saying, "No room here."

Yes, in the lowliest place in the world—a barn—the sinless King was born. For the Son of God, the Prince of Peace, there was no room!

G. S.

In his book entitled *When Iron Gates Yield,* author Geoffrey Bull tells of spending Christmas Eve in a Tibetan inn, en route to a communist prison camp. As he walked into the stable to feed the horses and mules, he says, "My boots squashed in the manure and straw. The horrible smell of the animals was nauseating, and I thought, 'to think Christ came all the way from heaven to some wretched, eastern stable, and what is more, He came for me.' "

G. S.

No fact in history is so well attested as is the birth, life, and death of Jesus Christ. *Encyclopaedia Britannica* devotes more words to Jesus than to Aristotle, Cicero, Julius Caesar, or the great Napoleon. No life has been so carefully examined, so carefully noted. No life has reached down so many centuries with so great an impact on so many millions of people.

fair

G. S.

I imagine the wise men were asked, "Well, why do you want to take this foolish and dangerous trip? Why are you going to all this trouble?" "Why?" the wise men must have replied. "Because we have heard a story from Scripture; we have seen the star in the sky; and we have felt a stirring in our souls."

Like Abraham of old, the wise men went out, not knowing whither they went. And wise men of every generation have done the same. William Carey, an English shoemaker, read our Lord's Great Commission. He realized the responsibility of taking the Gospel to every creature. In the face of severe opposition and ridicule, he traveled to that far-off land of India and labored seven years before he saw even one soul won to Christ. He worked relentlessly and translated the Bible into several languages. And he became known as the "father of modern missions."

David Livingstone demonstrated the same venture of faith as he pioneered with the Gospel message throughout the continent of Africa. C. T. Studd, an all-star cricketer from Cambridge, England, forsook fame and fortune and poured out his life in missionary work. He, too, traveled by faith. When Jim Elliot and four other men were murdered by the Auca Indians, some were critical of their attempts to penetrate that savage people with the Gospel. "What a waste," some people cry. "How foolish to throw your life away for nothing." But when the book of God is finally opened, all of these will be listed as wise men, men who ventured forth in faith.

Good 12-24-89

G. S.

God walked down the stairs of heaven with a Baby in his arms.

PAUL SCHERER

> O Father, may that Holy star
> Grow every year more bright,
> And send its glorious beams afar
> To fill the world with light.

WILLIAM CULLEN BRYANT

> In the pure soul, although it sing or pray,
> The Christ is born anew from day to day;
> The life that knoweth Him shall bide apart
> And keep eternal Christmas in the heart.

ELIZABETH STUART PHELPS

The purpose and cause of the incarnation was that He might illuminate the world by His wisdom and excite it to the love of Himself.

PETER ABÉLARD

Good

Christ was born in the first century, yet He belongs to all centuries. He was born a Jew, yet He belongs to all races. He was born in Bethlehem, yet He belongs to all countries.   *12-24-89*

GEORGE W. TRUETT

fait   12-24-89

> Whatever else be lost among the years,
> Let us keep Christmas still a shining thing:
> Whatever doubts assail us, or what fears,
> Let us hold close one day, remembering
> Its poignant meaning for the hearts of men.
> Let us get back our childlike faith again.

GRACE NOLL CROWELL, From *Let Us Keep Christmas*

fait

Christmas waves a magic wand over this world, and behold, everything is softer and more beautiful.

NORMAN VINCENT PEALE

He who has not Christmas in his heart will never find it under a tree.

ROY L. SMITH

Church

The Church is not a gallery for the exhibition of eminent Christians, but a school for the education of imperfect ones.

HENRY WARD BEECHER

Though the church has many critics, it has no rivals.

ANONYMOUS

The Bible knows nothing of solitary religion.

JOHN WESLEY

Church attendance is as vital to a disciple as a transfusion of rich, healthy blood to a sick man.

D. L. MOODY

[The local church is] the outcrop of the church universal.

P. T. FORSYTH

One day the telephone rang in the Rector's office of the Washington church which President Franklin Roosevelt attended. An eager voice inquired, "Tell me, do you expect the President to be in church this Sunday?"

"That," the Rector explained patiently, "I cannot promise. But we expect God to be there, and we fancy that will be incentive enough for a reasonably large attendance."

JOHN T. WATSON

The Church cannot be content to live in its stained-glass house and throw stones through the picture window of modern culture.

ROBERT MCAFEE BROWN

People with problems need the Church just like sick people need a hospital.

G. S.

One of the problems of the Church is that it is made up of people like you and me. The Church is a *divine institution,* founded by Jesus, but it is also a *human institution.* It is not a hothouse operating under ideal conditions.

G. S.

One hundred religious persons knit into a unity by careful organization do not constitute a church any more than eleven dead men make a football team. The first requisite is life, always.

A. W. TOZER

The greatest hindrances to the evangelization of the world are those within the church.

JOHN R. MOTT

A languid church breeds unbelief as surely as a decaying oak fungus. In a condition of depressed vitality, the seeds of disease, which a full vigour would shake off, are fatal. Raise the temperature, and you kill the insect germs.

ALEXANDER MACLAREN

Wherever we find the Word of God surely preached and heard, and the sacraments administered according to the institution of Christ, there, it is not to be doubted, is a church of God.

JOHN CALVIN, *The Institutes*

The (Early) Church was not an organization merely, not a movement, but a walking incarnation of spiritual energy. The Church began in power, moved in power and moved just as long as she had power.

When she no longer had power she dug in for safety and sought to conserve her gains. But her blessings were like the manna: when they tried to keep it overnight it bred worms and stank. So we have had monasticism, scholasticism, institutionalism; and they have all been indicative of the same thing: absence of spiritual power. In Church history, every return to New Testament power has marked a new advance somewhere, and every diminution of power has seen the rise of some new mechanism for conservation and defence. If this analysis is reasonably correct, then we are today in a state of very low spiritual energy.

A. W. TOZER

The difference between listening to a radio sermon and going to church . . . is almost like the difference between calling your girl on the phone and spending an evening with her.

Moody Monthly

The church is so subnormal that if it ever got back to the New Testament normal it would seem to people to be abnormal.

VANCE HAVNER

The Christian church is the only society in the world in which membership is based upon the qualification that the candidate shall be unworthy of membership.

CHARLES C. MORRISON

You can have the largest church auditorium, the biggest Sunday School, and run up a steeple on the church so high that it interferes with astronauts circling the earth, but the angels in heaven won't give a holy grunt until some old sinner comes down the aisle and gets right with Jesus.

BOB HARRINGTON

In the 1880s the nation's best-known infidel, Robert Ingersoll, announced that "the churches are dying out all over the land." Charles McCabe of the Methodist Church Extension Society replied by telegram:

Dear Robert: All hail the power of Jesus' name—we are building more than one Methodist church for every day in the year, and propose to make it two a day!

G. S.

The church exists to train its members through the practice of the presence of God to be servants of others, to the end that Christlikeness may become common property.

WILLIAM ADAMS BROWN

The Christian church is a society of sinners. It is the only society in the world, membership in which is based upon the single qualification that the candidate shall be unworthy of membership.

CHARLES C. MORRISON

An instinctive taste teaches men to build their churches with spire steeples which point as with a silent finger to the sky and stars.

SAMUEL T. COLERIDGE

All is holy where devotion kneels.

OLIVER WENDELL HOLMES, SR.

Cities

In his work *The Meaning of the City* (Wm. B. Eerdmans, 1970), the French social critic and commentator, Jacques Ellul, points out that the first biblically recorded cities were founded by men who rejected God. They were the products of self-will and self-ambition.

But Ellul goes on to acknowledge, "Our task is therefore to represent Him [God] in the heart of the city."

G. S.

It is significant that when our Lord, in His earthly ministry, sent out the twelve and later the seventy, He sent them to cities. And in a prophetic footnote, looking down to the end of the age, He added, "Ye shall not have gone over the cities of Israel, till the Son of man be come" (Matt. 10:23).

G. S.

As we follow the expansion of the first-century church, we see how it follows the contours of the urbanized Roman empire. This church faced mountainous problems. But its members put their complete confidence in God. "God is able!" was their password into the very strongholds of paganism.

G. S.

Either these [unsaved] people are to be evangelized, or the leaven of communism and infidelity will assume such enormous proportions that it will break out in a reign of terror such as this country has never known.

D. L. MOODY

I have never felt salvation in nature. I love cities above all.

MICHELANGELO

We will neglect our cities to our peril, for in neglecting them we neglect the nation.

JOHN F. KENNEDY, Message to Congress, 30 January 1962

There was never an hour when the opportunities of the church were what they are at this moment. There never was a moment since Calvary when the city cried for the help of Christians as it is crying now. The heart of the modern metropolis has been largely abandoned by the modern churches and the new theologians; and these great centers—threatening to become the black holes of our cities—have been flung at our feet as our special charges. Evangelical ministers and evangelistic churches will either shine there or darkness will reign; we will either be the salt to the city, or corruption and decay are its destiny. If we put Christ upon the throne of our affections, if we make His church the medium of our endeavors, if we tithe our time and tithe our income, we will conquer. Thousands will yet throng the courts of the Lord, the walls of His church will be compelled to widen by their incoming, and into every dark spot of the city we will send our young men and maidens, carrying the torchlight of life, and our mission stations will become the lighthouses for the storm-tossed of every region, and hospitals for those suffering from moral hurts, yea, homes into which Christ shall walk, and with His voice raise the dead.

WILLIAM B. RILEY

The city may have started with Cain, but it will climax with Christ. We need to keep in mind that the destiny of the redeemed is a city.

G. S.

Man's course begins in a garden, but it ends in a city.

ALEXANDER MACLAREN

Protestantism has somehow inherited a false perspective which says, "God made the country; man made the city." Even the names of many churches bear this out: Pleasantdale Community Church, Brookside Baptist, Shady Rest Presbyterian, Mountainside Methodist. Sometimes we get so restful we give the impression of a cemetery! We smile and nod and avoid the closeness within our fellowship that discloses flaws and problems and conflicts. The appearance from the outside may very well be one of living in a trance, a dream world where life is unreal.

G. S.

I like the cadence of the jackhammer. I like the sight of a huge crane hoisting steel beams into place. I like the flow of concrete, the clacking of a million heels on finished pavement. I like the feel of sweat, of

61

tears, and flesh. Here is action; here is life. In the crush of multitudes, the power of the living Jesus can still be sensed. Let us not limit our spiritual experience to the Grand Canyon.

G. S.

Why should we minister in the city centers? The churches of the New Testament set the example.

The apostles concentrated their efforts in the throbbing cities of their day. The ministries in those metropolitan areas were life-and-death struggles. The environment was not easy or compatible with the revolutionary new values introduced by the disciples of Christ.

Ephesus, located at the mouth of the Cayster River, was notorious for its luxury and moral looseness. Diana was the chief object of worship, and opposition to the gospel was fierce.

Corinth, with a population of 600,000, was the largest city in Greece. It was an important seaport, a garrison town, and a strategic highway junction. The Corinthians were particularly prone to sexual promiscuity and enjoyed dragging each other off to court over any little difference of opinion. The city seethed with a mass of merchants, philosophers, ex-soldiers, and peddlers of vice.

Rome, metropolitan center of the Roman empire, was riddled with perversions, court plots, and murders. Its prosperity and immorality eventually brought about its downfall.

In these centers of life, Christianity took root and flowered throughout the known world. The disciples went neither to the fringes of the towns nor to the tents of the migrants. They saw no future for the gospel in isolation.

G. S.

Scripture makes it clear that God's compassion reaches out to the great centers of population.

Remember how God sent Lot and the angels to warn the people of Sodom? Then, God's concern was reflected in the burden of Abraham as he interceded with God for Sodom.

Again we see God's compassion for another great city when He sent Jonah to Nineveh, and in the end spared the city after its repentance. We sense something of God's great pity when He asked Jonah, "And should not I have compassion on Nineveh, the great city in which there are more than 120,000 people who do not know the difference between their right and left hand . . .?" (Jonah 4:11).

G. S.

Civil Disobedience

Guidelines for Civil Disobedience

1. Disobedience, if necessary, must be without violence. To be violent and to hurt someone is contrary to the teaching of the Word of God.

2. The law being disobeyed must be clearly contrary to the Word of God. This was Peter and John's situation. They were commanded by their Lord to bear witness to the things they had seen and heard. The command of the authorities to be silent was clearly in conflict with God's word to them.

3. In general, disobedience must not be against civil rulers, because these rulers (both good ones and bad ones) fall within God's permissive and directive will.

Peter and Paul lived and served while wicked Nero held sway, yet both commanded believers to be submissive to the government. The direct teaching of Scripture requires civil obedience (Rom. 13:1–7; 1 Pet. 2:13–17).

Henry David Thoreau is often referred to by present-day dissenters. Thoreau stated, "It is not desirable to cultivate a respect for the law, so much as for the right." But, we must ask, who decides what is right? The government may make a mistake, but so may the people. If seven people disobey, that is one thing. But if seven million disobey, that is anarchy.

4. Christians must be willing to bear the consequences that disobedience to civil authority involves. Peter and John, and Paul, too, were so committed to Jesus Christ that they were willing to suffer ridicule, jail, and death to get out the gospel.

The Scriptures imply that ordinarily the commandments of God and the commandments of men should not be in conflict. But it also establishes that God is the Lord of the Christian's conscience. However, for the most part, *obedience is in* and *disobedience is out.* If we are forbidden to bear witness to salvation in Christ, we must disobey that command. If we are ordered by authorities to do evil in the sight of God, we must disobey.

But there is so much which can be done without disobeying! We must ask, what is the church willing to do today to get out the gospel? Can we be complacent when the world is in such great need?

G. S.

The workers have nothing to lose but their chains. They have a world to win. Workers of the world, unite!

KARL MARX

Civilization, Comfort

Have respect for authority. Jesus Christ was under the authority of His Father in heaven. . . . He lived for one thing: to fulfill the will of the Father. Everyone is subject to some kind of authority. There is one chain of command and the ultimate authority is God at the top. What is the authority in your life? Is it your selfishness? Your lust? Your greed? Or have you turned it all over to God and said, "Lord, You are going to be my authority"? . . . When you are under authority, you are then able to assume authority.

BILLY GRAHAM

Civilization

Civilization is a movement and not a condition, a voyage and not a harbor.

ARNOLD TOYNBEE

Civilization is a stream with banks. The stream is sometimes filled with blood from people killing, stealing, shouting and doing things historians usually record, while on the banks, unnoticed, people build homes, make love, raise children, sing songs, write poetry and even whittle statues. The story of civilization is the story of what happened on the banks. Historians are pessimists because they ignore the banks for the river.

WILL AND ARIEL DURANT

To be able to fill leisure intelligently is the last product of civilization.

ARNOLD TOYNBEE

Comfort

God does not comfort us to make us comfortable but to make us comforters. 8-12-90

J. H. JOWETT

So, amid the conflict, whether great or small,
Do not be discouraged, God is over all;
Count your many blessings, angels will attend,
Help and comfort give you to your journey's end.

JOHNSON OATMAN, JR.

God often comforts us, not by changing the circumstances of our lives, but by changing our attitude toward them.

S. H. B. MASTERMAN

And He that doth the ravens feed,
Yea, providently caters for the sparrow,
Be comfort to my age!

WILLIAM SHAKESPEARE, *As You Like It*

Commitment, Committees, Communication

Commitment

Take my life, and let it be/Consecrated, Lord, to thee.

FRANCES RIDLEY HAVERGAL

God calls us to be 100 percent committed. His resources can make us willing to take a stand with our friends and neighbors against abortion. We can write our senators and oppose laws legalizing pornography and homosexuality. Ours need not be the day of the placid pulpit and the comfortable pew. Dante said, "The hottest place in hell is reserved for those who, in times of crisis, preserved their neutrality."

G. S.

What an opportunity to realize that our generation, which lauds the excellence of its scientific accomplishments, perceives God—and the validity of His existence—by our actions! One basis of our judgment before God is the quality of life we live: "The fire will test each one's work, of what sort it is" (1 Cor. 3:13).

G. S.

Men must have goals which, in their eyes, merit effort and commitment; and they must believe that their efforts will win them self-respect and the respect of others.

JOHN W. GARDNER

Committees

One of the reasons why the Ten Commandments are so short and to the point is the fact they were given direct and did not come out of committees.

H. G. HUTCHESON

Committee—a group of men who keep minutes and waste hours.

MILTON BERLE

A committee is a thing which takes a week to do what one good man can do in an hour.

ELBERT HUBBARD

A camel looks like a horse that was planned by a committee.

ANONYMOUS

Communication

If you cry "Forward" you must be sure to make clear the direction in which to go. Don't you see that if you fail to do that and simply call out the word to a monk and a revolutionary, they will go in precisely opposite directions?

ANTON CHEKHOV

It must be that evil communications corrupt good dispositions.

MENANDER

Good, the more communicated, more abundant grows.

JOHN MILTON

Genuine poetry can communicate before it is understood.

T. S. ELIOT

Communication is depositing a part of yourself in another person.

ANONYMOUS

Pure truth cannot be assimilated by the crowd; it must be communicated by contagion.

HENRI-FRÉDÉRIC AMIEL

Community (or Society)

We need society, and we need solitude also, as we need summer and winter, day and night, exercise and rest.

PHILIP GILBERT HAMERTON, *The Intellectual Life*

Every man is like the company he is wont to keep.

EURIPIDES

Sociale animal est—[Man] is a social animal.

SENECA

Compromise

A new Decalogue has been adopted by the neo-Christians of our day, the first words of which reads "Thou shalt not disagree," and a new set of Beatitudes too, which begins "Blessed are they that tolerate everything, for they shall not be made accountable for anything." It is now the accepted thing to talk over religious differences in public with the understanding that no one will try to convert another or point out errors in his belief. Imagine Moses agreeing to take part in a panel discussion with Israel over the golden calf; or Elijah engaging in a gentlemanly dialogue with the prophets of Baal. Or try to picture our Lord Jesus Christ seeking a meeting of minds with the Pharisees to iron out differences.

The blessing of God is promised to the peacemaker, but the religious negotiator had better watch his step. Darkness and light can never be brought together by talk. Some things are not negotiable.

A. W. TOZER

Some Christians who once championed sound doctrine beat a retreat once in a while and from stratospheric heights announce that they will not "stoop to controversy." When a man contends for the faith in New Testament style, he does not stoop! . . . Contending for the faith is not easy. It is not pleasant business. It has many perils. It is a thankless job, and it is highly unpopular in this age of moral fogs and spiritual twilights. This is a day of diplomats, not prophets. It is nicer to be an appeaser than an opposer. It is the day of Erasmus, not Luther; of Gamaliel, not Paul.

VANCE HAVNER

In the year 1939, the Spanish Civil War was almost over. Just outside Madrid, the rebel General Mola prepared to attack. Someone asked which of his four columns would be the first to enter the besieged city. To the inquirer's surprise, he replied, "The fifth." General Mola was simply saying that his most important forces were the band of rebel sympathizers already in the city, already fighting for him behind the loyalist lines.

General Mola's remark coined the term "fifth column," a synonym for traitorous forces. During World War II, it was a fifth column in Norway that brought about that country's collapse. Norway's leader, Vidkun Quisling, became a puppet premier of Adolf Hitler's German Nazis, and when, at the end of the way, Norway was freed, Quisling was put to death for treason.

Betrayal is an ugly business and yet very common in history. Down through the centuries, even the church has had its Quislings.

G. S.

The instances are exceedingly rare of man immediately passing over a clear marked line from virtue into declared vice and corruption. There are middle tints and shades between the two extremes; there is something uncertain on the confines of the two empires which they must pass through, and which renders the change easy and imperceptible.

EDMUND BURKE

The greatness of Christianity did not arise from attempts to make compromises with those philosophical opinions of the ancient world which had some resemblance to its own doctrine, but from the unrelenting and fanatical proclamation and defense of its own teaching.

ADOLF HITLER, *Mein Kampf*

Confession

"Blessed art thou, Simon Barjonas." Yes, He blessed him right there because he confessed Him to be the Son of God. He was hungry to get someone to confess Him. Then let everyone take his stand on the side of the Lord; confess Him here on earth, and He will confess you when you get to heaven. He will look around upon you with pride, because you stood up for Him here. If you want the blessing of heaven, and the peace that passeth all understanding, you must be ready and willing to confess Him. Do you know how Peter fell? He fell as a thousand people fall, because they don't confess the Son of God.

D. L. MOODY

Confession of our faults is the next thing to innocence.

PUBLIUS SYRUS

There is no refuge from confession but suicide; and suicide is confession.

DANIEL WEBSTER

We confess to little faults only to persuade ourselves that we have no great ones.

FRANÇOIS, DUC DE LA ROCHEFOUCAULD

Confidence

Supreme confidence in one's ability to "deliver" in times of crisis or need is a quality much to be desired. It is possessed by all too few of us. Our tendency is to yield, to retreat, or to crack up when the going gets too tough. Each of us has his or her "breaking point," dependent upon the degree of courage and faith and resolution . . . built into our lives. Where one person gives up, another person may be just beginning. If you are not going forward, you are going backward. Nothing stands still in life. You must keep on putting forth the best efforts of which you are capable to maintain the position you have gained.

HAROLD SHERMAN

Self-confidence is the first requisite to great undertakings.

SAMUEL JOHNSON

God knows best; he hasn't arranged your anatomy so as to make it easy for you to pat yourself on the back.

ANONYMOUS

It's fine to believe in ourselves, but we mustn't be too easily convinced.
Better Homes and Gardens

Conflict

I believe in getting into hot water. I think it keeps you clean.

G. K. CHESTERTON

The best armor is to keep out of range.

ITALIAN PROVERB

A quarrel is quickly settled when deserted by one party; there is no battle unless there be two.

SENECA

The key to solving conflict is found in affirming God's will. When we do this, our desires become God's desires, and then His power becomes our power.

G. S.

> Let dogs delight to bark and bite,
> For God hath made them so;
> Let bears and lions growl and fight,
> For 'tis their nature too. . . .
> But children you should never let
> Such angry passions rise,
> Your little hands were never made
> To tear each other's eyes.

ISAAC WATTS

Conscience

Two things fill me with constantly increasing admiration and awe, the longer and more earnestly I reflect on them: the starry heavens without and the moral law within.

IMMANUEL KANT

A seared conscience is one whose warning voice has been suppressed and perverted habitually, so that eventually instead of serving as a guide, it only confirms the person in his premeditatedly evil course.

ROBERT J. LITTLE

Though the dungeon, the scourge, and the executioner be absent, the guilty mind can apply the goad and scorch with blows.

LUCRETIUS

What is conscience? God put within each one of us something that cries aloud against us, whenever we do that which we know to be wrong. Conscience is the detective that watches the direction of our steps and decries every conscious transgression. Conscience is a vigilant eye before which each imagination, thought, and act is held up for either censure or approval. I believe there is no greater argument for the existence of God in the world today than conscience. There is no greater proof of the existence of a moral law and lawgiver in the universe than this little light of the soul. It is God's voice to the inner man. Conscience is our wisest counselor and teacher, our most faithful and most patient friend.

BILLY GRAHAM

A man's conscience, like a warning line on the highway, tells him what he shouldn't do—but it does not keep him from doing it.

FRANK A. CLARK

Consecration

The mark of a saint is not perfection, but consecration. A saint is not a man without faults, but a man who has given himself without reserve to God.

BROOKE FOSS WESTCOTT

The greatness of a man's power is the measure of his surrender.

WILLIAM BOOTH

God is not so much concerned with your ability as with your availability.

The Bible Friend

I go out to preach with two propositions in mind. First, everyone ought to give his life to Christ. Second, whether or not anyone gives Him his life, I will give Him mine.

JONATHAN EDWARDS

Contentment

Being "contented" ought to mean in English, as it does in French, being pleased. Being content with an attic ought not to mean being unable to move from it and resigned to living in it: it ought to mean appreciating all there is in such a position.

G. K. CHESTERTON

True contentment is the power of getting out of any situation all that there is in it.

G. K. CHESTERTON

What's the use of worrying?
It never was worthwhile,
So, pack up your troubles in your old kit-bag
And smile, smile, smile.

GEORGE ASAF (GEORGE H. POWELL)

Is your place a small place?
Tend it with care!
He set you there.

Is your place a large place?
Guard it with care!
He set you there.

Whatever your place, it is
Not yours alone, but His,
Who set you there.

JOHN OXENHAM

"I have learned in whatsoever state I am, therewith to be content"
(Phil. 4:11).

Christ is enough to satisfy the hearts of all who confide in Him
and who leave everything in His hands. Such need never be cast down
by seeming misfortunes.

A Christian asked another how he was getting along. Dolefully his
friend replied, "Oh, fairly well, under the circumstances."

"I am sorry," exclaimed the other, "that you are under the circumstances. The Lord would have us living above all circumstances, where
He Himself can satisfy our hearts and meet our every need for time
and eternity."

H. A. IRONSIDE

If we noticed little pleasures,
    As we notice little pains—
If we quite forgot our losses
    And remembered all our gains.

If we looked for people's virtues
    And their faults refused to see.
What a comfortable, happy, cheerful place
    This world would be!

Forbes Magazine of Business

Be happy with what you have and are,
be generous with both,
and you won't have to hunt for happiness.

WILLIAM E. GLADSTONE

All the misfortunes of men spring from their not knowing how to
live quietly at home in their own rooms.

BLAISE PASCAL

Contrition

During a long life I have had to eat my own words many times, and
I have found it a very nourishing diet.

WINSTON CHURCHILL

> Four things which are not in thy treasury,
> I lay before thee, Lord, with this petition:—
>   My nothingness, my wants,
>   My sins, and my contrition.
>
> ROBERT SOUTHEY

> If you bethink yourself of any crime
> Unreconcil'd as yet to heaven and grace,
> Solicit for it straight.
>
> WILLIAM SHAKESPEARE, *Othello*

> Man, wretched man, whene'er he stoops to sin,
> Feels, with the act, a strong remorse within.
>
> JUVENAL

To err is human; but contrition felt for the crime distinguishes the virtuous from the wicked.

> VITTORIO ALFIERI

Countenance

A solemn, unsmiling, sanctimonious old iceberg that looked like he was waiting for a vacancy in the Trinity.

> MARK TWAIN

One of Abraham Lincoln's advisers urgently recommended a certain man for a post in the President's cabinet. When Lincoln declined to follow the suggestion, he was asked to give his reasons.

"I don't like the man's face," the President explained.

"But the poor man isn't responsible for his face," his advocate insisted.

"Every man over 40 is responsible for his face," Lincoln replied.

> FRANCES PARKINSON KEYES

He had a face like a benediction.

> MIGUEL DE CERVANTES

One ABC of Christianity: "Always Be Cheerful" (1 Thessalonians 5:16, Berkeley).

> ANONYMOUS

Courage

Courage
The courage that my mother had
  Went with her, and is with her still;
Rock from New England quarried;
  Now granite in a granite hill.

The golden brooch my mother wore
She left behind for me to wear;
I have no thing I treasure more;
Yet, it is something I could spare.
Oh, if instead she'd left to me
The thing she took into the grave!—
That courage like a rock, which she
Has no more need of, and I have.

EDNA ST. VINCENT MILLAY, *Mine the Harvest*

Today many people are living in the bondage of fear. In a recent study, a psychiatrist said that the greatest problem facing his patients was fear. Afraid of going insane, committing suicide, being alone, or afraid of heart disease, cancer, disaster, or death. We are becoming a nation of fearful people. Down through the centuries in times of trouble, temptation, trial, bereavement, and crisis, God has brought courage to the hearts of those who love Him. The Bible is crowded with assurances of God's help and comfort in every kind of trouble which might cause fears to arise in the human heart. Today the Christian can come to the Scriptures with full assurance that God is going to deliver the person who puts his trust and confidence in God. Christians can look into the future with promise, hope, and joy, and without fear, discouragement, or despondency.

BILLY GRAHAM

Here is the answer which I will give to President Roosevelt. . . . Give us the tools, and we will finish the job.

WINSTON CHURCHILL, Broadcast: 9 February 1941

Courage is the first of human qualities because it is the quality which guarantees all others.

WINSTON CHURCHILL

Without belittling the courage with which men have died, we should not forget those acts of courage with which men . . . have lived. The courage of life is often a less dramatic spectacle than the courage of a final moment; but it is no less a magnificent mixture of triumph and tragedy. A man does what he must . . . in spite of personal consequences, in spite of obstacles and damages and pressures—and that is the basis of all human morality.

JOHN F. KENNEDY, *Profiles in Courage*

When John Huss was about to be burned to death, they asked him to give up his teachings. Huss answered, "What I have taught with my lips, I now seal with my blood."
That is courage.

G. S.

Courtesy

The signing of the Declaration of Independence took courage. When Charles Carroll signed his name, someone asked, "How will anyone know which Charles Carroll is meant among all those with that name?"

"Well, let there be no mistake," said the courageous patriot, and he signed in bold letters, "Charles Carroll of Carrollton."

G. S.

Theodore Roosevelt is attributed to have said about his predecessor to the presidency, William McKinley, "As much backbone as a chocolate eclair."

G. S.

Courtesy

The test of good manners is to be able to put up pleasantly with bad ones.

WENDELL WILLKIE

There is no such thing as being a gentleman at important moments; it is at unimportant moments that a man is a gentleman. . . . If once his mind is possessed in any strong degree with the knowledge that he is a gentleman he will soon cease to be one.

G. K. CHESTERTON

Life is short, but there is always time for courtesy.

RALPH WALDO EMERSON

Love does not behave in a discourteous manner. Greed does; selfishness does; fear does—but not love.

G. S.

It is almost a definition of a gentleman to say that he is one who never inflicts pain.

JOHN HENRY NEWMAN

If you would win the world, melt it, do not hammer it.

ALEXANDER MACLAREN

"One of the most tactful men I ever knew," says a California manufacturer, "was the man who fired me from my first job. He called me in and said, 'Son, I don't know how we're ever going to get along without you, but starting Monday we're going to try.' "

JAMES M. BRAUDE

Covetousness

The man who covets is always poor.

CLAUDIAN

Envy is thin because it bites but never eats.

SPANISH PROVERB

Abraham Lincoln once walked down the street with his two sons, both of whom were crying. "What's the matter with your boys?" asked a passerby. "Exactly what is wrong with the whole world," said Lincoln. "I have three walnuts, and each boy wants two."

Lust in one form or another is the common sin that plagues all of mankind.

G. S.

Those that much covet are with gain so fond,
For what they have not, that which they possess
They scatter and unloose it from their bond,
And so, by hoping more, they have but less.

WILLIAM SHAKESPEARE, *The Rape of Lucrece*

Creation

I asked the whole frame of the world about my God; and he answered me, "I am not He, but He made me."

SAINT AUGUSTINE, *Confessions*

All created things are living in the Hand of God. The senses see only the action of the creatures; but faith sees in everything the action of God.

J. P. DE CAUSSADE, *Abandonments to Divine Providence*

Either God is in the whole of nature, with no gaps, or He's not there at all.

L. A. COULSON, *Science & Christian Belief*

Criticism

Here we write well when we expose frauds and hypocrites. We are great at counting warts and blemishes and weighing feet of clay. In expressing love, we belong among the undeveloped countries.

SAUL BELLOW

People ask you for criticism, but they only want praise.

W. SOMERSET MAUGHAM

He who throws dirt always loses ground.

ANONYMOUS

If what they are saying about you is true, mend your ways. If it isn't true, forget it, and go on and serve the Lord.

H. A. IRONSIDE

A thick skin is a gift from God.

KONRAD ADENAUER

Draw deep from the well of Biblical criticism, but do not give your congregation too much of the rope to chew.

W. R. MALTBY

Cross

If I see aright, the cross of popular evangelicalism is not the cross of the New Testament. It is, rather, a new bright ornament upon the bosom of a self-assured and carnal Christianity. The old cross slew men, the new cross entertains them. The old cross condemned; the new cross amuses. The old cross destroyed confidence in the flesh; the new cross encourages it.

A. W. TOZER

God is generous. The cross is the sign of addition.

G. S.

Once when Lord Tennyson was on vacation in a country village he asked an old Methodist woman, "Is there any news?"

"Well," she replied, "there is only one piece of news that I know, and that is that Christ died for my sins."

Tennyson responded, "That is old news, and good news, and new news."

G. S.

The most crucial event of all history, the one crisis that forms a watershed by which we number our years, write all our history, and reckon our relationship with God—the crucifixion of Christ—was one of those events that passed without much notice. Yet it is the cross of Christ to which all previous history looked forward and to which all history since looks back. It is the crucifixion that gives meaning to the flow of human history. It is Christ's death that makes sense of the pattern of events from the beginning of history.

Yes, the cross is the hinge of history. The great events that were compressed into the four days surrounding Christ's death touch the lives and hopes of everyone.

G. S.

Do you see the Person of the cross? He is the sinless one, the only man ever of whom it could accurately be said, "[He] did no sin, neither was guile found in his mouth" (1 Peter 2:22). He was "in all points tempted like as we are, yet without sin" (Hebrews 4:15). He was "holy, harmless, undefiled, separate from sinners" (Hebrews 7:26).

He was perfectly righteous, perfectly holy, and sinless; yet He died willingly for our sin. First Peter 2:23–24 tells us, "When he was reviled, [he] reviled not again; when he suffered, he threatened not; but committed himself to him that judgeth righteously: Who his own self bare our sins in his own body on the tree, that we, being dead to sins, should live unto righteousness."

G. S.

C. I. Scofield once wrote, "God was not changed, for He had always loved the world; nor was the world changed, for it continued in sinful rebellion against God. But by the death of Christ the relationship between God and the world was changed." God took away the wall between Himself and man the day Christ died.

G. S.

The Cross of Christ must be either the darkest spot of all in the mystery of existence or a searchlight by the aid of which we may penetrate the surrounding gloom.

BURNETT H. STREETER

Christ, who, being the holiest among the mighty, and mightiest among the holy, lifted with His pierced hands empires off their hinges and turned the stream of centuries out of its channel, and still governs the ages.

JEAN PAUL RICHTER

We are not saved by theories, but by fact, and what is the fact? For whom did Christ die? Christ died for sinners. Well, then, He died for me.

ARTHUR STANTON

God made a show of the powers of evil and darkness and at Calvary He put them to rout.

JAMES S. STEWART

The Cross is the ladder to heaven.

THOMAS DRAKE

> No pain, no palm;
> No thorns, no throne;
> No gall, no glory;
> No cross, no crown.

WILLIAM PENN

Cross

Upon a life I have not lived,
Upon a death I have not died—
Another's life, Another's death,
I stake my whole eternity.

ANONYMOUS

How soon would faith freeze without a cross!

SAMUEL RUTHERFORD

The cross is the center of the world's history. The incarnation of Christ and the crucifixion of our Lord are the pivot round which all the events of the ages revolve. The testimony of Christ was the spirit of prophecy, and the growing power of Jesus is the spirit of history.

ALEXANDER MACLAREN

The Cross is not only the symbol for the life of man; it is equally the symbol for the life of God, and it may indeed be said that the Cross is in the heart of God.

JOHN WATSON

Then said Jesus unto his disciples, If any man will come after me, let him deny himself, and take up his cross, and follow me.

MATTHEW 16:24

Then Jesus beholding him loved him, and said unto him, One thing thou lackest: go thy way, sell whatsoever thou hast, and give to the poor, and thou shalt have treasure in heaven: and come, take up the cross, and follow me.

MARK 10:21

I am crucified with Christ: nevertheless I live; yet not I, but Christ liveth in me: and the life which I now live in the flesh I live by the faith of the Son of God, who loved me, and gave himself for me.

GALATIANS 2:20

But God forbid that I should glory, save in the cross of our Lord Jesus Christ, by whom the world is crucified unto me, and I unto the world.

GALATIANS 6:14

There are no crown-wearers in heaven who were not cross-bearers here below.

CHARLES H. SPURGEON

← D →

Death

"Speculations!" said the dying man in astonishment. "I know nothing about speculations; I'm resting on certainties. 'I know whom I have believed, and am persuaded that he is able to keep that which I have committed unto him against that day' " (2 Tim. 1:12).

MICHAEL FARADAY

Death may be the King of terrors . . . but Jesus is the King of Kings!

D. L. MOODY

Death is but a passage. It is not a house, it is only a vestibule. The grave has a door on its inner side.

ALEXANDER MACLAREN

Death is the most democratic experience in life for we all participate in it. We think of its happening only to other people. We don't like to grow old and we don't like to die. The Bible teaches that death is an enemy of man and God. But it also teaches that this enemy, death, will ultimately be destroyed forever; that in fact it has already been defeated at the Cross and resurrection of Jesus Christ. Death, for a Christian, brings permanent freedom from evil. It also means the believer will be like Jesus. We shall be like Christ in love. So much of self is involved in what we do here; but one day, in Christ, we will have perfect love. What a glorious time it will be when we get to heaven!

BILLY GRAHAM

When Michelangelo, already well along in years, was discussing life with an old friend, the latter commented, "Yes, after such a good life, it's hard to look death in the eye."

"Not at all!" contradicted Michelangelo. "Since life was such a pleasure, death coming from the same great Source cannot displease us."

Temmler Werke

Truth sits upon the lips of dying men.

MATTHEW ARNOLD

I am ready to meet God face to face tonight and look into those eyes of infinite holiness, for all my sins are covered by the atoning blood.

R. A. TORREY

Death

I Have a Rendezvous with Death
I have a rendezvous with Death
At some disputed barricade,
When Spring comes back with rustling shade
And apple blossoms fill the air—
I have a rendezvous with Death
When Spring brings back blue days and fair.

It may be he shall take my hand,
And lead me into his dark land,
And close my eyes and quench my breath—
It may be I shall pass him still.
I have a rendezvous with Death
On some scarred slope of battered hill,
When Spring comes round again this year
And the first meadow flowers appear.

God knows 'twere better to be deep
Pillowed in silk and scented down,
Where Love throbs out in blissful sleep,
Pulse nigh to pulse, and breath to breath,
Where hushed awakenings are dear . . .
But I've a rendezvous with Death
At midnight in some flaming town,
When Spring trips north again this year;
And I to my pledged word am true,
I shall not fail that rendezvous.

ALAN SEEGER, AMERICAN VOLUNTEER
(killed in France while serving with
the French Foreign Legion, 1916, age 28)

All publicity is good, except an obituary notice.

BRENDAN BEHAN

Death always waits. The door of the hearse is never closed.

JOSEPH BAYLY, *The View from a Hearse*

The conquest of death is the final achievement of religion. No religion
is worth its name unless it can prove itself more than a match for
death.

L. P. JACKS, *The Inner Sentinel*

One short sleep past, we wake eternall,/And Death shall be no more:/
Death, thou shalt die!

JOHN DONNE

When I am dead, my dearest,/Sing no sad songs for me.

CHRISTINA ROSSETTI

To die is landing on some distant shore.

JOHN DRYDEN

Old man, exhausted by ordeal, detached from human deeds, feeling the approach of the eternal cold, but always watching in the shadows for the gleam of hope.

CHARLES DE GAULLE

Good-by world . . . Good-by to clocks ticking . . . and Mama's sunflowers. And food and coffee. And new-ironed dresses and hot baths . . . and sleeping and waking up. Oh, earth, you're too wonderful for anybody to realize you.

THORNTON WILDER

Yea, though I walk through the valley of the shadow of death, I will fear no evil: for thou art with me; thy rod and thy staff they comfort me.

PSALM 23:4

Mark the perfect man, and behold the upright: for the end of that man is peace.

PSALM 37:37

Precious in the sight of the Lord is the death of his saints.

PSALM 116:15

The wicked is driven away in his wickedness: but the righteous hath hope in his death.

PROVERBS 14:32

And fear not them which kill the body, but are not able to kill the soul: but rather fear him which is able to destroy both soul and body in hell.

MATTHEW 10:28

But she that liveth in pleasure is dead while she liveth.

1 TIMOTHY 5:6

For we brought nothing into this world, and it is certain we can carry nothing out.

1 TIMOTHY 6:7

And as it is appointed unto men once to die, but after this the judgment.

HEBREWS 9:27

He that hath the Son hath life; and he that hath not the Son of God hath not life.

1 JOHN 5:12

And God shall wipe away all tears from their eyes; and there shall be no more death, neither sorrow, nor crying, neither shall there be any more pain: for the former things are passed away.

REVELATION 21:4

Decay and Decline

History teaches us that when a barbarian race confronts a sleeping culture, the barbarian always wins.

ARNOLD TOYNBEE

Within the Roman empire, law and order prevailed, and never (before) did almost everybody "have it so good" . . . no foreign power could challenge Rome. . . . Why did this . . . civilization decline at all? and why did it decline so rapidly that, within another 100 years, the Roman Empire was plunged irreversibly into anarchy and penury, ravaged by foreign aggressors and doomed to extinction?

ROBERT STRAUSS-HUPE

According to Edward Gibbon, in his classic work, *The Decline and Fall of the Roman Empire,* there were five major causes for the decline and fall of the Roman empire.
1. The breakdown of the family and the increase of divorce.
2. The spiraling rise of taxes and extravagant spending.
3. The mounting desire for pleasure and the brutalization of sports.
4. The continual production of armaments to face everincreasing threats of enemy attacks.
5. The decay of religion into many confusing forms, leaving the people without a uniform faith.
It is very significant that these factors exist today.

G. S.

Decisions

There is no more miserable human being than one in whom nothing is habitual but indecision.

WILLIAM JAMES

The great thing in the world is not so much where we stand, as in what direction we are moving.

OLIVER WENDELL HOLMES, SR.

[They are] decided only to be undecided, resolved to be irresolute, adamant for drift, solid for fluidity, all-powerful to be impotent.

WINSTON CHURCHILL, *While England Slept*

A man with a half volition goes backwards and forwards, and makes no way on the smoothest road; a man with a whole volition advances on the roughest, and will reach his purpose, if there be even a little worthiness in it. The man without a purpose is like a ship without a rudder—a waif, a nothing, a no man. Have a purpose in life and having it, throw such strength of mind and muscle into your work as God has given you.

THOMAS CARLYLE

Formula for Achievement
Plan more work than you can do;
  Then do it.
Bite off more than you can chew;
  Then chew it.
Hitch your wagon to a star;
  Keep your seat;
And there you are!

ANONYMOUS

. . . the refusal to choose is a form of choice; disbelief is a form of belief.

FRANK BARRON

No answer is also an answer.

GERMAN PROVERB

In making our decisions, we must use the brains that God has given us. But we must also use our hearts which He also gave us.

FULTON OURSLER

How few of us could honestly crystallise the aims that guide our life into any single sentence? We try the impossible feat of riding on two horses at once. We resolve and retract, and hesitate and compromise. The ship heads now one way and now another, and that not because we are wisely *tacking*—that is to say, seeking to reach one point by widely varying courses—but because our hand is so weak on the helm that we drift wherever the wash of the waves and the buffets of the wind carry us.

ALEXANDER MacLAREN

Decisions

A man so various, that he seem'd to be
Not one, but all Mankind's Epitome:
Stiff in Opinions, always in the wrong;
Was everything by starts, and Nothing long:
But, in the course of one revolving moon,
Was Chymist, Fidler, Statesman, and Buffoon.

JOHN DRYDEN

A man who has not learned to say, "No"—who is not resolved that he *will* take God's way, in spite of every dog that can bay or bark at him, in spite of every silvery voice that woos him aside—will be a weak and a wretched man till he dies.

ALEXANDER MACLAREN

I'm glad for the Bible. It gives me a chance to see how other men chose—and the results. There's the contrast between Abraham's choice and Lot's choice before Sodom. There's Moses' choice of his fellows rather than the riches of Egypt. There's Joseph's choice in the prison house of Potiphar, and Daniel's choice of the king's vegetables rather than his meats. Paul paid a glorious price when he chose his lot with the early Christians. Christ made marvelous choices when he set his face toward Jerusalem, at the Garden of Gethsemane, and in the Judgment Hall.

Adam's choice cost him Eden; Esau's, his birthright; Achan's, his life; Lot's, his home and herds; Absalom's, his father's throne; Saul's, his kingdom; the rich young ruler's, the companionship of Christ. Judas lost his apostleship; Demas, his discipleship. Pilate, Agrippa, and Felix chose wrong and missed immortality. Ananias' choice fooled no one but himself. Caleb and Joshua chose well, while Jonah's first choice nearly shipwrecked himself and the crew.

Ye older ones, what would your answer be as a father, as a mother, as a Christian leader, if, concerning our young people, God would say to you today, "Ask what I shall make of these young people"? Would your answer prove you know how to choose the things that matter most? Would your answer prove you are a wise leader—for them?

ROBERT G. LEE

I determined never to stop until I had come to the end and achieved my purpose.

DAVID LIVINGSTONE

Destiny is not a matter of chance, it is a matter of choice; it is not a thing to be waited for, it is a thing to be achieved.

WILLIAM JENNINGS BRYAN

Dedication

You will not be carried to Heaven lying at ease upon a feather bed.
SAMUEL RUTHERFORD

The condition of an enlightened mind is a surrendered heart.
ALAN REDPATH

> What can I give Him,
> Poor as I am?
> If I were a shepherd
> I would bring a lamb.
> If I were a wise man
> I would do my part—
> Yet what can I give Him,
> Give him my heart.
CHRISTINA ROSSETTI

Obedience is the fruit of faith.
CHRISTINA ROSSETTI

It is a great deal easier to do that which God gives us to do, no matter how hard it is, than to face the responsibilities of not doing it.
J. R. MILLER

The world has yet to see what God will do with a man who is fully and wholly consecrated to the Holy Spirit.
HENRY VARLEY

By the grace of God, I'll be that man.
D. L. MOODY

If Jesus Christ died and died for me, then no sacrifice can be too great for me to make for Him.
C. T. STUDD

I wish to preach, not the doctrine of ignoble ease, but the doctrine of the strenuous life.
THEODORE ROOSEVELT

The Christian life is a positive allegiance to Jesus Christ. It is becoming so occupied with Him that the values and standards of the world around us have little influence.
G. S.

Nothing earthly will make me give up my work in despair.
DAVID LIVINGSTONE

Dedication

The fall of man has created a perpetual crisis. It will last until sin has been put down and Christ reigns over a redeemed and restored world. Until that time the earth remains a disaster area and its inhabitants live in a state of extraordinary emergency.

To me it has always been difficult to understand those evangelical Christians who insist upon living in the crisis as if no crisis existed. They say they serve the Lord, but they divide their days so as to leave plenty of time to play and loaf and enjoy the pleasures of the world as well. They are at ease while the world burns.

A. W. Tozer

I will place no value on anything I have or may possess except in relation to the kingdom of Christ.

David Livingstone

Men join the church. They take that Holy Name upon themselves. They enter into covenant with each other in the name of the Father and of the Son and of the Holy Spirit, inviting Holy Trinity to witness and support their purpose of faithfulness, purity, love, cooperation, liberality, of personal effort to win a lost world to Christ. Yet American churches are filled with men and women who flagrantly and frivolously and constantly ignore the obligations of their voluntary covenants. Thousands of church members have changed residence without changing church membership. They stand aloof from the local church. They take no local responsibility for Christ. They settle into becoming church drifters and sermon drifters and sermon tasters. God will not hold such guiltless. He has declared it in His Word.

J. C. Massee

Some people object to taking vows, but in the Bible you will find many great men of God directed by covenants, promises, vows and pledges. A carnal man refuses the discipline of such commitments. He says, "I want to be free. It is legalism." There are many religious tramps in the world who will not be bound by anything.

Now there are five vows I have in mind which we do well to make and keep.

1. *Deal thoroughly with sin.*
2. *Never own anything*—get rid of the sense of possessing.
3. *Never defend yourself.*
4. *Never pass anything on about anybody else that will hurt him.*
5. *Never accept any glory.*

Remember that these five vows are not something you write in the back of your Bible and forget. They have got to be written in your own blood.

A. W. Tozer

God doesn't seek for golden vessels, and does not ask for silver ones, but He must have clean ones.

D. L. MOODY

"Resolved: Very much to exercise myself in this, all my life long, namely, with the greatest openness of which I am capable, to declare my ways to God, and lay open my soul to Him, all my sins, temptations, difficulties, sorrows, fears, hopes, desires, and everything, and every circumstance."

JONATHAN EDWARDS

Your powers are dead or dedicated. If they are dedicated, they are alive with God and tingle with surprising power. If they are saved up, taken care of for their own ends, they are dead.

E. STANLEY JONES

Each believer stands on one side or the other of dedication. Either we have made this lifelong commitment or we have not. Either we have faced the issue of who is to be the master of our lives or we have been plucking up one sin at a time.

CHARLES CALDWELL RYRIE, *Balancing the Christian Life*

There are two kinds of people: those who say to God, "Thy will be done," and those to whom God says, "All right, then, have it your way."

C. S. LEWIS, *The Great Divorce*

Deeds

Every man feels instinctively that all the beautiful sentiments in the world weigh less than a single lovely action.

JAMES RUSSELL LOWELL

I expect to pass through this world but once. Any good therefore that I can do, or any kindness that I can show to any fellow creature, let me do it now. Let me not defer or neglect it, for I shall not pass this way again.

ANONYMOUS

O Lord, how many read the Word, and yet from vice are not deterred.

ANONYMOUS

People forget how *fast* you did a job—but they remember how *well* you did it.

HOWARD W. NEWTON

Defeat

We are told that the palmyra is the most useful plant in the world. Upward of eight hundred uses are recorded for its various parts.

Are we palmyra Christians—good for many things? Are we possessed of the spirit that will make us good for many things—or good for nothing?

It was D. L. Moody who quoted from a tombstone these words:

> Do all the good you can,
> To all the people you can,
> In all the ways you can,
> As long as ever you can.

If that were engraved on our hearts and were to find expression in our lives, we would be palmyra-palm servants of Christ.

ROBERT G. LEE

Nothing can be made of nothing; he who has laid up no material can produce no combination.

JOSHUA REYNOLDS

The man who has accomplished all that he thinks worthwhile has begun to die.

E. T. TRIGG

Chop your own wood, and it will warm you twice.

HENRY FORD'S FIREPLACE MOTTO

A good deed is never lost. He who sows courtesy, reaps friendship; he who plants kindness, gathers love; pleasure bestowed on a grateful mind was never sterile, but generally gratitude begets reward.

BASIL

> Sitting still and wishing
> Makes no person great.
> The good Lord sends the fishing
> But you must dig the bait.

ANONYMOUS

Defeat

> If you think you are beaten, you are,
> If you think that you dare not, you don't,
> If you'd like to win, but you think you can't,
> It's almost certain you won't.
>
> If you think you'll lose, you've lost,
> For out in the world you'll find
> Success begins with a fellow's will—
> It's all in the state of mind.

If you think you are out-classed, you are;
You've got to think high to rise;
You've got to be sure of yourself before
You can ever win a prize.

Life's battles don't always go
To the stronger or faster man;
But soon or late the man who wins
Is the man who thinks he can.

ANONYMOUS

When the Confederate army retreated after Gettysburg, General Lee wrote to Jefferson Davis a remarkable letter in which he said: "We must expect reverses, even defeats. They are sent to teach us wisdom and prudence, to call forth greater energies, and to prevent our falling into greater disasters." True of a nation's life, this is also profoundly true of the life of the individual. And what shall we say of sickness, sorrow, and affliction? Shall these things overwhelm us, or shall we be able to say, with that great spirit who kept both his soul and his body under the dominion of a great and holy purpose, "Nay, in all these things we are more than conquerors through him that loved us" (Rom. 8:37)?

CLARENCE E. MACARTNEY

A man is not defeated by his opponents but by himself.

JAN CHRISTIAN SMUTS

My lowest days as a Christian (and there were low ones—seven months' worth of them in prison, to be exact) have been more fulfilling and rewarding than all the days of glory in the White House.

CHARLES COLSON

Most human organizations that fall short of their goals do so not because of stupidity or faulty doctrines, but because of internal decay and rigidification. They grow stiff in the joints. They get in a rut. They go to seed.

JAMES GARDNER

Delay

Defer no time, delays have dangerous ends.

WILLIAM SHAKESPEARE, King Henry VI

Throughout history, it has been the inaction of those who could have acted, the indifference of those who should have known better, the silence of the voice of justice when it mattered most, that has made it possible for evil to triumph.

HAILE SELASSIE

He was going to be all that a mortal should be—
  Tomorrow.
No one would be better than he—
  Tomorrow.
Each morning he stacked up the letters he'd write—
  Tomorrow.
It was too bad indeed he was too busy to see Bill,
but he promised to do it—
  Tomorrow.
The greatest of workers this man would have been—
  Tomorrow.
The world would have known him had he ever seen—
  Tomorrow.
But the fact is he died and faded from view,
and all that was left when living was through
Was a mountain of things he intended to do—
  Tomorrow.

ANONYMOUS

Procrastination is my sin.
It brings me naught but sorrow.
I know that I should stop it.
In fact, I will—tomorrow!

GLORIA PITZER

Depression, Despair, Determination

The Christian's chief occupational hazards are depression and discouragement.

JOHN STOTT

Now, God be prais'd, that to believing souls
Gives light in darkness, comfort in despair!

WILLIAM SHAKESPEARE, *King Henry VI*

Despair of ever being saved, "except thou be born again," or of seeing God "without holiness," or of having part in Christ except thou "love him above father, mother, or thy own life." This kind of despair is one of the first steps to heaven.

RICHARD BAXTER

Determination

One cold February day a snail started climbing an apple tree. As he inched slowly upward, a worm stuck its head from a crevice in the bark to offer some advice. "You're wasting your energy. There isn't a single apple up there."

The snail kept up his slow climb. "There will be when I get there," he said.

ANONYMOUS

Once while St. Francis of Assisi was hoeing his garden, he was asked, "What would you do if you were suddenly to learn that you were to die at sunset today?" He replied, "I would finish hoeing my garden."

ANONYMOUS

Millions of people in our culture make decisions for Christ, but there is a dreadful attrition rate. . . . In our kind of culture anything, even news about God, can be sold if it is packaged freshly; but when it loses its novelty, it goes on the garbage heap. There is a great market for religious experience in our world; there is little enthusiasm for the patient acquisition of virtue, little inclination to sign up for a long apprenticeship.

EUGENE PETERSON

> When things go wrong as they sometimes will,
> When the road you're trudging seems all uphill,
> When the funds are low and the debts are high,
> And you want to smile, but you have to sigh.
>
> When care is pressing you down a bit,
> Rest if you must, but don't you quit.
> Life is queer with its twists and turns,
> As every one of us sometimes learns,
> And many a failure turns about
> When he might have won had he stuck it out.
> Don't give up though the pace seems slow—
> You may succeed with another blow!
>
> Success is failure turned inside out—
> The silver tint of the clouds of doubt,
> And you never can tell just how close you are,
> It may be near when it seems so far.
>
> So stick to the fight when you're hardest hit—
> It's when things seem worst that you must not quit.

ANONYMOUS

Devil

The devil is a better theologian than any of us and is a devil still.

A. W. TOZER

"Christ in you, the hope of glory." I'm not afraid of the devil. The devil can handle me—he's got judo I never heard of. But he can't handle the One to whom I'm joined; he can't handle the One to whom I'm united; he can't handle the One whose nature dwells in my nature.

A. W. TOZER

If the devil could be persuaded to write a bible, he would title it "You Only Live Once."

SYDNEY HARRIS

Satan is neither omnipotent nor free to do everything he pleases. Prince of the world he may be, but the Prince of Peace has come and dealt him a death blow.

HAROLD LINDSELL, *The World, the Flesh, and the Devil*

The devil can cite Scripture for his purpose.

WILLIAM SHAKESPEARE, *The Merchant of Venice*

The devil hath power to assume a pleasing shape.

WILLIAM SHAKESPEARE, *Hamlet*

The Devil does not stay where music is.

MARTIN LUTHER

As I see it, there are two possible mistakes to be made. One is to overestimate the power of Satan, and the other is to underestimate it.

A believer who overestimates Satan's power can live an entire lifetime in fear, always terrified of what Satan might do. Satan likes nothing better than to stir up that kind of fear in a believer, because it destroys his effectiveness for the Lord.

On the other hand, a person who underestimates the power and cunning of Satan may become unconcerned with Satan's activity and be lulled into complacency. That is where Satan can do his most damaging work.

G. S.

I would like to suggest three evil devices that make up most of Satan's repertoire.

The first is opposition. The very name *Satan* means opposer, and he has opposed the work of God from the day he fell. To the Christian he is the chief adversary. First Peter 5:8 says, "Be sober, be vigilant; because your adversary the devil, as a roaring lion, walketh about, seeking whom he may devour."

Another of Satan's devices is imitation. Often he is more successful at imitation than he could be with blatant opposition. Satan has always imitated God. It was his desire to be like God that led to his fall in the first place.

Whatever God does, Satan is sure to substitute his own imitation. When Moses demonstrated the power of God to Pharaoh with miracles, Satan enabled Pharaoh's magicians to imitate those miracles. Throughout the Old Testament when God raised up His prophets, Satan countered by raising up false prophets.

A third device of Satan is accusation. He is called the "accuser of our brethren" in Revelation 12:10. That same verse says that Satan accuses believers before God day and night. It is the picture of one pointing his finger at others, accusing of wrongdoing, shortcoming, false motives, and sin.

G. S.

Devotions

We are to be shut out from men, and shut in with God.

ANDREW MURRAY

I came to see that my relationship to my Lord Jesus Christ, with the passing years, had eroded away something like a marriage gone humdrum. What did I do when I found a little pocket of spare time, on a Sunday, or a holiday? I couldn't wait to get together with other people—people I liked, people with whom I had something in common—so we could share ideas and experiences. Or I read a stimulating book. Or I went out to enjoy nature. I even plunged further into my work, doing things that I normally didn't have time for. But to go to Jesus—to give Him first claim on even my spare time—that I did not do.

M. BASILEA SCHLINK

An essential condition of listening to God is that the mind should not be distracted by thoughts of resentment, ill-temper, hatred or vengeance, all of which are comprised in the general term *the wrath of man.*

R. V. G. TASKER

Whatever is your best time in the day, give that to communion with God.

HUDSON TAYLOR

I have only missed my morning watch once or twice this term. . . . I can easily believe that it is next in importance to accepting Christ. For I know that when I don't wait upon God in prayer and Bible study, things go wrong.

WILLIAM BORDEN

Difficulties

How rare it is to find a soul quiet enough to hear God speak.

FRANÇOIS FÉNELON

Cut your morning devotions into your personal grooming. You would not go out to work with a dirty face. Why start the day with the face of your soul unwashed?

ROBERT A. COOK

Andrew Bonar, a great man of God, had three rules that he lived by. Rule 1—Not to speak to any person before speaking to Jesus Christ. Rule 2—Not to do anything with his hands until he had been on his knees. Rule 3—Not to read the papers until he had read his Bible.

G. S.

To be a Christian without prayer is no more possible than to be alive without breathing.

MARTIN LUTHER

If we don't maintain a quiet time each day, it's not really because we are too busy; it's because we do not feel it is important enough. . . .

There's an old navy rule: when ships readjust their compass, they drop anchor in a quiet spot. . . .

Late nights kill the quiet time. . . . Quiet time is not just a helpful idea, it is absolutely necessary to spiritual growth.

G. S.

Difficulties

Nothing will ever be attempted if all possible objections must first be removed.

SAMUEL JOHNSON

When it is dark enough, men see the stars.

RALPH WALDO EMERSON

A Christian is like a teabag—he's not worth much until he's been through some hot water.

ANONYMOUS

> Out of the presses of pain
> Cometh the soul's best wine;
> The eyes that have shed no rain
> Can shed but little shine.

A. B. SIMPSON

94

Storms make oaks take deeper root.

GEORGE HERBERT

The lowest ebb is the turn of the tide.

HENRY WADSWORTH LONGFELLOW

Be assured that, if God waits longer than you could wish, it is only to make the blessing doubly precious! God waited four thousand years, till the fullness of time, ere He sent His Son. Our times are in His hands; He will avenge His elect speedily; He will make haste for our help, and not delay one hour too long.

ANDREW MURRAY

If we could see beyond today, as God can see,
If all the clouds should roll away, the shadows flee;
O'er present griefs we would not fret,
Each sorrow we would soon forget;
For many joys are waiting yet for you and me.
"If we could see, if we could know," we often say.
But God in love a veil doth throw across our way.
We cannot see what lies before
And so we cling to Him the more,
He leads us till this life is o'er;
Trust and obey.

ANONYMOUS

Many men owe the grandeur of their lives to their tremendous difficulties.

CHARLES H. SPURGEON

The eternal stars shine out as soon as it is dark enough.

THOMAS CARLYLE

Troubles are often the tools by which God fashions us for better things.

HENRY WARD BEECHER

Difficulties are stepping stones to success.

ANONYMOUS

Our greatest glory is not in never falling, but in rising each time we fall.

OLIVER GOLDSMITH

As in nature, as in art, so in grace; it is rough treatment that gives souls, as well as stones, their lustre. The more the diamond is cut the

95

Difficulties

brighter it sparkles; and in what seems hard dealing, there God has no end in view but to perfect His people.

THOMAS GUTHRIE

What is difficulty? Only a word indicating the degree of strength requisite for accomplishing particular objects; a mere notice of the necessity for exertion; a bugbear to children and fools; only a mere stimulus to men.

SAMUEL WARREN

God drives a deep share through many a wayside heart, and the coulter of affliction breaks up many a spirit that it may afterwards yield "the peaceable fruit of righteousness."

ALEXANDER MACLAREN

Into each life some rain must fall, some days be dark and dreary.

HENRY WADSWORTH LONGFELLOW

Jesus Christ is no security against storms, but He is perfect security in storms. He has never promised you an easy passage, only a safe landing.

ANONYMOUS

When the storms of life come down upon you, keep your eyes fixed on Jesus.

G. S.

Every life has dark tracts and long stretches of sombre tint, and no representation is true to fact which dips its pencil only in light, and flings no shadows on the canvas.

ALEXANDER MACLAREN

Job feels the Rod/Yet blesses GOD.

New England Primer

If you have God for your "enduring substance," you can face all varieties of condition, and be calm, saying—
> "Give what Thou canst, without Thee I am poor,
> And with Thee rich, take what Thou wilt away."

ALEXANDER MACLAREN

People have a natural tendency to flee to the mountains when things get tough.

STUART BRISCOE, *What Works*

Diplomacy, Discipline, Doubt

Diplomacy

Diplomacy is the art of saying "Nice doggie!" till you can find a rock.

WYNN CATLIN

A diplomat is a man who always remembers a woman's birthday but never remembers her age.

ROBERT FROST

[Advice to a young diplomat]: Tell the truth, and so puzzle and confound your adversaries.

HENRY WOTTON

Discipline

The diamond cannot be polished without friction, nor the man perfected without trials.

CHINESE PROVERB

I bear my willing witness that I owe more to the fire, and the hammer, and the file, than to anything else in my Lord's workshop. I sometimes question whether I have ever learned anything except through the rod. When my schoolroom is darkened, I see most.

CHARLES H. SPURGEON

Discipline is the soul of an army. It makes small numbers formidable; procures success to the weak, and esteem to all.

GEORGE WASHINGTON, Letter of instruction
to the Virginia regiments, 29 July 1759

You can judge the quality of their faith from the way they behave. Discipline is an index to doctrine.

TERTULLIAN

Doubt

Don't doubt in the dark what God has revealed in the light.

V. RAYMOND EDMAN

Hindu prayer: O God, if you are there, save me, if you can!

R. K. NARAYAN

8-16-92

All fanaticism is a strategy to prevent doubt from becoming conscious.

H. A. WILLIAMS, *The True Wilderness*

97

Doubt

It's shocking to realize how many people are made miserable by the disease called doubt. Uncertainty has robbed thousands of people of the joy of salvation.

People who even read their Bibles, earnestly pray, faithfully attend church, and live uprightly in all their dealings with others, may yet have no assurance of forgiveness and be living defeated lives.

Is assurance of salvation possible? What does the Bible say? In 2 Corinthians 13:5, Paul writes, "Examine yourselves, whether ye be in the faith." In 2 Peter 1:10 we are told, "Give diligence to make your calling and election sure." The assurance of salvation is one of God's beautiful gifts. Every believer ought to know that he possesses salvation.

G. S.

All of us at times have passed through the sea of doubt. Bunyan speaks of being "much tumbled up and down in his thoughts." However, without question we may know now that we have eternal life. Jesus said, "He that believeth on me hath everlasting life" (John 6:47). Anything that contradicts the words of Jesus is a lie. "Let God be true, but every man a liar" (Romans 3:4).

G. S.

At the conclusion of a mass meeting, I was greeting people when a distinguished-looking man approached me and asked, "May I talk with you about my salvation? I'm desperately confused." He went on to state that he had acknowledged the Lord as Saviour but had little peace and Christian confidence. "As I listened to your message, I decided I must settle it."

I replied. "First, look into your life to discover if all is right between yourself and the Lord. Carnal believers are usually full of doubts. If the Holy Spirit is grieved through self-will or sin, He cannot witness effectively to your salvation because there is contradiction. For this reason the witness of the Holy Spirit is often dimmed. Second, after discovering the wrong, openly confess it to the Lord. Third, deal with it and do works to prove your repentance."

"That's it," he interrupted. "I've grown careless; there's sin in my life, and I must make it right."

We bowed our heads in a holy hush as he sought God's gracious forgiveness. It was evident that the Lord was in the room, for when we arose from our knees the doctor was changed. His expression, his voice, his whole attitude radiated blessed assurance. Careless living will always create doubt, but the opposite is also true. Doubt leads to careless living.

G. S.

Dreams

We grow great by dreams. All big men are dreamers. They see things in the soft haze of a spring day or in the red fire of a long winter's evening. Some of us let these great dreams die, but others nourish and protect them; nurse them through bad days till they bring them to the sunshine and light which comes always to those who sincerely hope that their dreams will come true.

WOODROW WILSON

One of the most tragic things I know about human nature is that all of us tend to put off living. We are all dreaming of some magical rose garden over the horizon—instead of enjoying the roses that are blooming outside our windows today.

DALE CARNEGIE

I like the dreams of the future better than the history of the past.

THOMAS JEFFERSON

Dreams are the touchstones of our characters.

HENRY THOREAU

Duty

Let men laugh when you sacrifice desire to duty, if they will. You have time and eternity to rejoice in.

THEODORE PARKER

> The things which must be, must be for the best,
> God helps us do our duty and not shrink,
> And trust His mercy humbly for the rest.

OWEN MEREDITH

He who is false to present duty breaks a thread in the loom, and will find the flaw when he may have forgotten its cause.

HENRY WARD BEECHER

In doing what we ought we deserve no praise, because it is our duty.

SAINT AUGUSTINE

← **E** →

Easter

The simplest meaning of Easter is that we are living in a world in which God has the last word.

An Easter Carol
Tomb, thou shalt not hold Him longer;
Death is strong, but Life is stronger;
Stronger than the dark, the light;
Stronger than the wrong, the right;
Faith and Hope triumphant say,
Christ will rise on Easter Day.

PHILLIPS BROOKS

And He departed from our sight that we might return to our heart, and there find Him. For He departed, and behold, He is here.

SAINT AUGUSTINE

Look at the sequence: risen from the dead, therefore alive for ever; therefore our contemporary; therefore able to confront us face to face.

JAMES S. STEWART

He takes men out of time and makes them feel eternity.

RALPH WALDO EMERSON

And the graves were opened; and many bodies of the saints which slept arose, and came out of the graves after his resurrection, and appeared unto many.

MATTHEW 27:52-53

Education

Education is the knowledge of how to use the whole of oneself. Many men use but one or two faculties out of the score with which they are endowed. A man is educated who knows how to make a tool of every faculty—how to open it, how to keep it sharp, and how to apply it to all practical purposes.

HENRY WARD BEECHER

Educate men without religion and you make of them but clever Devils.

ARTHUR WELLESLEY

Talk to a man about himself and he will listen for hours.

BENJAMIN DISRAELI

Every man who knows how to read has it in his power to magnify himself, to multiply the ways in which he exists, to make his life full, significant and interesting.

ALDOUS HUXLEY

America's founding fathers did not intend to take religion out of education. Many of the nation's greatest universities were founded by evangelists and religious leaders; but many of these have lost the founders' concept and become secular institutions. Because of this attitude, secular education is stumbling and floundering.

BILLY GRAHAM

Egotism

Don't talk about yourself; it will be done when you leave.

WILSON MIZNER

He who does not think much of himself is much more esteemed than he imagines.

JOHANN WOLFGANG VON GOETHE

Be yourself is about the worst advice you can give some people.

ANONYMOUS

We reproach people for talking about themselves; but it is the subject they treat best.

ANATOLE FRANCE

He who falls in love with himself will have no rivals.

BENJAMIN FRANKLIN

Empathy

Sometimes I'm asked by kids why I condemn marijuana when I haven't tried it. The greatest obstetricians in the world have never been pregnant.

ART LINKLETTER

When James Burrill Angell, for thirty-eight years president of the University of Michigan, was asked for the secret of his success, he answered: "Grow antennae, not horns."

G. S.

When a good man is hurt all who would be called good must suffer with him.

EURIPIDES

World-wide apart, and yet akin,
As showing that the human heart,
Beats on forever as of old.

HENRY WADSWORTH LONGFELLOW

101

Encouragement, Enemies

Yet, taught by time, my heart has learned to glow/For other's good, and melt at other's woe.

HOMER

Encouragement

It takes so little to make us sad,
Just a slighting word or a doubting sneer,
Just a scornful smile on some lips held dear;
And our footsteps lag, though the goal seemed near,
And we lose the courage and hope we had—
So little it takes to make us sad.

It takes so little to make us glad,
Just a cheering clasp of a friendly hand,
Just a word from one who can understand;
And we finish the task we long had planned,
And we lose the doubt and the fear we had—
So little it takes to make us glad.

IDA GOLDSMITH MORRIS

Correction does much, but encouragement does more. Encouragement after censure is as the sun after a shower.

JOHANN WOLFGANG VON GOETHE

Enemies

I have had a lot of adversaries in my political life, but no enemies that I can remember.

GERALD FORD

The best way to destroy your enemy is to make him your friend.

ABRAHAM LINCOLN

One enemy can do more hurt than ten friends can do good.

JONATHAN SWIFT

One enemy is too much.

GEORGE HERBERT

Give us grace and strength to forbear and to persevere. Give us courage and gaiety and the quiet mind, spare to us our friends, soften to us our enemies.

ROBERT LOUIS STEVENSON

A man cannot be too careful in the choice of his enemies.

OSCAR WILDE

You shall judge a man by his foes as well as by his friends.

JOSEPH CONRAD

Enthusiasm

Nothing great was ever achieved without enthusiasm.

RALPH WALDO EMERSON

Enthusiasm makes ordinary people extraordinary.

ANONYMOUS

When I hear a man preach, I like to see him act as if he were fighting bees.

ABRAHAM LINCOLN

How poor a guide enthusiasm is when it is not informed with the mind and spirit of Christ.

JAMES STALKER, *The Trial and Death of Jesus Christ*

Fires can't be made with dead embers, nor can enthusiasm be stirred by spiritless men. Enthusiasm in our daily work lightens effort and turns even labor into pleasant tasks.

JAMES MARK BALDWIN

Enthusiasm is a telescope that yanks the misty, distant future into the radiant, tangible present.

ANONYMOUS

The word *enthusiasm* really means to be filled or inspired by God. If any people ought to radiate enthusiasm and joy, we should.

We read that the apostolic church was "Praising God, and having favour with all the people" (Acts 2:47). Their unanimous acceptance was related to their spirit of praise. There is a charisma in praise. "Praise is comely for the upright" (Psalm 33:1).

A sad, half-hearted, reluctant Christian is an enigma. But when the joy of the Lord is our strength, we must say with Peter, "We cannot but speak" what we know and believe. Ask the Lord to make you a winsome witness, and I guarantee you that you will win some. Enthusiasm isn't everything but it is important.

G. S.

Epitaph

Rev. Adoniram Judson,
Born August 9th, 1788,
Died April 12th, 1850.

Equality

> Malden his birthplace,
> The ocean his sepulchre,
> Converted Burmans and
> The Burman Bible
> His Monument
> His record is on high.
>
> ADONIRAM JUDSON

I hope for happiness beyond the grave.

THOMAS PAINE

He that doeth the will of God abideth forever.

D. L. MOODY

> Statesman, yet friend of truth,
> A soul sincere,
> In action faithful and in honor clear.
>
> WILLIAM JENNINGS BRYAN

> In heart a Lydia, and in tongue a Hanna,
> In zeal a Ruth, in wedlock a Susanna,
> Prudently simple, providentially wary.
> To the world a Martha, and to heaven a Mary.
>
> DAME DOROTHY SELBY

Here lies one whose name was writ in water.

JOHN KEATS

> This is the grave of Mike O'Day
> Who died maintaining his right of way.
> His right was clear, his will was strong,
> But he's just as dead as if he'd been wrong.
>
> AUTHOR UNKNOWN

Equality

If liberty and equality, as is thought by some, are chiefly to be found in democracy, they will be best attained when all persons alike share in the government to the utmost.

ARISTOTLE

It is the mark of the cultured man that he is aware of the fact that equality is an ethical and not a biological principle.

ASHLEY MONTAGU

For the colonel's lady an' Judy O'Grady,/Are sisters under their skins.

RUDYARD KIPLING

Equality is the life of conversation; and he is as much out who assumes to himself any part above another, as he who considers himself below the rest of society.

RICHARD STEELE

We hold these truths to be sacred and undeniable; that all men are created equal and independent, that from that equal creation they derive rights inherent and inalienable, among which are the preservation of life, and liberty, and the pursuit of happiness.

THOMAS JEFFERSON, Original draft for the
Declaration of Independence, June 1776

Eternity

I know what Eternity is, though I cannot define the word to satisfy a metaphysician. The little child taught by some grandmother Lois, in a cottage, knows what she means when she tells him "you will live forever," though both scholar and teacher would be puzzled to put it into other words.

ALEXANDER MACLAREN

Forever is a long bargain.

GERMAN PROVERB

> Life is real! Life is earnest!
> And the grave is not its goal;
> Dust thou art, to dust returnest,
> Was not spoken of the soul.

HENRY WADSWORTH LONGFELLOW

Puritan writer Thomas Watson said, "Eternity to the godly is a day that has no sunset; eternity to the wicked is a night that has no sunrise." Eternity is the grand climax of all history. It is the age to come when every person will acknowledge Jesus as Lord. Eternity will bring to this world all God intended for us. Sin will have been judged and banished. Rewards will have been presented. Life will continue with new vitality, meaning, and perfection. What an age that will be!

G. S.

Ethics

Evangelical faith without Christian ethics is a travesty on the gospel.

V. RAYMOND EDMAN

Actually, there is only one "first question" of government, and it is "How should we live?" or (this is the same question) "What kind of people do we want our citizens to be?"

GEORGE WILL

I say statecraft is soulcraft. Just as all education is moral education because learning conditions conduct, much legislation is moral legislation because it conditions the action and the thought of the nation in broad and important spheres in life.

GEORGE WILL

Ethics and equity and the principles of justice do not change with the calendar.

DAVID LAWRENCE

Nothing that is morally wrong can be politically right.

WILLIAM E. GLADSTONE

Let us raise a standard to which the wise and honest can repair; the rest is in the hands of God.

GEORGE WASHINGTON

Evangelism

Evangelism is just one beggar telling another beggar where to find bread.

D. T. NILES

The Holy Spirit can't save saints or seats. If we don't know any non-Christians, how can we introduce them to the Savior?

PAUL LITTLE, *How to Give Away Your Faith*

The world has more winnable people than ever before . . . but it is possible to come out of a ripe field empty-handed.

DONALD MCGAVRAN

Evangelism as the New Testament describes it is not child's play. Evangelism is work, often hard work. Yet it is not drudgery. It puts a person in good humor, and makes him truly human.

OSWALD C. J. HOFFMAN

Evangelism is the spontaneous overflow of a glad and free heart in Jesus Christ.

ROBERT MUNGER

Our business is to present the Christian faith clothed in modern terms, not to propagate modern thought clothed in Christian terms. . . . Confusion here is fatal.

J. I. PACKER

106

To call a man evangelical who is not evangelistic is an utter contradiction.

G. CAMPBELL MORGAN

While women weep, as they do now, I'll fight; while little children go hungry, I'll fight; while men go to prison, in and out, in and out, as they do now, I'll fight; while there is a drunkard left, while there is a poor lost girl upon the streets, where there remains one dark soul without the light of God—I'll fight! I'll fight to the very end!

GENERAL WILLIAM BOOTH,
The end of his very last speech

Evolution

After listening to a lecture on evolution by a science professor, a student wrote a poem and titled it "The Amazing Professor." The poem read:
Once I was a tadpole when I began to begin.
Then I was a frog with my tail tucked in.
Next I was a monkey on a coconut tree.
Now I am a doctor with a Ph.D.

ANONYMOUS

That old bastard theory of evolution. Jackass nonsense.

BILLY SUNDAY

One of the stupidest theories of Western life.

MALCOLM MUGGERIDGE, FROM THE SUNDAY TIMES,
i.e. *London Times* (newspaper) 17 February 1980

Example

Every life is a profession of faith, and exercises an inevitable and silent propaganda. As far as lies in its power, it tends to transform the universe and humanity into its own image. Thus we have all a cure of souls. Every man is a centre of perpetual radiation like a luminous body; he is, as it were, a beacon which entices a ship upon the rocks if it does not guide it into port. Every man is a priest, even involuntarily; his conduct is an unspoken sermon, which is for ever preaching to others—but there are priests of Baal, of Moloch, and of all the false gods. Such is the high importance of example.

HENRI FRÉDÉRIC AMIEL

A man who lives right, and is right, has more power in his silence than another has by his words.

PHILLIPS BROOKS

Excellence

The first great gift we can bestow on others is a good example.

THOMAS MORELL

He that gives good advice builds with one hand; he that gives good counsel and example builds with both; but he that gives good admonition and bad example builds with one hand and pulls down with the other.

FRANCIS BACON

It is easier to exemplify values than teach them.

THEODORE HESBURGH

Excellence

There never will exist anything permanently noble and excellent in the character which is a stranger to resolute self-denial.

SIR WALTER SCOTT

Lord, grant that I may always desire more than I can accomplish.

MICHELANGELO

Whoever I am or whatever I am doing, some kind of excellence is within my reach.

JOHN W. GARDNER

Some people have greatness thrust upon them. Very few have excellence thrust upon them. . . . They achieve it. They do not achieve it unwittingly by doing what comes naturally and they don't stumble into it in the course of amusing themselves. All excellence involves discipline and tenacity of purpose.

JOHN W. GARDNER

Excellence is never cheap. It is costly. Constant care, serious preparation, and continual application are required. Excellence involves desire plus discipline plus determination.

G. S.

Over my desk at home hangs a poster of an Olympic runner, and its caption reads, "Run in such a way that you may *WIN*" (1 Cor. 9:24, NASB).

G. S.

If a society holds conflicting views about excellence—or cannot rouse itself to the pursuit of excellence—the consequences will be felt in everything that it undertakes. The disease may not attack every organ, but the resulting debility will be felt in all parts of the system. Everything that it does and everything that it strives for will be affected.

JOHN W. GARDNER

Only a mediocre person is always at his best.

W. SOMERSET MAUGHAM

Great spirits have always found violent opposition from mediocrities.

ALBERT EINSTEIN

Quality is never an accident. It is always the result of intelligent effort. There must be the will to produce a superior thing.

JOHN RUSKIN

← F →

Failure

Not failure, but low aim, is a crime.

ERNEST HOLMES

Thomas Edison was taunted by some wag before he had successfully invented the incandescent light bulb, "Ten thousand experiments and you haven't learned a thing."

"You're wrong," responded Edison, "I've learned ten thousand ways not to invent the incandescent electric light."

G. S.

Watergate was worse than a crime, it was a blunder.

RICHARD M. NIXON

Failure is the line of least persistence.

ANONYMOUS

The glory is not in never failing, but in rising every time you fall.

ANONYMOUS

Faith

Faith makes all things possible . . . love makes all things easy.

D. L. MOODY

Faith

> Lord give me faith!—to live from day to day,
> With tranquil heart to do my simple part,
> And, with my hand in Thine, just go Thy way.
>
> Lord, give me faith!—to trust, if not to know;
> With quiet mind in all things Thee to find,
> And, child-like, to go where Thou wouldst have me go.
>
> Lord, give me faith!—to leave it all to Thee,
> The future is Thy gift, I would not lift
> The veil Thy love has hung 'twixt it and me.
>
> JOHN OXENHAM

It is a masterpiece of the devil to make us believe that children cannot understand religion. Would Christ have made a child the standard of faith if He had known that it was not capable of understanding His words?

D. L. MOODY

The apostolic church faced mountainous problems with complete confidence in God. "God is able" was their password into pagan territory. Only a fool would have attempted in human strength what they did. Ancient Israel met defeat at Kadesh-Barnea because the people doubted God's ability to see them through. They forgot too soon. The miracle of the Red Sea, the provision of the manna, all faded from their minds, as they considered their own weakness. Problems? Yes, they had problems. Each of us faces his own little custom-designed set of temptations and problems. Every one of us—at our own point of greatest weakness— has a magnificent chance to display God's power. "If God be for us, who can be against us?"

G. S.

The great evangelist George Whitefield once asked a coal miner in Cornwall, England, what he believed.
"Oh," said he, "I believe what my church believes."
Whitefield then inquired, "And what does your church believe?"
"Well," he answered, "the church believes what I believe."
Seeing that he was getting nowhere, Whitefield then asked, "What do you both believe?"
The coal worker answered, "We both believe the same thing."
This sort of unintelligent faith is pathetic and only perpetuates error.

G. S.

Faith, as Paul saw it, was a living, flaming thing leading to surrender and obedience to the commandments of Christ.

A. W. TOZER

You should not believe your conscience and your feelings more than the word which the Lord who receives sinners preaches to you.

MARTIN LUTHER

Sight is not faith, and hearing is not faith, neither is feeling faith; but believing when we neither see, hear, nor feel is faith; and everywhere the Bible tells us our salvation is to be by faith. Therefore we must believe before we feel, and often against our feelings, if we would honor God by our faith.

HANNAH WHITALL SMITH

We walk by faith, not by sight.

2 CORINTHIANS 5:7

The beginning of anxiety is the end of faith, and the beginning of true faith is the end of anxiety.

GEORGE MUELLER

Faith and obedience are bound up in the same bundle; he that obeys God trusts God; and he that trusts God obeys God. He that is without faith is without works, and he that is without works is without faith.

CHARLES H. SPURGEON

Faith is: dead to doubts, dumb to discouragements, blind to impossibilities.

ANONYMOUS

Faith makes: The uplook good, the outlook bright, the future glorious.

ANONYMOUS

Attempt something so impossible that unless God is in it, it is doomed to failure.

JOHN HAGGAI

Faith is a living, daring confidence in God's grace, so sure and certain that a man could stake his life on it a thousand times.

MARTIN LUTHER

Faith . . . is a steady and certain knowledge of the Divine benevolence towards us, which, being founded on the truth of the gratuitous promise in Christ, is both revealed to our minds, and confirmed to our hearts, by the Holy Spirit.

JOHN CALVIN

I believe though I do not comprehend, and I hold by faith what I cannot grasp with the mind.

SAINT BERNARD OF CLAIRVAUX

Family

Justifying faith implies, not only a divine evidence or conviction that "God was in Christ, reconciling the world unto Himself," but a sure trust and confidence that Christ died for my sins, that He loved me and gave Himself for me.

JOHN WESLEY

To have faith is to have wings.

JAMES M. BARRIE

There is no great future for any people whose faith has burned out.

RUFUS M. JONES

The only limit to our realization of tomorrow will be our doubts of today. Let us move forward with strong and active faith.

FRANKLIN D. ROOSEVELT

The steps of faith fall on the seeming void and find the rock beneath.

WALT WHITMAN

Family

In a broken nest there are few whole eggs.

CHINESE PROVERB

A man ought to live so that everybody knows he is a Christian . . . and most of all, his *family* ought to know.

D. L. MOODY

Divorces had multiplied, and the family seemed about to be dissolved. Augustus strove to arrest this downward tendency by edicts and laws in encouragement of marriage and in the restraint of divorces. But the trouble was too deep-seated in the failing moral and religious life of the times to be reached and remedied by any measures of the state.

PHILIP VAN NESS MYERS

The fine edge of character had been blunted in the Rome of the second century A.D. The stern face of the traditional father of the family had faded out; instead we see on every hand the flabby face of the son of the house, the eternal spoiled child of society, who has grown accustomed to luxury and lost all sense of discipline. . . .
Some evaded the duty of maternity for fear of losing their looks. Some were not content to live their lives by their husband's side.

JEROME CARCOPINO, *Daily Life in Ancient Rome*

Let France have good mothers and she will have good sons.

NAPOLEON BONAPARTE

What if God should place a diamond in your hand and tell you to inscribe on it a sentence which should be read at the Last Day and shown there as an index of your thoughts and feelings! What care, what caution would you exercise in the selection! (The diamond is your child.)

RUSSELL PAYSON

The family is the school of duties . . . founded on love.

FELIX ADLER

Apart from religious influence, the family is the most important unit of society. It would be well if every home were Christian, but we know that it is not so. The family and the home can never exert their proper influence while ignoring the Biblical standard. The Bible calls for discipline and a recognition of authority. If children do not learn this at home, they will go out into society without the proper attitude toward authority and law. There is always the exceptional child, but the average tells us that the child is largely what the home has made him. The only way to provide the right home for your children is to put the Lord above them, and fully instruct them in the ways of the Lord. You are responsible before God for the home you provide for them.

BILLY GRAHAM

If there is something one cannot do without, it is Mother. Father loves her, daughter imitates her, son ignores her, salesmen thrive on her, motorists hurry around her, teacher phones her, and the woman next door confides in her.

She can be sweeter than sugar, more sour than a lemon, all smiles, and crying her heart out all within any given two-minute period.

She likes sewing, detective stories, having her birthday remembered, church, a new dress, the cleaning woman, Father's praise, a little lipstick, flowers and plants, canasta, dinner out on Sunday, policemen, one whole day in bed, crossword puzzles, sunny days, tea, and the newspaper boy.

She dislikes doing the dishes, Father's boss, having her birthday forgotten, the motorist behind her, spring cleaning, Junior's report card, rainy days, the neighbor's dog, stairs, and the man who was supposed to cut the grass.

She can be found standing by, bending over, reaching for, kneeling under, and stretching around, but rarely sitting on.

She has the beauty of a spring day, the patience of a saint, the appetite of a small bird, and the memory of a large elephant.

She knows the lowest prices, everybody's birthday, what you should be doing, and all your secret thoughts.

Family

She is always straightening up after, reminding you to, and taking care of, but never asking for.

Yes, a Mother is one thing that nobody can do without. And when you have harassed her, buffeted her about, tried her patience, and worn her out, and it seems that the end of the world is about to descend upon you, then you can win her back with four little words, "Mom, I love you!"

WILLIAM A. GREENBAUM II

Parents wonder why the streams are bitter when they themselves have poisoned the fountain.

JOHN LOCKE

'Mid pleasures and palaces though we may roam,/Be it ever so humble, there's no place like home.

JOHN HOWARD PAYNE

Parents: persons who spend half their time worrying how a child will turn out, and the rest of the time wondering when a child will turn in.

TED COOK

At the bottom as it were of Roman society and forming its ultimate unit, was the family. . . . The typical Roman family consisted of the father . . . and mother, the sons, together with their wives and sons, and the unmarried daughters. . . . The most important feature or element of this family group was the authority of the father. It would be difficult to overestimate the influence of this group upon the history and destiny of Rome. It was the cradle of at least some of those splendid virtues of the early Romans that contributed so much to the strength and greatness of Rome, and that helped to give her the dominion of the world.

PHILIP VAN NESS MYERS

There is an old proverb: "The shoemaker's wife is always the worst shod." The families of many very busy Christian teachers suffer woefully for want of remembering "He first findeth his own brother."

ALEXANDER MACLAREN

All I am, or can be, I owe to my angel mother.

ABRAHAM LINCOLN

The babe at first feeds upon the mother's bosom, but it is always on her heart.

HENRY WARD BEECHER

God could not be everywhere, and therefore he made mothers.

OLD JEWISH SAYING

A man never sees all that his mother has been to him until it is too late.

W. D. HOWELLS

Who ran to help me when I fell,
And would some pretty story tell,
Or kiss the place to make it well? My mother.

JANE TAYLOR

When I was a boy of fourteen, my father was so ignorant I could hardly stand to have the old man around. But when I got to be twenty-one, I was astonished at how much the old man had learned.

MARK TWAIN

Fear

To hate and to fear is to be psychologically ill . . . it is, in fact, the consuming illness of our time.

H. A. OVERSTREET

The only thing we have to fear is fear itself.

FRANKLIN D. ROOSEVELT

Shame arises from the fear of men, conscience from the fear of God.

SAMUEL JOHNSON

Less base the fear of death than fear of life.

EDWARD YOUNG

Fellowship

A gentleman is one who puts more into the world than he takes out.

GEORGE BERNARD SHAW

Who practices hospitality entertains God himself.

ANONYMOUS

Fellowship with God means warfare with the world.

CHARLES E. FULLER

No man is an island.

JOHN DONNE

115

Forgiveness

A habit of devout fellowship with God is the spring of all our life, and the strength of it.

H. E. MANNING

Forgiveness

He who cannot forgive others breaks the bridge over which he must pass himself.

GEORGE HERBERT

God pardons like a mother, who kisses the offense into everlasting forgiveness.

HENRY WARD BEECHER

The best thing to give to your enemy is forgiveness; to an opponent, tolerance; to a friend, your heart; to your child, a good example; to a father, deference; to your mother, conduct that will make her proud of you; to yourself, respect; to all men, charity.

ARTHUR J. BALFOUR

"I can forgive, but I cannot forget," is only another way of saying, "I cannot forgive."

HENRY WARD BEECHER

This is certain, that a man that studieth revenge keeps his wounds green, which otherwise would heal and do well.

FRANCIS BACON

God has a big eraser.

BILLY ZEOLI

I will not permit any man to narrow and degrade my soul by making me hate him.

BOOKER T. WASHINGTON

When Andrew Jackson was being interviewed for church membership, the pastor said, "General, there is one more question which I must ask you. Can you forgive all your enemies?"

Andrew Jackson was silent as he recalled his stormy life of bitter fighting. Then he responded, "My political enemies I can freely forgive; but as for those who attacked me for serving my country and those who slandered my wife—Doctor, I cannot forgive them!"

The pastor made it clear to Jackson that before he could become a member of that church and partake of the broken bread and the cup,

116

his hatred and bitterness must be confessed and dealt with before God.

Again there was an awkward silence. Then Jackson affirmed that if God would help him, he would forgive his enemies.

G. S.

The discretion of a man deferreth his anger; and it is his glory to pass over a transgression.

PROVERBS 19:11

Rejoice not when thine enemy falleth, and let not thine heart be glad when he stumbleth.

PROVERBS 24:17

And forgive us our debts, as we forgive our debtors . . . . For if ye forgive men their trespasses, your heavenly Father will also forgive you: but if ye forgive not men their trespasses, neither will your Father forgive your trespasses.

MATTHEW 6:12, 14–15

And when ye stand praying, forgive, if ye have ought against any: that your Father also which is in heaven may forgive you your trespasses.

MARK 11:25

And be ye kind one to another, tenderhearted, forgiving one another, even as God for Christ's sake hath forgiven you.

EPHESIANS 4:32

Fortune

Fortune does not so much change men as it unmasks them.

ANONYMOUS

Fortune favors the prepared mind.

LOUIS PASTEUR

He that waits upon fortune is never sure of a dinner.

BENJAMIN FRANKLIN

Therefore if a man look sharply and attentively, he shall see Fortune: for though she be blind, yet she is not invisible.

FRANCIS BACON

Fortune truly helps those who are of good judgment.

EURIPIDES

If a man's fortune does not fit him, it is like the shoe in the story; if too large it trips him up, if too small it pinches him.

HORACE

Frankness

A trouble-making woman once told John Wesley, "God has given me the talent of speaking my mind."

Mr. Wesley snapped back, "God wouldn't mind if you buried that talent."

G. S.

We are franker towards others than towards ourselves.

FRIEDRICH NIETZSCHE

People who talk much say nothing.

ANONYMOUS

Freedom

Any nation that thinks more of its ease and comfort than its freedom will soon lose its freedom; and the ironical thing about it is that it will lose its ease and comfort too.

W. SOMERSET MAUGHAM

All theory is against freedom of the will; all experience for it.

SAMUEL JOHNSON

Liberty is the only thing you cannot have unless you are willing to give it to others.

WILLIAM ALLEN WHITE

I disapprove of what you say, but I will defend to the death your right to say it.

VOLTAIRE (ATTRIBUTED)

Yesterday the greatest question was decided which ever was debated in America; and a greater perhaps never was, nor will be, decided among men. A resolution was passed without one dissenting colony, "that these United Colonies are, and of right ought to be, free and independent States."

JOHN ADAMS, Letter to Abigail Adams, 3 July 1776

Friendship

Keep a fair-sized cemetery in your back yard, in which to bury the faults of your friends.

HENRY WARD BEECHER

To gather with God's people in united adoration of the Father is as necessary to the Christian life as prayer.

MARTIN LUTHER

We will win the world when we realize that fellowship, not evangelism, must be our primary emphasis. When we demonstrate the Big Miracle of Love, it won't be necessary for us to go out—they will come in.

JESS MOODY

You may poke a man's fire after you've known him for seven years.

ENGLISH PROVERB

Associate with men of good quality, if you esteem your own reputation; for it is better to be alone than in bad company.

GEORGE WASHINGTON

Old friends are best. King James used to call for his old shoes; they were easiest for his feet.

JOHN SELDEN

A friend should bear a friend's infirmities,/But Brutus makes mine greater than they are.

WILLIAM SHAKESPEARE, Cassius in *Julius Caesar*

You can't eat your friends and have them too.

BUDD SCHULBERG

There is a destiny that makes us brothers,
No one goes his way alone;
All that we send into the lives of others,
Comes back into our own.

EDWIN MARKHAM

He whose hand is clasped in friendship cannot throw mud.

ANONYMOUS

Ten Commandments of Human Relations
1. Speak to people. There is nothing as nice as a cheerful word of greeting.
2. Smile at people. It takes seventy-two muscles to frown, only fourteen to smile.
3. Call people by name. The sweetest music to anyone's ears is the sound of his own name.
4. Be friendly and helpful. If you would have friends, be friendly.

119

5. Be cordial. Speak and act as if everything you do is a genuine pleasure.
6. Be genuinely interested in people. You can like almost everybody if you try.
7. Be generous with praise—cautious with criticism.
8. Be considerate with the feelings of others. There are usually three sides to a controversy; yours, the other fellow's and the right one.
9. Be alert to give service. What counts most in life is what we do for others.
10. Add to this a good sense of humor, a big dose of patience and a dash of humility, and you will be rewarded many-fold.

ROBERT G. LEE

Friendship is one of the sweetest joys of life. Many might have failed beneath the bitterness of their trial had they not found a friend.

CHARLES H. SPURGEON

You can make more friends in two months by becoming interested in other people than you can in two years by trying to get other people interested in you.

DALE CARNEGIE

A friend attributed the secret of his popularity to one particular word. "Years ago," he said, "upon hearing a statement with which I disagreed, I used to say, 'Baloney,' and people began to avoid me like the plague. Now I substitute 'Amazing' for 'Baloney,' and my phone keeps ringing and my list of friends continues to grow."

Capper's Weekly

A friend is a present you give yourself.

ROBERT LOUIS STEVENSON

In the progress of personality, first comes a declaration of independence, then a recognition of interdependence.

HENRY VAN DYKE

We cannot tell the precise moment when friendship is formed. As in filling a vessel drop by drop, there is at last a drop which makes it run over, so in a series of kindnesses there is at last one that makes the heart run over.

SAMUEL JOHNSON

A friend is one to whom one may pour out all the contents of one's heart, chaff and grain together, knowing that the gentlest of hands will take and sift it, keep what is worth keeping, and with a breath of kindness, blow the rest away.

ANONYMOUS

It brings comfort to have companions in whatever happens.

SAINT JOHN CHRYSOSTOM

Three men are my friends: he that loves me, he that hates me, and he that is indifferent to me. Who loves me teaches me tenderness. Who hates me teaches me caution. Who is indifferent to me teaches me self-reliance.

These Times

Those who best knew Sir Walter Scott used to say of him, "He spoke to every man he met as if he were a blood relative."

G. S.

Future

Ignorance of God's prophetic outline, failure to know God's program for the Church, the nations, and Israel, is the cause of the overwhelming amount of error and misunderstanding of the events of the future.

M. R. DeHAAN

We should all be concerned about the future because we will have to spend the rest of our lives there.

CHARLES F. KETTERING

We Break New Seas Today

We break new seas today—
Our eager keels quest unaccustomed waters,
And, from the vast uncharted waste in front,
The mystic circles leap
To greet our prows with mightiest possibilities,
Bringing us—What?

Dread shoals and shifting banks?
And calms and storms?
And clouds and biting gales?
And wreck and loss?
And valiant fighting times?
And, maybe, death!—and so, the Larger Life!

For, should the Pilot deem it best
To cut the voyage short,
He sees beyond the sky-line, and
He'll bring us into Port!

JOHN OXENHAM

Giving

The nineteenth-century American preacher William Jackson once said, "Here on earth our greatest joys are empty and imperfect. But in the presence of God, we shall have fullness of joy. Our cup of joy will be full. There will be no room for sorrow. Here our sweetest pleasures are but momentary. They fly away, and are replaced by bitter disappointment. But at God's right hand, there are 'pleasures forevermore.'"

G. S.

In eternity all the promises of God for His children will be fulfilled. There will be no strife between nations, for all men will want God's will. All of creation and redeemed mankind will continue as God meant them to be, perfect in unity and working together for the glory of God.

G. S.

> One short life for watching with the Saviour,
> Eternal years to walk with Him in white,
> One short life to bravely meet disaster,
> Eternal years to reign with Him in light,
> One brief life for weary toils and trials,
> Eternal years for calm and peaceful rest,
> One brief life for patient self-denials,
> Eternal years for life, where life is best.

ANONYMOUS

Some men see things as they are and say why. I dream things that never were and say why not.

ROBERT F. KENNEDY

← G →

Giving

The nine-tenths prove man's love, but the one-tenth tests man's legal obedience.

HERSCHEL HOBBS

There never was a person who did anything worth doing, who did not receive more than he gave.

HENRY WARD BEECHER

I have somewhere met with the epitaph on a charitable man which has pleased me very much. I cannot recollect the words, but here is the sense of it: "What I spent I lost; what I possessed is left to others; what I gave away remains with me."

JOSEPH ADDISON

> Not what we give, but what we share—
> For the gift without the giver is bare;
> Who gives himself with his alms feeds three—
> Himself, his hungering neighbor, and me.

JAMES RUSSELL LOWELL, *The Vision of Sir Launfal*

He who bestows his goods upon the poor,/Shall have as much again, and ten times more.

JOHN BUNYAN, *Pilgrim's Progress*

Said a good man to me when I asked him, "How do you manage to give so much?"—"The Lord is all the time shoveling it on me, and I would be overwhelmed if I did not give." God shovels wealth upon us, and if we do not shovel it back, we will be buried beneath it as by an avalanche of ruin.

DASHIELL

I do not believe one can settle how much we ought to give. I am afraid the only safe rule is to give more than we can spare.

C. S. LEWIS, *Mere Christianity*

For the Macedonian Christians, giving was not a chore but a challenge, not a burden but a blessing. Giving was not something to be avoided, but a privilege to be desired.

G. S.

When we come to the end of life, the question will be, "How much have you given?" not "How much have you gotten?"

G. S.

Jesus Christ is the supreme Example of giving.

G. S.

The Dead Sea is a dead sea because it continually receives and never gives.

ANONYMOUS

God

Seek to cultivate a buoyant, joyous sense of the crowded kindnesses of God in your daily life.

ALEXANDER MACLAREN

123

God's Character

The most important thought that ever occupied my mind is that of my individual responsibility to God.

DANIEL WEBSTER

Man without God is a seed upon the wind.

ANONYMOUS

> Lord, the newness of this day
> Calls me to an untried way:
> Let me gladly take the road,
> Give me strength to bear my load,
> Thou my guide and helper be—
> I will travel through with Thee.

HENRY VAN DYKE

I find the doing of the will of God leaves me no time for disputing about His plans.

GEORGE MACDONALD

It is difficult to make a man miserable while he feels he is worthy of himself and claims kindred to the great God who made him.

ABRAHAM LINCOLN

God's Character

Having given us the package, do you think God will deny us the ribbon?

OSWALD C. J. HOFFMAN

If God is dead, then the great capitulation of the force standing over against man has been made, and man is free to move forward and to occupy the God-like positions.

Henceforth, man is free to make of himself what he will. . . . If God is dead everything is permitted, even the resort to the animality of an amoral natural force. The decision that the war is over, and man has won, and God is dead is the inspiration and despair of contemporary movements such as nihilism and existentialism.

LESLIE PAUL

It is not a difficult matter to learn what it means to delight ourselves in the Lord. It is to live so as to please Him, to honor everything we find in His Word, to do everything the way He would like to have it done, and for Him.

S. MAXWELL CODER

What do you conceive God to be like? Some would say that to believe at all in a personal God requires a giant leap of faith—but I am convinced that belief in God is a far more reasonable position than atheism. Nature, the personal experience of literally billions of people, and something innate in the heart of man all testify to the existence of God.

G. S.

Down through the years God's love has shined through misery, tears, and sin like a shaft of sunlight on a dark day. We see God's love in His revelation, in His mercy, in His patience, and in His redemption. We see the love of God as the infinite one becomes an infant in Bethlehem's manger. We see it in His life and ministry. And most of all we see it as He hangs on the cross, dying for our sins.

G. S.

I know not, but God knows;
Oh, blessed rest from fear!
All my unfolding days
To Him are plain and clear
Each anxious, puzzled "Why?"
From doubt or dread that grows,
Finds answer in this thought:
I know not, but He knows.

I cannot, but God can;
Oh, balm for all my care!
The burden that I drop
His hand will lift and bear,
Though eagle pinions tire—
I walk where once I ran,
This is my strength to know:
I cannot, but God can.

ANNIE JOHNSON FLINT

Yes, pine for thy God, fainting soul!
    ever pine;
O languish mid all that life brings thee of mirth;
Famished, thirsty, and restless—
    let such life be thine—
For what sigh is to heaven, desire is to earth.

God loves to be longed for, He loves to be sought,
For He sought us Himself with such longing and love;
He died for desire of us, marvellous thought!
And he yearns for us now to be with Him above.

FREDERICK WILLIAM FABER

God's Character

All people that on earth do dwell
  Sing to the Lord with cheerful voice. . . .
For why? the Lord our God is good:
  His mercy is for ever sure;
His truth at all times firmly stood,
  And shall from age to age endure.

WILLIAM KETHE

Dios tarda pero no olvida—God delays but doesn't forget.

SPANISH PROVERB

O God, our help in ages past,
  Our hope for years to come,
Our shelter from the stormy blast,
  And our eternal home.

A thousand ages in thy sight
  Are like an evening gone,
Short as the watch that ends the night
  Before the rising sun.

Time, like an ever-rolling stream,
  Bears all its sons away;
They fly forgotten, as a dream
  Dies at the opening day.

ISAAC WATTS

The trouble with our modern thinking is that we have a conception that God is a haphazard God with no set rules of life and salvation. Ask the astronomer if God is a haphazard God. He will tell you that every star moves with precision in its celestial path. Ask the scientist if God is a haphazard God. He will tell you that His formulas and equations are fixed, and that to ignore the laws of science would be a fool's folly. If the laws in the material realm are so fixed and exact, is it reasonable that God could afford to be haphazard in the spiritual realm when eternal destinies of souls are at stake? Just as God has equations and rules in the material realm, God has equations and rules in the spiritual.

BILLY GRAHAM

An infinite God can give all of Himself to each of His children. He does not distribute Himself that each may have a part, but to each one He gives all of Himself as fully as if there were no others.

A. W. TOZER

126

If the Lord be with us, we have no cause of fear. His eye is upon us, His arm over us, His ear open to our prayer—His grace sufficient, His promise unchangeable.

JOHN NEWTON

I find that doing the will of God leaves me no time for disputing about His plans.

GEORGE MACDONALD

God's Will

I was frustrated out of my mind, trying to figure out the will of God. I was doing everything but getting into the presence of God and asking Him to show me. . . .

PAUL LITTLE

Some people think that God peers over the balcony of heaven trying to find anybody who is enjoying life. And when He spots a happy person, He yells, "Now cut that out!" That concept of God should make us shudder because it's blasphemous!. . .

PAUL LITTLE

Others think it's a choice between doing what we want to do and being happy, and doing what God wants us to do and being miserable.

PAUL LITTLE

In His will is our peace.

DANTE ALIGHIERI

> Thy way, not mine, O Lord,
>   However dark it be!
> Lead me by thine own hand;
>   Choose thou the path for me.
>
> Smooth let it be or rough,
>   It will be still the best;
> Winding or straight, it leads
>   Right onward to thy rest.
>
> I dare not choose my lot;
>   I would not if I might;
> Choose thou for me, my God:
>   So shall I walk aright.
>
> Take thou my cup and it
>   With joy or sorrow fill,
> As best to thee may seem;
>   Choose thou my good and ill.

God's Will

> Choose thou for me my friends,
>   My sickness or my health;
> Choose thou my cares for me,
>   My poverty or wealth.
>
> Not mine, not mine the choice,
>   In things or great or small:
> Be thou my guide, my strength,
>   My wisdom, and my all.
>
> HORATIUS BONAR

Can you think of a father who has no will or plan for the life of his son? Can you imagine a mother who has no clear will or definite ambition for her daughter? Can you imagine a man who has no special desire or pattern in the one he chooses to be his wife? Can you conceive of a king or ruler who has no will or desire or law to govern the conduct of his people? A captain who has no plan for his soldiery? An employer who has no plan or pattern to guide the labor of his workers? If so, then you may also think that God does not have a plan for your life, for every one of these symbols is used in the Bible to represent the relation the Christian bears to his Lord.

G. CHRISTIAN WEISS, The Perfect Will of God

To know the will of God is the greatest knowledge! To do the will of God is the greatest achievement!

GEORGE W. TRUETT

If God gives you a watch, are you honoring Him more by asking Him what time it is or by simply consulting the watch?

A. W. TOZER

In almost everything that touches our everyday life on earth, God is pleased when we're pleased. He wills that we be as free as birds to soar and sing our maker's praise without anxiety.

A. W. TOZER

Has it ever struck you that the vast majority of the will of God for your life has already been revealed in the Bible? That is a crucial thing to grasp.

PAUL LITTLE

Perhaps some of our teaching about God's will could be made more helpful if we supplemented it by additional figures of speech. It is useful . . . for example, to think of God's will as an area in a television wave guide or tube. As I understand it, the waves in this tube bounce back anywhere within the tube that they "want" to go, completely free so long as they remain in the tube. They are not channeled to a thin line—they just can't go outside of the wave guide.

KENNETH PIKE

When we want to know God's will, there are three things which always concur: the inward impulse, the Word of God and the trend of circumstances. . . . Never act until these three things agree.

F. B. MEYER

My Jesus, as Thou wilt: O may Thy will be mine!
Into Thy hand of love I would my all resign.
Through sorrow or thro' joy, Conduct me as Thine own,
And help me still to say, "My Lord, Thy will be done!"

My Jesus, as Thou wilt: All shall be well for me;
Each changing future scene I gladly trust with Thee.
Straight to my home above I travel calmly on,
And sing in life or death, "My Lord, Thy will be done!"

BENJAMIN SCHMOLCK

I like to interpose in all of my appointments, if the Lord wills.

A. B. SIMPSON

The man or woman who is wholly or joyously surrendered to Christ can't make a wrong choice—any choice will be the right one.

A. W. TOZER

The history of all the great characters of the Bible is summed up in this one sentence: They acquainted themselves with God, and acquiesced His will in all things.

RICHARD CECIL

Man proposes, but God disposes.

THOMAS À KEMPIS

Blessed is the man who finds out which way God is moving and then gets going in the same direction.

ANONYMOUS

Six Steps to Knowing God's Will
1. I seek at the beginning to get my heart into such a state that it has no will of its own in regard to a given matter. Nine-tenths of the trouble with people is just here. Nine-tenths of the difficulties are overcome when our hearts are ready to do the Lord's will,

whatever it may be. When one is truly in this state, it is usually but a little way to the knowledge of what His will is.

2. Having done this, I do not leave the result to feeling or simple impression. If I do so, I make myself liable to great delusions.

3. I see the will of the Spirit of God through, or in connection with, the Word of God. The Spirit and the Word must be combined. If I look to the Spirit alone without the Word, I lay myself open to great delusions also. If the Holy Spirit guides us at all, He wills according to the Scriptures and never contrary to them.

4. Next I take into account providential circumstances. These often plainly indicate God's will in connection with His Word and Spirit.

5. I ask God in prayer to reveal His will to me aright.

6. Thus, through prayer to God, the study of the Word, and reflection, I come to a deliberate judgment according to the best of my ability and knowledge; and if my mind is thus at peace, and continues so after two or three more petitions, I proceed accordingly. In trivial matters, and in transactions involving more important issues, I have found this method always effective.

GEORGE MUELLER

That the Almighty does make use of human agencies and directly intervenes in human affairs is one of the plainest statements in the Bible. I have had so many evidences of His direction, so many instances when I have been controlled by some other power than my own will, that I cannot doubt that this power comes from above.

ABRAHAM LINCOLN

Gospel

Religions are man's search for God; the Gospel is God's search for man. There are many religions, but one Gospel.

E. STANLEY JONES

The inclusive gospel cannot be shared by an exclusive people.

G. S.

The gospel is not merely a message of deliverance, it is also a rule of conduct. It is not merely theology, it is also ethics. Like some of the ancient municipal charters, the grant of privileges and proclamation of freedom is also the sovereign code which imposes duties and shapes life.

ALEXANDER MACLAREN

Each generation of the church in each setting has the responsibility of communicating the gospel in understandable terms, considering the language and thought-forms of that setting.

FRANCIS SCHAEFFER, *Escape from Reason*

Gossip and Slander

The real truth is that while He came to preach the gospel, His chief object in coming was that there might be a gospel to preach.

R. W. DALE

Men may not read the gospel in sealskin, or the gospel in morocco, or the gospel in cloth covers, but they can't get away from the gospel in shoe leather.

DONALD GREY BARNHOUSE

Philosophical argument has sometimes shaken my reason for the faith that was in me; but my heart has always assured me that the Gospel of Jesus Christ must be reality.

DANIEL WEBSTER

Gossip and Slander

The secret of a governable tongue is not self-control but Christ-control.

G. S.

Thy friend has a friend, and thy friend's friend has a friend; be discreet.

The Talmud

Remember, every time you open your mouth to talk, your mind walks out and parades up and down the words.

EDWIN H. STUART

So live that you wouldn't be ashamed to sell the family parrot to the town gossip.

WILL ROGERS

Language is the apparel in which your thoughts parade before the public. Never clothe them in vulgar or shoddy attire.

GEORGE CRANE

I am more deadly than the screaming shell from the howitzer. I win without killing. I tear down homes, break hearts, and wreck lives. I travel on the wings of the wind. No innocence is strong enough to intimidate me, no purity pure enough to daunt me. I have no regard for truth, no respect for justice, no mercy for the defenseless. My victims are as numerous as the sands of the sea, and often as innocent. I never forget and seldom forgive. My name is Gossip.

MORGAN BLAKE, *Atlanta Journal*

The tongue can be a beautiful angel or a hideous demon. The tongue can be as honey or vinegar. The tongue can be pure or vile. The tongue

Grace

can caress or cut. The tongue can rouse men to act as well as it can subdue their emotions. A false whisper can infuriate a nation, but the power of eloquence can quell the fury of a multitude. A word of anger can wound while a word of kindness can win. Words of hate can kill and words of love can kiss. God says: "Death and life are in the power of the tongue" (Proverbs 18:21).

G. S.

Girl like her mother: Clip off the old soundtrack.

G. S.

Three boys were playing when one noticed a large gossipy man coming down the sidewalk. "Clear the roadway," said one. "Here comes the sound truck."

G. S.

Methodist evangelist Sam Jones said he knew a woman with a tongue so long she could sit in the parlor and lick the skillet in the kitchen.

G. S.

I would rather play with forked lightning, or take in my hand living wires with their fiery current, than speak a reckless word against any servant of Christ, or idly repeat the slanderous darts which thousands of Christians are hurling on others, to the hurt of their own souls and bodies.

A. B. SIMPSON

Grace

"The grace of God," says Luther, "is like a flying summer shower." It has fallen upon more than one land, and passed on. Judaea had it, and lies barren and dry. These Asiatic coasts had it, and flung it away.

ALEXANDER MACLAREN

I remember a rough parable of Luther's, grafted on an older legend, which runs somewhat in this fashion:—A man's heart is like a foul stable. Wheelbarrows and shovels are of little use, except to remove some of the surface filth, and to litter all the passages in the process. What is to be done with it? "Turn the Elbe into it," says he. The flood will sweep away all the pollution. Not my own efforts, but the influx of that pardoning, cleansing grace which is in Christ will wash away the accumulations of years, and the ingrained evil which has stained every part of my being.

ALEXANDER MACLAREN

There, but for the grace of God, goes John Bradford.

JOHN BRADFORD

Grace means the free, unmerited, unexpected love of God, and all the benefits, delights, and comforts which flow from it. It means that while we were sinners and enemies we have been treated as sons and heirs.

R. P. C. HANSON

Salvation is from our side a choice, from the divine side it is a seizing upon, an apprehending, a conquest by the Most High God. Our "accepting" and "willing" are reactions rather than actions. The right of determination must always remain with God.

A. W. TOZER

[Grace is] free sovereign favor to the ill-deserving.

BENJAMIN WARFIELD

Growth, Guidance

The unexamined life is not worth living.

SOCRATES

The strongest principle of growth lies in human choice.

GEORGE ELIOT

Youth is happy because it has the ability to see beauty. Anyone who keeps the ability to see beauty never grows old.

FRANZ KAFKA

The harvest of old age is the memory and rich store of blessings laid up earlier in life.

CICERO

To know where you are is a good thing; but it is as important and perhaps more so, to know where you are going.

Quarterly Magazine

What is the present, after all, but a growth out of the past?

WALT WHITMAN

Guidance

Lead, kindly Light, amid the encircling gloom,
　Lead thou me on;
The night is dark, and I am far from home;
　Lead thou me on.

JOHN HENRY NEWMAN

> Guide me, O thou great Redeemer,
>   Pilgrim through this barren land;
> I am weak, but thou art mighty,
>   Hold me with thy powerful hand;
>   Bread of heaven,
> Feed me till I want no more.

WILLIAM WILLIAMS

> Abide with me, fast falls the eventide;
> The darkness deepens; Lord, with me abide!
> When other helpers fail, and comforts flee,
> Help of the helpless, O abide with me.
>
> Swift to its close ebbs out life's little day;
> Earth's joys grow dim; its glories pass away;
> Change and decay in all around I see;
> O thou who changest not, abide with me.
>
> I need Thy presence every passing hour;
> What but Thy grace can foil the tempter's power?
> Who like Thyself my guide and stay can be?
> Through cloud and sunshine, O abide with me!
>
> I fear no foe, with Thee at hand to bless;
> Ills have no weight, and tears no bitterness.
> Where is death's sting? Where, grave, thy victory?
> I triumph still, if Thou abide with me.
>
> Hold Thou Thy word before my closing eyes;
> Shine through the gloom, and point me to the skies;
> Heaven's morning breaks, and earth's vain shadows flee—
> In life, in death, O Lord, abide with me.

HENRY FRANCIS LYTE

You can't drive straight on a twisting lane.

RUSSIAN PROVERB

← **H** →

Happiness (See Cheerfulness)

Happiness is a perfume you cannot pour on others without getting a few drops on yourself.

ANONYMOUS

Happiness is no laughing matter.

RICHARD WHATELY

134

God cannot give us a happiness and peace apart from Himself, because it is not there. There is no such thing.

C. S. LEWIS, *Mere Christianity*

If happiness truly consisted in physical ease and freedom from care, then the happiest individual would not be either a man or a woman; it would be, I think, an American cow.

WILLIAM LYON PHELPS

Heart

Caras vemos, corazones no sabemos—Faces we see, hearts we know not.

SPANISH PROVERB

Le coeur a ses raisons que la raison ne connaît point—The heart has its reasons which reason knows nothing of.

BLAISE PASCAL

There never was any heart truly great and generous, that was not also tender and compassionate.

ROBERT FROST

In making our decisions, we must use the brains that God has given us. But we must also use our hearts which He also gave us.

FULTON OURSLER

The eyes see what the heart loves. If the heart loves God and is single in this devotion, then the eyes will see God whether others see Him or not.

WARREN WIERSBE, *Live Like a King*

Heaven

We talk about heaven being so far away. It is within speaking distance to those who belong there. . . . Heaven is a prepared place for a prepared people.

D. L. MOODY

I would rather go to heaven alone than go to hell in company.

R. A. TORREY

What is heaven going to be like? Just as there is a mystery to hell, so there is a mystery to heaven. Yet I believe the Bible teaches that heaven

Hell

is a literal place. Is it one of the stars? I don't know. I can't even speculate. The Bible doesn't inform us. I believe that out there in space where there are one thousand million galaxies, each a hundred thousand light years or more in diameter, God can find some place to put us in heaven. I'm not worried about where it is. I know it is going to be where Jesus is. Christians don't have to go around discouraged and despondent with their shoulders bent. Think of it—the joy, the peace, the sense of forgiveness that He gives you, and then heaven too.

BILLY GRAHAM

In heaven, after "ages of ages" of growing glory, we shall have to say, as each new wave of the shoreless, sunlit sea bears us onward, "It doth not yet appear what we shall be."

ALEXANDER MACLAREN

4-1-90

If you read history you will find that the Christians who did most for the present world were precisely those who thought most of the next. It is since Christians have largely ceased to think of the other world that they have become so ineffective in this.

C. S. LEWIS, *Mere Christianity*

Aim at heaven and you will get earth thrown in. Aim at earth and you will get neither.

C. S. LEWIS, *Living Quotations*

Has this world been so kind to you that you should leave with regret? There are better things ahead than any we leave behind.

C. S. LEWIS, *Living Quotations*

4-1-90

Christ's grave was the birthplace of an indestructible belief that death is vanquished and there is life eternal.

ADOLPH HARNACK

Those are dead even for this life who hope for no other.

JOHANN WOLFGANG VON GOETHE

No man must go to heaven who hath not sent his heart thither before.

THOMAS WILSON

Hell

On one occasion Colonel Robert G. Ingersoll, the agnostic lecturer of the last century, was announced to give an address on hell. He declared he would prove conclusively that hell was a wild dream of some scheming theologians who invented it to terrify credulous people. As he was launching into his subject, a half-drunken man arose in the audience and exclaimed, "Make it strong, Bob. There's a lot of us poor fellows depending on you. If you are wrong, we are all lost. So be sure you can prove it clear and plain."

No amount of reasoning can nullify God's sure Word. He has spoken as plainly of a hell for the finally impenitent as of a heaven for those who are saved.

G. S.

The safest road to Hell is the gradual one—the gentle slope, soft underfoot, without sudden turnings, without milestones, without signposts.
C. S. LEWIS, *The Screwtape Letters*

The vague and tenuous hope that God is too kind to punish the ungodly has become a deadly opiate for the consciences of millions.
A. W. TOZER

One of the horrors of hell is the undying memory of a misspent life—"Son, remember" (Luke 16:25).

ANONYMOUS

It does not require a decision to go to hell.

ANONYMOUS

Heritage

I desire no future that will break the ties of the past.
GEORGE ELIOT

What from your fathers' heritage is lent,
Earn it anew to really possess it.
JOHANN WOLFGANG VON GOETHE

The young, whether they know it or not, live on borrowed property.
RICHARD W. LIVINGSTONE

Wisdom is to be gained only as we stand upon the shoulders of those who have gone before.

LEARNED HAND

History

How shall we labour with any effect to build up the Church, if we have no thorough knowledge of her history, or fail to apprehend it

137

from the proper point of observation? History is, and must ever continue to be, next to God's word, the richest foundation of wisdom, and sweet guide to all successful practical activity.

PHILIP SCHAFF

History is about the most cruel of all goddesses, and she leads her triumphal car over heaps of corpses, not only in war, but also in "peaceful" economic development. And we men and women are unfortunately so stupid that we never pluck up courage for real progress unless urged to it by sufferings that seem almost out of proportion.

FRIEDRICH ENGELS

In Guatemala and southern Mexico one can observe the Indians who are without doubt the lineal descendants of those who created the Mayan civilization. Today they are a humble people, not asking much of themselves or of the world, and not getting much. A light went out.

JOHN W. GARDNER

Rome remained great as long as she had enemies who forced her to unity, vision, and heroism. When she had overcome them all, she flourished for a moment and then began to die.

WILL DURANT, *Caesar & Christ*

Those who disregard the past are bound to repeat it.

GEORGE SANTAYANA

Consciousness of the past alone can make us understand the present.

HERBERT LUETHY

History is a bucket of ashes.

CARL SANDBURG

History is indeed little more than the register of the crimes, follies, and misfortunes of mankind.

EDWARD GIBBON

History is bunk!

HENRY FORD

The rich experience of history teaches that up to now not a single class has voluntarily made war for another class.

JOSEPH STALIN

. . . a page of history is worth a volume of logic.

OLIVER WENDELL HOLMES, JR.

Hobbies and Leisure

It is a sad thing when a man has only a vocation, with no avocation whatsoever. An avocation can very well save the situation if we are condemned to the monotonous work which may be the by-product of some large productive process. Then our sense of creativity should be derived from our avocation or hobby. If a man can have a hobby, he can retain vigor and vitality.

HAROLD OCKENGA

Every now and then go away, have a little relaxation. For when you come back to your work, your judgment will be surer, since to remain constantly at work, you lose power of judgment. Go some distance away because then the work appears smaller, and more of it can be taken in at a glance, and a lack of harmony or proportion is more readily seen.

LEONARDO DA VINCI

No man is really happy or safe without a hobby, and it makes precious little difference what the outside interest may be—botany, beetles or butterflies, roses, tulips or irises; fishing, mountaineering or antiquities— anything will do so long as he straddles a hobby and rides it hard.

SIR WILLIAM OSLER

Retired Leisure,/That in trim gardens takes his pleasure.

JOHN MILTON

One ought, every day at least, to hear a little song, read a good poem, see a fine picture, and, if it were possible, to speak a few reasonable words.

JOHANN WOLFGANG VON GOETHE

Holy Spirit

God commands us to be filled with the Spirit; and if we aren't filled, it's because we're living beneath our privileges.

D. L. MOODY

If you have been born of the Holy Spirit, you will not *have* to serve God . . . it will become the natural thing to do.

D. L. MOODY

How would you like to live with somebody who was everlastingly grieving your heart by his conduct?

G. CAMPBELL MORGAN

Holy Spirit

The Spirit of God was the spirit of conviction while sin worked itself out from Fall to Flood; He was a Spirit of detailed service while the people of God were being organized into a nationality; He was a Spirit of strength while the people were fighting for the land, and were casting out those who had deeply sinned; and He became a Spirit of hope when the peculiar people had passed into a condition of apostasy and wandering. He lit the horizon with the glow of approaching day.

G. CAMPBELL MORGAN, *The Spirit of God*

Watch out for any ministry or person who claims to be led by the Holy Spirit but acts contrary to the Word of God. And beware of any movement or group whose focus is the Holy Spirit. The Holy Spirit points not to Himself but to the Lord Jesus.

G. S.

Though every believer has the Holy Spirit, the Holy Spirit does not have every believer.

A. W. TOZER

When we rely on organization, we get what organization can do. When we rely upon education, we get what education can do. When we rely on eloquence, we get what eloquence can do. But when we rely on the Holy Spirit, *we get what God can do.*

A. C. DIXON

The doctrine of the Spirit as it relates to the believer has over the last half-century been shrouded in a mist such as lies upon a mountain in stormy weather. A world of confusion has surrounded this truth. This confusion has not come by accident. An enemy has done this. Satan knows that Spiritless evangelicalism is as deadly as Modernism or heresy, and he has done everything in his power to prevent us from enjoying our true Christian heritage.

A. W. TOZER

It is impossible for that man to despair who remembers that his Helper is omnipotent.

JEREMY TAYLOR

When the Spirit presents Christ to our inner vision it has an exhilarating effect on the soul much as wine has on the body. The Spirit-filled man may literally dwell in a state of spiritual fervour amounting to a mild and pure inebriation. God dwells in a state of perpetual enthusiasm. He pursues His labours always in a fulness of holy zeal.

A. W. TOZER

It is curious to remark, that wherever the Holy Ghost is spoken of in the Bible, he is spoken of in terms of gentleness and love. We often read of "the wrath of God" the Father, as Romans 1:18; and we read of the wrath of God the Son, as Psalms 2:12, but we nowhere read of the wrath of God the Holy Ghost.

ROBERT M. MCCHEYNE

Notice three important facts about Ephesians 5:18. First, it is in the imperative mood. It is not a suggestion or an appeal, but a command. Anything less than the fullness of the Spirit is disobedience to the Word of God.

Second, it is a present tense verb. We are to be filled with the Holy Spirit now. And it is a continuous action verb. It could be translated, "Be being filled with the Spirit." We must be filled daily, constantly, moment by moment. Yesterday's blessings are not sufficient for today or tomorrow.

Third, it is a passive verb. That means that being filled with the Spirit is not something we do, but something that is done for us. We must be yielded. We must be willing. We must be believing. But God does the filling. We simply receive it by faith.

G. S.

Imagine, if you will, a brand-new factory filled with the finest modern equipment—everything that is needed to manufacture quality products.

Then suppose a visitor enters the factory and comments on the beauty of the machines but wonders why the machines are not running. No one is sure, he is told, "Why not oil the machines?" the man suggests. They do. But still nothing happens.

A little later another visitor comes in and comments on the splendid layout of the facilities. But there is no action. "I think you need some drapes and a few pictures on the wall," he says. So these are added. The place looks better, but still none of the equipment moves.

Other suggestions follow one by one—stained glass windows, an organ, even a steeple, but nothing works. The machinery still remains idle.

Finally, someone asks, "Did anyone turn on the power?"

Turn on the power? Of course, that's it! Sure enough, when the master control panels are switched on, the machines begin to roll. Soon the materials are fashioned and processed and the factory begins to produce.

"How simple," you say. You are absolutely right. But what the power was to that factory, the Holy Spirit is in the life of each believer. Just as the factory must have power to produce, so we need the Holy Spirit and the power He gives to live successfully in the Christian life.

G. S.

Home

I believe firmly that the moment our hearts are emptied of pride and selfishness and ambition and everything that is contrary to God's law, the Holy Spirit will fill every corner of our hearts. But if we are full of pride and conceit and ambition and the world, there is no room for the Spirit of God.

D. L. MOODY

There must be an emptying before there can be a filling. Your life may be powerless because you have never given complete control to God's Spirit.

G. S.

The world has yet to see what God can do with and for and through and in a man who is fully and wholly consecrated to Him.

HENRY VARLEY

We do not use the Holy Spirit; he uses us.

WARREN WIERSBE

Home

An ideal wife is any woman who has an ideal husband.

BOOTH TARKINGTON

The little child digs his well in the seashore sand, and the great Atlantic, miles deep, miles wide, is stirred all through and through to fill it for him.

PHILLIPS BROOKS

The happiness of the domestic fireplace is the first boon of heaven.

THOMAS JEFFERSON

Home is where the heart is.

PLINY THE ELDER

Home should be a place of mutual responsibility and respect, of encouragement and cooperation and counsel, of integrity, of willingness to work, of discipline when necessary, with the tempering quality of love added to it, with a sense of belonging, and with someone to talk to.

RICHARD L. EVANS

Home that our feet may leave, but not our hearts.

ANONYMOUS

142

Honesty

Ay, sir; to be honest, as the world goes, is to be one man picked out of ten thousand.

WILLIAM SHAKESPEARE, *Hamlet*

"Honesty is the best policy," but he who acts on that principle is not an honest man.

RICHARD WHATELY, *Apophthegms*

I hope I shall possess firmness and virtue enough to maintain what I consider the most enviable of all titles, the character of an honest man.

GEORGE WASHINGTON

A jug is never carried under one's coat for an honest reason.

LATIN PROVERB

The louder he talked of his honor, the faster we counted our spoons.

RALPH WALDO EMERSON

Hope

It has been said that man can live about forty days without food, about three days without water, and about eight minutes without air—but only one second without HOPE.

ANONYMOUS

Hope means expectancy when things are otherwise hopeless.

G. K. CHESTERTON

Dr. Victor Frankl, an Austrian psychiatrist, observed that a prisoner did not continue to live very long after hope was lost. But even the slightest ray of hope—the rumor of better food, a whisper about an escape—helped some of the camp inmates to continue living even under systematic horror (*Man's Search for Meaning*).

G. S.

The word *hope* in Scripture is a term of certainty. To say that we hope for the return of the Lord is not to say that we are uncertain about His coming. His coming for His own is certain.

The Greek word translated "hope" in the New Testament is *elpizō*, which means "to anticipate with confident expectation." *Elpizō* is also translated "trust" in several New Testament verses. Hope is one of the three evidences of salvation—faith, hope, and love—referred to by the apostle Paul throughout the epistles (see 1 Corinthians 13:13; Colossians 1:4–5; 1 Thessalonians 1:3).

G. S.

"Totally without hope one cannot live." To live without hope is to cease to live. Hell is hopelessness. It is no accident that above the entrance to Dante's hell is the inscription: "Leave behind all hope, you who enter here."

FEODOR DOSTOEVSKI

The world is full of experiments for bringing deliverance to the race, but on the authority of the New Testament and in the light of nineteen centuries of history, I declare my conviction that the only hope of this world is the return of Christ to reign over the earth and to establish universal peace.

A. J. GORDON

Hope is wishing for a thing to come true; faith is believing that it will come true.

NORMAN VINCENT PEALE

He who plants a tree plants a hope.

LUCY LARCOM

There is not enough darkness in all the world to put out the light of one small candle.

ANONYMOUS

Humanism, Secular

No morality can be founded on authority even if the authority were divine.

A. J. AYER, *Essays on Humanism*

The New Testament is certainly not a blue-print for twentieth-century Christian behaviour.

F. R. BARRY, *Christian Ethics & Secular Society*

Humanism asserts that the nature of the universe depicted by modern science makes unacceptable any supernatural or cosmic guarantees of human values.

THE HUMANIST MANIFESTO I

The cosmos is all that is or ever was or ever will be.

CARL SAGAN, in the public television show, Cosmos

As in 1933 (the date of the Humanist Manifesto I) humanists still believe that traditional theism, especially faith in the prayer-hearing God, assumed to love and care for persons, to hear and understand their prayers, and to be able to do something about them, is an unproved and outmoded faith. Salvationism, based on mere affirmation, still appears as harmful, diverting people with false hopes of heaven hereafter. Reasonable minds look to other means for survival.

THE HUMANIST MANIFESTO II

Man can will nothing unless he has first understood that he must count on no one but himself; that he is alone, abandoned on earth in the midst of his infinite responsibilities, without help, with no other aim than the one he sets himself, with no other destiny than the one he forges for himself on this earth.

JEAN PAUL SARTRE

We have grasped the mystery of the atom and rejected the Sermon on the Mount. . . . Ours is a world of nuclear giants and ethical infants.

OMAR BRADLEY

What marks our own generation? It is the fact that modern man thinks there is nobody home in the universe.

FRANCIS SCHAEFFER, *Death in the City*

Humanism, man beginning only from himself, had destroyed the old basis of values, and could find no way to generate with certainty any new values. In the resulting vacuum the impoverished values of personal peace and affluence had come to stand supreme.

FRANCIS SCHAEFFER, *How Should We Then Live?*

Humility

Do you want to enter what people call "the higher life"? Then go a step lower down.

ANDREW MURRAY

The ears of barley that bear the richest grain always hang the lowest.

ANONYMOUS

They that know God will be humble, and they that know themselves cannot be proud.

JOHN FLAVEL

The meek man is not a human mouse afflicted with a sense of his own inferiority. Rather he may be in his moral life as bold as a lion and as strong as Samson; but he has stopped being fooled about himself. He has accepted God's estimate of his own life. He knows he is as weak and helpless as God declared him to be, but paradoxically, he knows at the same time that he is in the sight of God of more importance than angels. In himself, nothing; in God, everything. That is his motto.

A. W. TOZER

Walk humbly before God.

WILLIAM CULBERTSON

I used to think that God's gifts were on shelves one above the other, and that the taller we grew in Christian character the easier we could reach them. I now find that God's gifts are on shelves one beneath the other. It is not a question of growing taller, but of stooping down, to get His best gifts.

F. B. MEYER, *Alliance Weekly*

3-11-01 The higher a man is in grace, the lower he will be in his own esteem.

CHARLES H. SPURGEON

"Become nothing if you would *become something."* In His rules of success, you must *stoop* to *rise, go down* to *get up,* and *shrink* to *grow.*

ANONYMOUS

I have never accepted what many people have kindly said, namely that I inspired the nation. It was the nation and the race dwelling all round the globe that had the lion heart. I had the luck to be called upon to give the roar.

WINSTON CHURCHILL

3-11-01 Humility is to make a right estimate of one's self.

CHARLES H. SPURGEON

To be poor in spirit means knowing yourself, accepting yourself, and being yourself to the glory of God.

WARREN WIERSBE, *Live Like a King*

Life is a long lesson in humility.

JAMES M. BARRIE

I believe the first test of a truly great man is his humility.

JOHN RUSKIN

Hunger

We cannot exist as a little island of well-being in a world where two-thirds of the people go to bed hungry every night.

ELEANOR ROOSEVELT

Hungry bellies have no ears.

FRANÇOIS RABELAIS

They that die by famine die by inches.

MATTHEW HENRY

Our policy is not directed against any country or doctrine, but against hunger, poverty, desperation and chaos.

GEORGE C. MARSHALL

Is it only the mouth and belly which are injured by hunger and thirst? Men's minds are also injured by them.

MENCIUS

A hungry man is not a free man.

ADLAI STEVENSON

Hypocrisy

May God deliver us from a ho-hum attitude. Young people can read their parents. They can see right through their teachers, and they turn away in disgust from a make-believe faith.

G. S.

I am afraid we modern Christians are long on talk and short on conduct. We use the language of power but our deeds are the deeds of weakness. We settle for words in religion because deeds are too costly. It is easier to pray, "Lord, help me to carry my cross daily" than to pick up the cross and carry it; but since the mere request for help to do something we do not actually intend to do has a certain degree of religious comfort, we are content with repetition of the words.

A. W. TOZER

Honey in his mouth, knives in his heart.

CHINESE PROVERB

← I →

Ideals

Sometimes a person's mind is stretched by a new idea and never does go back to its old dimensions.

OLIVER WENDELL HOLMES, SR.

Never tell a young person that something cannot be done. God may have been waiting for countless centuries for somebody ignorant enough of the impossibility to do that thing.

ANONYMOUS

The power of ideals is incalculable. We see no power in a drop of water. But let it get into a crack in the rock and be turned to ice, and it splits the rock; turned into steam, it drives the pistons of the most powerful engines. Something has happened to it which makes active and effective the power that is latent in it.

ALBERT SCHWEITZER

I know of no more encouraging fact than the unquestionable ability of man to elevate his life by a conscious endeavor.

HENRY THOREAU

Character is singularly contagious.

SAMUEL A. ELIOT

Ideas

False ideas are the greatest obstacles to the reception of the gospel. We may preach with all the fervor of a reformer and yet succeed only in winning a straggler here and there, if we permit the whole collective thought of the nation or of the world to be controlled by ideas which, by the resistless force of logic, prevent Christianity from being regarded as anything more than a harmless delusion. Under such circumstances, what God desires us to do is to destroy the obstacle at its root. . . . What is today a matter of academic speculation begins tomorrow to move armies and pull down empires.

J. GRESHAM MACHEN

A fair idea put to use is better than a good idea kept on the polishing wheel.

ALEX OSBORN

Nothing is as powerful as an idea whose time has come.

VICTOR HUGO

Ideas rule life and in the long run shape the ages.

ANONYMOUS

There is something inevitable about an idea whose hour has struck.

JOHANN WOLFGANG VON GOETHE

Idolatry

The worship of the false in any form is idolatry.

WILLIAM PURCELL

You don't have to go to heathen lands today to find false gods. America is full of them. Whatever you love more than God is your idol.

D. L. MOODY

Indeed the Idols I have loved so long
Have done my credit in this World much wrong:
Have drown'd my Glory in a shallow Cup
And sold my reputation for a Song.

OMAR KHAYYÁM, *Rubyaiyat,* Fitzgerald translation

. . . the triumph of my art is in thoroughly examining whether the thought which the mind of the young man brings forth is a false idol or a noble and true birth.

PLATO

How glad the heathens would have been,/That worship idols, wood and stone,/If they the book of God had seen.

ISAAC WATTS

Man is certainly stark mad; he cannot make a worm, and yet he will be making gods by dozens.

MICHEL DE MONTAIGNE

Imagination

The soul without imagination is what an observatory would be without a telescope.

HENRY WARD BEECHER

When I could not sleep for cold
I had fire enough in my brain,
And builded with roofs of gold
My beautiful castles in Spain!

JAMES RUSSELL LOWELL

Immortality, Incarnation

The human race is governed by its imagination.

NAPOLEON BONAPARTE

Imagination is the air of the mind.

PHILIP JAMES BAILEY

Immortality

God created man for immortality, and made him the image of his own eternal self.

WISD. 2:23

I perceived that in kinship with wisdom lies immortality.

ANONYMOUS

A few years ago when I was in Northfield, Massachusetts, to conduct evangelistic services, I visited "Roundtop" where D. L. Moody is buried. As I knelt in prayer, I recalled vividly Mr. Moody's eloquent words:
"Someday you will read in the papers that D. L. Moody is dead. Don't you believe a word of it. At that moment I shall have gone up higher; that is all; out of this old clay tenement, into a house that is immortal—a body that death cannot touch, that sin cannot taint; a body fashioned like unto His glorious body. I was born of the flesh in 1837. I was born of the spirit in 1856. That which is born of the flesh may die. That which is born of the spirit will live forever."
Mr. Moody was right. And I expect to meet him one day in a glorified body that will never die.

G. S.

Incarnation

For in Christ all the fullness of the Deity lives in bodily form. . . .

COLOSSIANS 2:9, NIV

The Incarnation would be equally a miracle however Jesus entered the world.

P. T. FORSYTH

He was made what we are that He might make us what He is Himself.

SAINT IRENAEUS

Whoever thinks God is most freely revealed in the impersonal movements of the stellar galaxies must reckon yet with Jesus Christ as the incarnation of righteousness, goodness and love, and with the well-nigh irresistible impression that the eternal God is best seen in his personality and life.

CARL F. H. HENRY

Influence

Let no man imagine that he has no influence.

HENRY GEORGE

The good person increases the value of every other person whom he influences in any way.

ANONYMOUS

Young people set their watches, for right time or wrong, by the watches of their elders.

ANONYMOUS

But evil men and seducers shall wax worse and worse, deceiving and being deceived.

2 TIMOTHY 3:13

The serene, silent beauty of a holy life is the most powerful influence in the world, next to the might of God.

BLAISE PASCAL

The length and breadth of our influence upon others depends upon the depth of our concern for others.

ANONYMOUS

You cannot antagonize and influence at the same time.

JOHN KNOX

Intelligence

He [Christ] wants a child's heart, but a grown-up's head. He wants us to be simple, single-minded, affectionate, and teachable, as good children are; but He also wants every bit of intelligence we have to be alert at its job, and in first-class fighting trim.

C. S. LEWIS, *Mere Christianity*

Anyone who is honestly trying to be a Christian will soon find his intelligence being sharpened: one of the reasons why it needs no special education to be a Christian is that Christianity is an education itself. That is why an uneducated believer like Bunyan was able to write a book that has astonished the whole world.

C. S. LEWIS, *Mere Christianity*

If you are thinking of becoming a Christian, I warn you you are embarking on something which is going to take the whole of you, brains and all.

C. S. LEWIS

I do not feel obliged to believe that that same God who has endowed us with sense, reason, and intellect has intended us to forego their use.

GALILEO

I tremble for my country when I think that schools may be sending forth into government people who are too proudly "practical" to take ideas seriously.

GEORGE WILL, *Statecraft As Soulcraft*

Every powerful movement has had its philosophy which has gripped the mind, fired the imagination and captured the devotion of its adherents.

JOHN STOTT, *Your Mind Matters*

Ideas have consequences.

RICHARD WEAVER, *Ideas Have Consequences*

There is no longer a Christian mind. It is common place that the mind of modern man has been secularized. . . . But unfortunately the Christian mind has succumbed to the secular drift with a degree of weakness and nervelessness unmatched in Christian history.

HARRY BLAMIRES, *The Christian Mind*

← **J** →

Jesus

Napoleon was right when he said, "I know men, and I tell you, Jesus is more than a man. Comparison is impossible between Him and any other human being who ever lived, because He was the Son of God." Emerson was right when he replied to those who asked him why he did not include Jesus among his *Representative Men,* "Jesus was not just a man." Arnold Toynbee was right when he said, "As we stand and gaze with our eyes fixed upon the farther shore a simple figure rises from the flood and straightway fills the whole horizon of history. There is the Savior."

BILLY GRAHAM

The hand that holds the seven stars is as loving as the hand that was laid in blessing upon the little children; the face that is as the sun shining in its strength beams with as much love as when it drew publicans and harlots to His feet. The breast that is girt with the golden girdle is the same breast upon which John leaned his happy head.

ALEXANDER MACLAREN

To tie Jesus Christ to the very best human system is to tie a star, light years distant, to a dead horse here on earth. Neither star nor Christ will thus be bound.

JOE BAYLY

Jesus clothes the Beatitudes with his own life.

CARL F. H. HENRY

"I'm ready to accept Jesus as a great moral teacher, but I don't accept his claim to be God." That is the one thing we must not say. A man who was merely a man and said the sort of things Jesus said would not be a great moral teacher. He would either be a lunatic—on a level with the man who says he is a poached egg—or else he would be the Devil of Hell. You must make your choice. Either this man was, and is, the Son of God; or else a madman or something worse. You can shut him up for a fool, you can spit at him and kill him as a demon, or you can fall at his feet and call him Lord and God. But let us not come with any patronizing nonsense about his being a great human teacher. He has not left that open to us. He did not intend to.

C. S. LEWIS, *Mere Christianity*

His zeal never degenerated into passion, nor His constancy into obstinacy, nor His benevolence into weakness, nor His tenderness into sentimentality. His unworldliness was free from indifference and unsociability, His dignity from pride and presumption, His affectability from undue familiarity, His self-denial from moroseness, His temperance from austerity. He combined child-like innocency with manly strength, absorbing devotion to God with untiring interest in the welfare of man, tender love to the sinner with uncompromising severity against sin, commanding dignity with winning humility, fearless courage with wise caution, unyielding firmness with sweet gentleness!

PHILIP SCHAFF

Jews

"Can you give me one single irrefutable proof of God?"
"Yes, your majesty, the Jews."

MARQUIS D'ARGENS TO FREDERICK THE GREAT

Religious or secularized, the Jew remains a Jew—*malgré lui*—a voluntary or involuntary witness to the truth that is symbolized in the story of God's covenant with Abraham.

ALAN RICHARDSON, *Christian Apologetics*

No nation is more significant in the future of world politics than the nation of Israel. That is a meaningful statement in light of the fact that less than fifty years ago some believed that the Jewish people could never again hope to return to their land as a sovereign nation. Today the headlines show that what was once scoffed at as a ludicrous idea has indeed taken place. Israel has returned to the world scene and is now more important, more strategic, and more crucial to future events than ever seemed possible. The rebirth of the nation Israel has been like the key piece of a jigsaw puzzle, enabling the other pieces to fall quickly in place.

G. S.

Certainly as Israel's promises are being fulfilled before our eyes other aspects of prophecy such as the resurrection of the dead in Christ and the translation of living saints become a real and an imminent possibility.

JOHN F. WALVOORD

More than any other of the world's races and nations, the Jewish people can trace their history with accuracy. The origin of most nations is wrapped in surmise and conjecture, but Scripture clearly records the beginning of the Hebrews. In Genesis 12, the Lord said to Abraham, "Get thee out of thy country, and from thy kindred, and from thy father's house, unto a land that I will shew thee: And I will make of thee *a great nation,* and I will bless thee, and make thy name great; and thou shalt be a blessing: and I will bless them that bless thee, and curse him that curseth thee: and in thee shall all families of the earth be blessed" (vv. 1–3, italics added).

G. S.

There is a bright and exciting future for the nation of Israel. Jeremiah 31:10 says, "He that scattered Israel will gather him." God is going to continue bringing the people of Israel back to their land for the fulfillment of the promises He made to Abraham many years ago. The Jewish nation, despite the stated intentions of many of her enemies, is indestructible. This is God's promise: "I am with thee, saith the Lord, to save thee: though I make a full end of all nations whither I have scattered thee, yet will I not make a full end of thee" (Jeremiah 30:11).

G. S.

Joy

Those whose sins have perished, whose doubts are destroyed, who are self-restrained, and are intent on the welfare of all other beings, these obtain God's everlasting joy.

The Bhagavad Gita (Hindu)

This is the land of sin and death and tears . . . but up yonder is unceasing joy.

D. L. MOODY

There is more joy in Jesus in twenty-four hours than there is in the world in 365 days. I have tried them both.

R. A. TORREY

Joy is never in our power and pleasure often is.

C. S. LEWIS, *Surprised by Joy*

Joy makes us giddy, dizzy.

GOTTHOLD EPHRAIM LESSING

> Joy, in Nature's wide dominion,
> Mightiest cause of all is found;
> And 'tis joy that moves the pinion
> When the wheel of time goes round.

JOHANN VON SCHILLER

There is a sweet joy which comes to us through sorrow.

CHARLES H. SPURGEON

Joy is the gigantic secret of the Christian.

G. K. CHESTERTON

Any man can again have the joy of his first meeting with God if he will go back over the same road.

ROY L. SMITH

Cheerfulness and content are great beautifiers and are famous preservers of youthful looks.

CHARLES DICKENS

Love, in the divine alchemy of life, transmutes all duties into privileges, all responsibilities into joys.

WILLIAM GEORGE JORDAN

Judgment

Nothing great was ever achieved without enthusiasm.

RALPH WALDO EMERSON

Judgment

Heaven is above all yet; there sits a judge/That no king can corrupt.

WILLIAM SHAKESPEARE, *Henry VIII*

The time was the 19th of May 1780. The place was Hartford, Connecticut. The day has gone down in New England history as a terrible foretaste of Judgment Day. For at noon the skies turned from blue to grey and by mid-afternoon had blackened over so densely that, in that religious age, men fell on their knees and begged a final blessing before the end came. The Connecticut House of Representatives was in session. And as some of the men fell down and others clamored for an immediate adjournment, the speaker of the House, one Colonel Davenport, came to his feet. He silenced them and said these words: "The day of judgment is either approaching or it is not. If it is not, there is no cause for adjournment. If it is, I choose to be found doing my duty. I wish therefore that candles may be brought."

ALISTAIR COOKE

Though the mills of God grind slowly, yet they grind exceeding small;
Though with patience He stands waiting, with exactness grinds He all.

FRIEDRICH VON LOGAU, Translated by
Henry Wadsworth Longfellow

At the day of Doom men shall be judged according to their fruits. It will not be said then, Did you believe? but, Were you doers, or talkers only?

JOHN BUNYAN

The final chapter of human history is solely God's decision, and even now He is everywhere active in grace or judgment. Never in all history have men spoken so much of end-time, yet been so shrouded in ignorance of God's impending doomsday.

CARL F. H. HENRY

I shall tell you a great secret, my friend. Do not wait for the last judgment, it takes place every day.

ALBERT CAMUS

Sometimes those of us who hold that the Lord Jesus Christ is coming again are spoken of as pessimists. I think it can be truly said that we are really the only ones who have any right to be optimistic.

WILLIAM CULBERTSON

One of the greatest paintings of all time is Michelangelo's *The Last Judgment.* The action of the painting centers on Christ as He raises His arm in a gesture of damnation. Though some elements of the painting appear unbiblical, at that time its message reminded people of God's holy presence, which had been forgotten in the humanism of the day.

The painting pictures the dead as they are resurrected to be judged. As hell releases its captives, the Judge of Heaven reviews their works. The entire painting reflects the despair of that generation.

When the painting was unveiled, a storm of conviction fell upon the viewers. All Europe trembled as the story of the power of *The Last Judgment* traveled from city to city.

G. S.

God gives Jesus Christ authority to judge all men *because of who He is.* Jesus is uniquely qualified to judge because He is God and has existed from eternity (John 1:1). As God, He knows everything, can be everywhere at once, and has unlimited power and authority. He knows everything we think and sees everything we do. Thus He can judge perfectly, with wisdom and full understanding and without error or partiality.

Christ is also uniquely qualified to judge *because of what He has done.* By dying for our sins on the cross, He demonstrated perfect love for all men. Thus, when He judges, His perfect righteousness is balanced by His perfect love.

G. S.

[About Andrew Jackson] I have great respect for the President but all men need to be restored, and unless our good President repents of his sin, he will be judged by God.

PETER CARTWRIGHT

Some seem to think that if we are Christians, God is not going to bring up anything done in this life. It is all under the blood. Put everything on Jesus and live any way you please. Surely that cannot be right.

KEITH L. BROOKS

Justice

. . . the Christian's goal is not power, but justice. We are to seek to make the institutions of power just, without being corrupted by the process necessary to do this.

CHARLES COLSON

I will look, your Honor, and endeavor to find a precedent, if you require it; though it would seem to be a pity that the Court should lose the honor of being the first to establish so just a rule.

RUFUS CHOATE

There is no virtue so truly great and godlike as justice.

JOSEPH ADDISON

If we have to choose between making men Christian and making the social order more Christian, we must choose the former. But there is no such antithesis. . . . There is no hope of establishing a more Christian social order except through the labour and sacrifice of those in whom the Spirit of Christ is active, and the first necessity for progress is more and better Christians taking full responsibility as citizens for the political, social and economic system under which they and their fellows live.

WILLIAM TEMPLE

Justification

Now the article of justification, which is our sole defense, not only against all the force and craft of man, but also against the gates of hell, is this: that by faith only in Christ, and without works, we are pronounced righteous and saved.

MARTIN LUTHER

Virtue debases itself in justifying itself.

VOLTAIRE

That in such righteousness
To them by faith imparted they may find
Justification towards God, and peace
Of conscience.

JOHN MILTON

← K →

Kindness

Kindness is a language which the blind can see and the deaf can hear.

ANONYMOUS

Kindness is the golden chain by which society is bound together.

JOHANN WOLFGANG VON GOETHE

The best place to find a good helping hand is at the end of your arm.

MARTIN VANBEE

158

Humanitarianism is a grand-sounding word, but it can sometimes mean something very much thinner than human kindness.

A. C. CRAIG

There is a grace of kind listening, as well as a grace of kind speaking.

FREDERICK WILLIAM FABER

Getting money is not all a man's business: to cultivate kindness is a valuable part of the business of life.

SAMUEL JOHNSON

That best portion of a good man's life,/His little, nameless, unremembered acts/Of kindness and love.

WILLIAM WORDSWORTH, *Lines above Tintern Abbey*

Kingdoms

He has rescued us out of the darkness and gloom of Satan's kingdom and brought us into the kingdom of his dear Son.

COLOSSIANS 1:13, LB

And if thou be not in the kingdom of Christ, it is certain that thou belongest to the kingdom of Satan, which is this evil world.

MARTIN LUTHER

Goodness is a realm; and there is a realm of evil. Each is spiritually against the other. If the other world has a king, there is also a prince of this world; and there can be no peace except in a complete victory, so that such a war shall never be again.

P. T. FORSYTH

The fundamental biblical opposition is not between flesh and Spirit, creature and Creator, but between the Creator of the flesh and its destroyer, between God and the devil, Christ and Satan, the Holy Spirit and the Unholy.

PHILIP S. WATSON

Knowledge

Knowledge comes by eyes always open and working hands, and there is no knowledge that is not power.

JEREMY TAYLOR

The farther one pursues knowledge, the less one knows.

LAO-TZU

We must observe that the knowledge of God which we are invited to cultivate is not that which, resting satisfied with empty speculation, only flutters in the brain, but a knowledge which will prove substantial and fruitful whenever it is duly perceived and rooted in the heart.

JOHN CALVIN

← L →

Last Words

See in what peace a Christian can die.

JOSEPH ADDISON

Et tu, Brute fili—you also, O son Brutus.

JULIUS CAESAR (ATTRIBUTED)

Turn up the lights; I don't want to go home in the dark.

O. HENRY

I am about to take my last voyage, a great leap in the dark.

THOMAS HOBBES

How were the circus receipts at Madison Square Garden?

P. T. BARNUM

. . . the fog is rising.

EMILY DICKINSON

Just before his death on March 2, 1791, John Wesley opened his eyes and exclaimed in a strong, clear voice, "The best of it is, God is with us."

G. S.

Let us cross over the river and rest under the shade of the trees.

THOMAS J. "STONEWALL" JACKSON

Laughter

Laugh, and the world laughs with you;
    Weep, and you weep alone.
For the sad old earth must borrow its mirth,
    But has troubles enough of its own.

ELLA WHEELER WILCOX

160

I laugh because I must not cry. . . . With the fearful strain that is on me night and day, if I did not laugh I should die.

ABRAHAM LINCOLN

He who laughs—lasts.

NORWEGIAN PROVERB

People who laugh actually live longer than people who don't laugh. Few persons realize that health actually varies according to the amount of laughter.

JAMES S. WALSH

A man isn't poor if he can still laugh.

RAYMOND HITCHCOCK

One should take good care not to grow too wise for so great a pleasure of life as laughter.

JOSEPH ADDISON

I am not in the show business alone to make money. I feel it my mission, as long as I live, to provide clean, moral, and healthful recreation for the public to which I have so long catered.

P. T. BARNUM

Laziness

We have so many labor-saving devices today that we go broke keeping them repaired. Everything is easier, but requires greater maintenance.

LORNE SANNY

Absorption in ease is one of the most reliable signs of present or impending decay.

RICHARD WEAVER

Laziness grows on people; it begins in cobwebs and ends in iron chains. The more one has to do, the more he is able to accomplish.

THOMAS BUXTON

The lazier a man is, the more he plans to do tomorrow.

NORWEGIAN PROVERB

He also that is slothful in his work is brother to him that is a great waster.

PROVERBS 18:9

Leaders

The sluggard will not plough by reason of the cold; therefore shall he beg in harvest, and have nothing.

PROVERBS 20:4

Not slothful in business; fervent in spirit; serving the Lord.

ROMANS 12:11

Leaders

We need a baptism of clear seeing. We desperately need seers who can see through the mist—Christian leaders with prophetic vision. Unless they come soon it will be too late for this generation. And if they do come we will no doubt crucify a few of them in the name of our worldly orthodoxy.

A. W. TOZER

A leader is best
When people barely know that he exists,
Not so good when people obey and acclaim him,
Worse when they despise him.
"Fail to honor people,
They fail to honor you";
But of a good leader, who talks little,
When his work is done, his aim fulfilled,
They will all say, "We did this ourselves."

LAO-TZU

A great leader never sets himself above his followers except in carrying responsibilities.

JULES ORMONT

The penalty of leadership is loneliness.

H. WHEELER ROBINSON

Energy is the dynamo, the power plant of personality, the driving force upon which all other traits depend. It is the Alpha but not the Omega of leadership.

E. S. BOGARDUS

George Washington, kneeling in prayer at Valley Forge, tells something about the heartbeat of the founders of America. We need to remember that the method of all leadership is humble, modest service. What else makes a nation great?

G. S.

162

Learning

Our safety does not lie in the present perfection of our knowledge of the will of God, but in our sincerity in obeying the light we have, and in seeking for more.

EDWARD WORSDELL

The greatest discovery of my generation is that human beings can alter their lives by altering their attitudes of mind.

WILLIAM JAMES

Of the two purposes of education—to make a person fit for the world as it is and to make him able to change it—the second is the more important.

C. DELISLE BURNS

The doorstep to the temple of wisdom is the knowledge of our own ignorance.

CHARLES H. SPURGEON

Teaching that would lay any claim at all to distinction, if not to actual greatness, is the influence of personality upon personality, rather than the mere imparting of a set of facts.

FRANK E. GAEBELEIN

I grow old learning something new every day.

SOLON

Whosoever would understand what he hears must hasten to put into practice what he has heard.

SAINT GREGORY

There are no foolish questions and no man becomes a fool until he has stopped asking questions.

CHARLES P. STEINMETZ

As we acquire more knowledge, things do not become more comprehensible but more mysterious.

ALBERT SCHWEITZER

Lies

Slander, lies, character assassination—these things are a threat to every single citizen everywhere in this country. When even one American—

who has done nothing wrong—is forced by fear to shut his mind and close his mouth, then all Americans are in peril. It is the job of all of us—of every American who loves his country and his freedom—to rise up and put a stop to this terrible business.

HARRY S. TRUMAN, Speech on McCarthyism

There are people who exaggerate so much that they can't tell the truth without lying.

H. W. SHAW

As ten millions of circles can never make a square, so the united voice of myriads cannot lend the smallest foundation to falsehood.

OLIVER GOLDSMITH

So near is falsehood to truth that a wise man would do well not to trust himself on the narrow edge.

CICERO

Who is not sure of his memory should not attempt lying.

MICHEL DE MONTAIGNE

And he that does one fault at first,/And tries to hide it, makes it two.

ISAAC WATTS

Life Views

Life at the longest is amazingly short. The Bible uses several metaphors to convey just how brief it is.

Job says, "My life is wind" (Job 7:7), and, "My days are swifter than a weaver's shuttle" (Job 7:6). Have you ever watched a weaver's shuttle? It moves so fast that you can't distinguish its movement. It's just a blur.

The psalmist compares life to a fading flower or a falling leaf: "As for man, his days are as grass; as a flower of the field, so he flourisheth. For the wind passeth over it, and it is gone" (Ps. 103:15–16).

The writer of Chronicles says, "Our days on the earth are as a shadow, and there is none abiding" (1 Chron. 29:15).

And Psalm 90:9 reminds, "We spend our years as a tale that is told."

James (4:14) asks, "What is your life? It is even a vapor, that appeareth for a little time, and then vanisheth away."

Life is so short that the wood of the cradle rubs up tight against the marble of the tomb.

G. S.

We can fly like the bird,
And swim like the fish,
If we could only learn
To behave like men—we'd
Be doing something.

VANCE HAVNER

Always take hold of things by the smooth handle.

THOMAS JEFFERSON

Life is like riding a bicycle. You don't fall off until you stop pedaling.

CLAUDE PEPPER

There is no need to run outside
For better seeing. . . .
Rather abide
At the center of your being;
For the more you leave it, the less you learn.
Search your heart and see . . .
The way to do is to be.

LAO-TZU

Life is not a spectacle or a feast; it is a predicament.

GEORGE SANTAYANA

Life is an onion and one cries while peeling it.

FRENCH PROVERB

We are born crying, live complaining, and die disappointed.

THOMAS FULLER

All I maintain is that on this earth there are pestilences and there are victims, and it's up to us, as far as possible, not to join forces with the pestilences.

ALBERT CAMUS

In the land of lobelias and tennis flannels
The rabbit shall burrow and the thorn revisit,
The nettle shall flourish on the gravel court,
And the wind shall say: "Here were decent godless people:
Their only monument the asphalt road
And a thousand lost golf balls."

T. S. ELIOT

Life is one long process of getting tired.

SAMUEL BUTLER

Life Views

Life is the art of drawing sufficient conclusions from insufficient premises.

SAMUEL BUTLER

Life is made up of sobs, sniffles, and smiles, with sniffles predominating.

O. HENRY

There is such a thing as the very perfection of arrangement without life, like cabinets in a museum, where all the specimens are duly classified and dead.

ALEXANDER MACLAREN

It seems to me that we're all in the same boat with Christopher Columbus. He didn't know where he was going when he started. When he got there he didn't know where he was, and when he got back he didn't know where he had been.

JAMES M. BRAUDE

> Farewell, a long farewell, to all my greatness!
> This is the state of man: today he puts forth
> The tender leaves of hope; tomorrow blossoms,
> And bears his blushing honors thick upon him;
> The third day comes a frost, a killing frost;
> And when he thinks, good easy man, full surely
> His greatness is a-ripening, nips his root,
> And then he falls, as I do.

WILLIAM SHAKESPEARE, Wolsey in *Henry VIII*

Life is a hard fight, a struggle, a wrestling with the principle of evil, hand to hand, foot to foot. Every inch of the way is disputed. The night is given us to take breath, to pray, to drink deep at the fountain of power. The day, to use the strength which has been given us, to go forth to work with it till the evening.

FLORENCE NIGHTINGALE

Any twenty-year-old who isn't a liberal doesn't have a heart, and any forty-year-old who isn't a conservative doesn't have a brain.

WINSTON CHURCHILL

A man is rich in proportion to the number of things which he can afford to let alone.

HENRY THOREAU

The great thing is to be found at one's post as a child of God, living each day as though it were our last, but planning as though our world might last a hundred years.

C. S. LEWIS, *God in the Dock*

Little Things, Loneliness

When I consider the short duration of my life, swallowed up in the eternity before and after, the little space which I fill, and even can see, engulfed in the infinite immensity of space of which I am ignorant, and which knows me not, I am frightened, and am astonished being here rather than there, why now rather than then.

BLAISE PASCAL

Where is the Life we have lost in living?

T. S. ELIOT

There is more to life than increasing its speed.

MOHANDAS GANDHI

Little Things

Little words are the sweetest to hear; little charities fly furthest and stay longest on the wing; little lakes are the stillest; little hearts are the fullest, and little farms are the best tilled. Little books are read the most and little songs the dearest loved. And when Nature would make anything especially rare and beautiful, she makes it little; little pearls, little diamonds, little dews. Agar's is a model prayer but then it is a little one; and the burden of the petition is for but the little. The Sermon on the Mount is little, but the last dedication discourse was an hour long. Life is made up of little things that count, and death is what remains of them all. Day is made up of little beams, and night is glorious with little stars.

ANONYMOUS

Little pots soon boil over.

ANONYMOUS

Better to light one small candle than to curse the darkness.

CHINESE PROVERB

Regarding the lever: "Give me a firm place to stand, and I will move the earth."

ARCHIMEDES

If you add a little to a little and do this often, soon the little will become great.

HESIOD, *Works and Days*

Loneliness

Few of us have reached middle life who do not, looking back, see our track strewn with the gaunt skeletons of dead friendships, and

Lost Man

dotted with "oaks of weeping," waving green and mournful over graves, and saddened by footprints striking away from the line of march, and leaving us the more solitary for their departure.

ALEXANDER MACLAREN

People are lonely because they build walls instead of bridges.

JOSEPH FORT NEWTON

One of the prominent symptoms of our times . . . is loneliness. Isn't it ironic that in an age of the greatest population explosion the world has ever known, more people are desperately lonely than ever before? . . . Even the high-rise apartments in our big cities are monuments to loneliness. There is aching loneliness behind those doors for many people. I know of those, both in the city and in the suburb, who go to the large shopping centers simply for the opportunity to talk to somebody in the store. At least the checker will speak to them as they go out. Loneliness is one of the desperate problems of our age.

PAUL LITTLE

The central purpose of Christ's life . . . is to destroy the life of loneliness and to establish here on earth the life of love.

THOMAS WOLFE

Loneliness is stamped on the American face; it rises like an exhalation from the American landscape.

VAN WYCK BROOKS

Cannot the heart in the midst of crowds feel frightfully alone?

CHARLES LAMB

Lost Man

All man's miseries derive from not being able to sit quiet in a room alone.

BLAISE PASCAL

There is a God-shaped vacuum in every heart.

BLAISE PASCAL

There is no exit from the human dilemma.

JEAN PAUL SARTRE

All my life I have been seeking to climb out of the pit of my besetting sins and I cannot do it and I never will unless a hand is let down to draw me up.

SENECA

Man is the product of causes which had no prevision of the end they were achieving . . . his origin, his growth, his hopes and fears, his loves and his beliefs, are but the outcome of accidental collocations of atoms . . . no fire, no heroism, no intensity of thought and feeling, can preserve an individual life beyond the grave . . . and the whole temple of man's achievement must inevitably be buried beneath the debris of a universe in ruins.

BERTRAND RUSSELL

The mass of men live lives of quiet desperation.

HENRY THOREAU

I cannot find my way: there is no star/In all the shrouded heavens anywhere.

EDWIN ARLINGTON ROBINSON

I am a fallen, lost creature.

SAMUEL COLERIDGE

The world is . . . a kind of spiritual kindergarten where millions of bewildered infants are trying to spell "God" with the wrong blocks.

EDWIN ARLINGTON ROBINSON

> Mock on, mock on, Voltaire, Rousseau;
> Mock on, mock on; 'tis all in vain!
> You throw the sand against the wind,
> And the wind blows it back again.

WILLIAM BLAKE

Man is lost because he is separated from God, his true reference point, by true moral guilt. But he never will be nothing. Therein lies the horror of his lostness. For man to be lost, in all his uniqueness and wonder, is tragic.

FRANCIS SCHAEFFER

God does not die on the day when we cease to believe in a personal deity, but we die on the day when our lives cease to be illuminated by the steady radiance, renewed daily, of a wonder, the source of which is beyond all reason.

DAG HAMMARSKJöld

Modern writers depict the pessimism of our time and many of them throw up their hands in despair and say, "There is no answer to man's dilemma." Hemingway once said, "I live in a vacuum that is as lonely as a radio tube when the batteries are dead, and there is no current to plug into." Eugene O'Neill in "Long Day's Journey Into Night" typifies the philosophical attitude of our day. He says, "Life's only meaning is death." I say to Hemingway and O'Neill, who have already gone on, "There is more to life than death." There is more to life than a radio tube that needs a place to plug into. Jesus taught us the dignity and importance of being a person. God put us on this earth for a purpose, and our purpose is fellowship with God and to glorify God.

BILLY GRAHAM

Dr. Rollo May in his book, *Man's Search for Himself,* quotes Friedrich Nietzsche who wrote a parable about the "death of God." It is a haunting story about a madman who ran into the village square shouting, "Where is God?"

The people around him did not believe in God; they laughed and said that perhaps God had gone on a voyage or emigrated. The madman then shouted: "Where is God? I shall tell you! We have killed Him—you and I—yet how have we done this? . . . Who gave us the sponge to wipe away the whole horizon? What did we do when we unchained this earth from its sun? . . . Whither shall we move now? Away from all suns? Do we not fall incessantly? Backward, sideward, forward, in all directions? Is there yet any up and down?"

G. S.

I fled Him, down the nights and down the days;
I fled Him, down the arches of the years;
I fled Him, down the labyrinthine ways
Of my own mind; and in the mist of tears
I hid from Him, and under running laughter.
Up vistaed hopes, I sped;
And shot, precipitated,
Adown Titanic glooms of chasmed fears,
From those strong Feet that followed, followed after.

FRANCIS THOMPSON, *The Hound of Heaven*

Love

You called, you cried, you shattered my deafness, you sparkled, you blazed, you drove away my blindness, you shed your fragrance, and I drew in my breath, and I pant for you.

SAINT AUGUSTINE

For though thou didst know the whole Bible by heart and the sayings of the philosophers, what doth it profit thee without the love of God?

. . . Surely a humble husbandman that serveth God is better than a proud philosopher who, neglecting himself, labours to understand the movements of the heavens.

THOMAS À KEMPIS

A wise lover values not so much the gift of the lover as the love of the giver.

THOMAS À KEMPIS

What a vast distance there is between knowing God and loving him!

BLAISE PASCAL

Let everyone understand that real love of God does not consist in tear-shedding, nor in that sweetness and tenderness for which we usually long, just because they console us, but in serving God in justice, fortitude of soul and humility.

SAINT THERESA OF AVILA

You wish to hear from me why and how God is to be loved? My answer is: the reason for loving God is God himself, and the measure in which we should love him is to love him without measure.

SAINT BERNARD OF CLAIRVAUX

Love so amazing, so divine, demands my soul, my life, my all.

ISAAC WATTS

I never knew up to that time that God loved us so much. This heart of mine began to thaw out; I could not keep back the tears. I just drank it in. . . . I tell you there is one thing that draws above everything else in the world and that is love.

D. L. MOODY

Satan separates; God unites; love binds us together.

D. L. MOODY

Love is the best thing in the world, and the thing that lives longest.

HENRY VAN DYKE

Love is friendship set on fire.

JEREMY TAYLOR

Yes, love is the magic key of life—not to get what we want but to become what we ought to be.

EILEEN GUDER

Love

Only the loving will have any understanding of love—just as only the good will understand goodness. When one has gotten only a little way into loving, one learns that what understanding we do attain, poor and partial as it must be, is not gotten by thinking about it. It comes by receiving and giving love, as a part of the process of living.

EILEEN GUDER

Love is exclusively a Person. *2-5-89*

NORMAN GRUBB

No cord nor cable can so forcibly draw, or hold so fast, as love can do with a twined thread.

ROBERT BURTON

For where love is wanting, the beauty of all virtue is mere tinsel, is empty sound, is not worth a straw, nay more, is offensive and disgusting.

JOHN CALVIN

There are more people who wish to be loved than there are willing to love.

S. R. N. CHAMFORT

And the moral of that is—"Oh, 'tis love, 'tis love, that makes the world go round!"

LEWIS CARROLL, *Alice's Adventures in Wonderland*

Respect is what we owe; love, what we give.

PHILIP JAMES BAILEY

> I think true love is never blind,
>   But rather brings an added light,
> An inner vision quick to find
>   The beauties hid from common sight.

PHOEBE CARY

A friendship like love is warm;/A love like friendship steady.

THOMAS MOORE

Music is Love in search of a word.

SIDNEY LANIER

Required in every good lover . . . the whole alphabet . . . Agreeable, Bountiful, Constant, Dutiful, Easy, Faithful, Gallant, Honourable, Ingenious, Joyful, Kind, Loyal, Mild, Noble, Officious, Prudent, Quiet,

Rich, Secret, True, Understanding, Valiant, Wise . . . Young and Zealous.

MIGUEL DE CERVANTES

> Across the gateway of my heart
> I wrote "No Thoroughfare,"
> But love came laughing by, and cried:
> "I enter everywhere."

HERBERT SHIPMAN

How vast a memory has Love!

ALEXANDER POPE

God, from a beautiful necessity, is Love.

MARTIN FARQUHAR TUPPER

Love is ever the beginning of Knowledge, as fire is of light!

THOMAS CARLYLE

True love is like ghosts, which everybody talks about and few have seen.

FRANÇOIS, DUC DE LA ROCHEFOUCAULD

X I think that love is the only spiritual power that can overcome the self-centeredness that is inherent in being alive. Love is the thing that makes life possible or, indeed, tolerable.

ARNOLD TOYNBEE

Real love is the universal language—understood by all. You may have every accomplishment or give your body to be burned; but, if love is lacking, all this will profit you and the cause of Christ nothing.

HENRY DRUMMOND

Love would put a new face on this weary old world in which we dwell as pagans and enemies too long, and it would warm the heart to see how fast the vain diplomacy of statesmen, the impotence of armies, and navies, and lines of defence, would be superseded by this unarmed child. Love will creep where it cannot go, will accomplish that by imperceptible methods—being its own level, fulcrum, and power—which force could never achieve.

RALPH WALDO EMERSON

Infantile love follows the principle: "I love because I am loved." Mature love follows the principle: "I am loved because I love." Immature love says: "I love you because I need you." Mature love says: "I need you because I love you."

ERICH FROMM

The desire of power in excess caused the angels to fall; the desire of knowledge in excess caused man to fall, but in love there is no excess, neither can angel or man come in danger by it.

FRANCIS BACON

Love does not die easily. It is a living thing. It thrives in the face of all life's hazards, save one—neglect.

JAMES D. BRYDEN

> Do you know the world is dying
> For a little bit of love?
> Everywhere we hear them sighing,
> For a little bit of love.

ANONYMOUS

It is possible to have compassion without love, and it is possible to have kindness without love; but it is impossible for one who has put on love to be unkind and without compassion, for love itself is not just an accessory garment. Love is the complete garment that has all the others built into it, so that love is a total way of life.

RAY ANDERSON

Love is appealing, but its practice is appallingly difficult.

ANONYMOUS

I took up that word Love, and I do not know how many weeks I spent in studying the passages in which it occurs, till at last I could not help loving people. I had been feeding on love so long that I was anxious to do everybody good I came in contact with. I got full of it. It ran out my fingers. You take up the subject of love in the Bible! You will get so full of it that all you have to do is to open your lips, and a flood of the Love of God flows out.

D. L. MOODY

The churches would soon be filled if outsiders could find that people in them loved them when they came. This love draws sinners! We must win them to us first, then we can win them to Christ. We must get people to love us, and then turn them over to Christ.

D. L. MOODY

If you haven't love in your heart, you should throw your hope to the four winds, and go and get a better one.

D. L. MOODY

Persons are to be loved; things are to be used.

REUEL HOWE

People don't go where the action is, they go where love is.

JESS MOODY

O, there is nothing holier, in this life of ours, than the first consciousness of love—the first fluttering of its silken wings.

HENRY WADSWORTH LONGFELLOW

> Blest be the tie that binds,
> Our hearts in Christian love;
> The fellowship of kindred minds,
> Is like to that above.

JOHN FAWCETT

This "first love" seeks not people, but a Person, the One who alone merits our first love. The "first love" is the intimate personal relationship of love which one has with our Lord Jesus Christ.

M. BASILEA SCHLINK

No one can live without being a debtor; no one should live without being a creditor.

N. J. PANIN

No single factor has so limited the Christian church down through the years as man's inhumanity to man—sometimes outright cruelty, but far more often, sheer lovelessness.

G. S.

Without God's help, our other loves cannot even remain what they start out to be, or become what they promise.

G. S.

X Life minus love equals zero!

G. S.

Five steps in knowing how to love:
1. Receive Christ as your Saviour. He is God's gift of love to you. "God is love" (1 John 4:8).
2. Experience the power of God's love in your life. "The love of God is shed abroad in our hearts" (Rom. 5:5).
3. Seek the fruit of the Spirit (Gal. 5:22).
4. Pray for an abounding love (Phil. 1:9).

Love

5. Begin to love by faith. Believe God for the love you cannot muster in yourself.

G. S.

Love is not big-headed; it is big-hearted.

G. S.

Living without loving is merely existing!

G. S.

The call to love is not for the halfhearted. It is a full-time, life-long vocation.

G. S.

First love looks at the grand possibilities, not the weight of the problems. . . . First love is warm, radiant, and real.

G. S.

> I asked a river, "What is love?"
> And it replied: "The sea."
> I asked the question of the trees:
> "The wind," they answered me.
> I asked a mountain and it cried:
> "The stars!" And I asked a field of grain;
> It quickly sang: "The rain! The rain!"
> The shore told me it was the tide.
> And when I asked my soul, it said:
> "Love is the shining key
> To that fair golden temple
> Of my immortality."
>
> ADELAIDE P. LOVE

Love, like the creeping vine, withers if it has nothing to embrace.

NISUMI

Our Lord told His disciples that love and obedience were organically united. The final test of love is obedience.

A. W. TOZER

Love is the only fire that is hot enough to melt the iron obstinacy of a creature's will.

ALEXANDER MACLAREN

Young people talk a lot about love. Most of their songs are about love. . . . "The supreme happiness of life," Victor Hugo said long

176

ago, "is the conviction that we are loved." "Love is the first requirement for mental health," declared Sigmund Freud. The Bible teaches that "God is love" and that God loves you. To realize that is of paramount importance. Nothing else matters so much. And loving you, God has wonderful plans for your life. Who else could plan and guide your life so well?

BILLY GRAHAM

Love and a cough cannot be hid.

GEORGE HERBERT

Our souls, by reason of sin, are "like sweet bells jangled, harsh and out of tune." Love's master hand laid upon them restores to them their part in "the fair music that all creatures make to their great Lord," and brings us into such accord with God that "We on earth with undiscording voice,/May rightly answer" even the awful harmonies of His lips.

ALEXANDER MacLAREN

Love is optimistic; it looks at people in the best light. Love thinks constructively as it senses the grand possibilities in other people.

G. S.

What does love look like? It has the hands to help others. It has the feet to hasten to the poor and needy. It has eyes to see misery and want. It has the ears to hear the sighs and sorrows of men. That is what love looks like.

SAINT AUGUSTINE

If monotony tries me, and I cannot stand drudgery; if stupid people fret me and little ruffles set me on edge; if I make much of the trifles of life, then I know nothing of Calvary love.

AMY CARMICHAEL

I visited the 110-story, 1,454-foot Sears Tower, the tallest man-made structure on earth. It is a fantastic architectural feat, but someday its tons of concrete will be broken and its designer's name will be forgotten. And yet a cup of cold water, given in love, will break on the shores of eternity. In a world gone mad with greed and hate, how wonderful to know that love never dies! Love is never obsolete.

G. S.

> He prayeth best, who loveth best
> All things both great and small;
> For the dear God who loveth us,
> He made and loveth all.

SAMUEL T. COLERIDGE

A part of kindness consists in loving people more than they deserve.

JOSEPH JOUBERT

It is not a question of how much we know, how clever we are, nor even how good; it all depends upon the heart's love. External actions are the results of love, the fruit it bears; but the source, the root, is in the deep of the heart.

FRANÇOIS FÉNELON

← M →

Man

"Slightly lower than the angels" is a whole lot better than slightly higher than the apes. Let's get the order straight. God, angelic beings, man, animals, and vegetables.

STUART BRISCOE

God tells man who he is. God tells us that He created man in His image. So man is something wonderful.

FRANCIS SCHAEFFER, *Escape from Reason*

There is nothing autonomous—nothing apart from the lordship of Jesus Christ and the authority of the Scriptures. God made the whole man and is interested in the whole man, and the result is a unity.

FRANCIS SCHAEFFER, *Escape from Reason*

What an absurd thing it is to pass over all the valuable parts of a man, and fix our attention on his infirmities.

JOSEPH ADDISON

The great man is he who does not lose his child's heart.

MENCIUS

The ideal man is his own best friend and takes delight in privacy.

ARISTOTLE

If we let ourselves believe that man began with divine grace, that he forfeited this by sin, and that he can be redeemed only by divine grace through the crucified Christ then we shall find a peace of mind never granted to philosophers. He who cannot believe is cursed, for he reveals by his unbelief that God has not chosen to give him grace.

BLAISE PASCAL

Man is but a reed, the most weak in nature, but he is a thinking reed.

BLAISE PASCAL

The more I see of man, the more I like dogs.

MADAME DE STAËL

The release of atom power has changed everything except our way of thinking, and thus we are being driven unarmed towards a catastrophe. . . . The solution of this problem lies in the heart of humankind.

ALBERT EINSTEIN

There will be no major solution to the suffering of mankind until we reach some understanding of who we are, what the purpose of creation was, what happens after death. Until these questions are resolved we are caught.

WOODY ALLEN

Up till now, man derived his coherence from his Creator. But from the moment that he consecrates his rupture with him, he finds himself delivered over to the fleeting moment, to the passing days, and to wasted sensibility.

ALBERT CAMUS

Man's chief end is to glorify God, and to enjoy Him forever.

SHORTER WESTMINSTER CATECHISM

What a piece of work is a man! How noble in reason! how infinite in faculty! in form, in moving, how express and admirable! in action, how like an angel! in apprehension, how like a god! the beauty of the world! the paragon of animals! And yet, to me, what is this quintessence of dust? man delights not me; no, nor woman neither.

WILLIAM SHAKESPEARE, *Hamlet*

Marriage

To keep your marriage brimming,
With love in the loving cup,
Whenever you're wrong, admit it,
Whenever you're right, shut up.

OGDEN NASH

By all means marry. If you get a good wife, you will become very happy; if you get a bad one, you will become a philosopher—and that is good for any man.

SOCRATES

Marriage

Marriage is never finished. The lesson is never learned. The effort is never at an end. Marriage, like life, is a matter of solving the little things. The big ones generally take care of themselves. It is a matter of surrendering small, personal preferences.

RANDOLPH RAY

Three guidelines for a Christian marriage
First of all, and foundational to a biblical understanding of marriage, is the truth that *marriage is a permanent relationship.* In Mark 10:6–7, Jesus said, "From the beginning of the creation God made them male and female. For this cause shall a man leave his father and mother, and cleave to his wife." And then in verse nine we read, "What therefore God hath joined together, let not man put asunder."

A second biblical guideline is that *marriage is a harmonious partnership.* The Bible speaks of the union of the husband and wife as harmonious. Jesus said, "And they twain shall be one flesh: so then *they are no more twain,* but one flesh" (Mark 10:8, italics added).

I have never known of a broken marriage where the husband and wife had enjoyed a true partnership that had been harmonious and mutually sacrificial. But God established marriage to be just that, and His Word gives guidelines about how to keep harmony in the home.

But there is a truth that is even greater than the truths that marriage is a permanent relationship and a harmonious partnership. And that is the biblical teaching that *marriage is a spiritual companionship.*

Christian marriage should be a companionship where each helps the other to grow in Christ. The Bible tells us that in the marriage relationship, the husband and wife become one. It is my conviction that that speaks not only of a physical union, but of a spiritual union as well.

G. S.

They divorce in order to remarry. They marry in order to divorce.

SENECA

It is not marriage that fails; it is people that fail. All that marriage does is show people up.

ANONYMOUS

Success in marriage consists not only in finding the right mate, but also in being the right mate.

ANONYMOUS

A bachelor is a fellow who doesn't think the bonds of matrimony are a good investment.

MAURICE SEITTER

Meaning

If God exists and we are made in His image we can have real meaning, and we can have real knowledge through what he has communicated to us.

FRANCIS SCHAEFFER, *The God Who Is There*

There is a land of the living and a land of the dead and the bridge is love, the only survival, the only meaning.

THORNTON WILDER

Eternal truths will be neither true nor eternal unless they have fresh meaning for every new social situation.

FRANKLIN D. ROOSEVELT

Hold every moment sacred. Give each clarity and meaning, each the weight of thine awareness, each its true and due fulfillment.

THOMAS MANN

You must lie upon the daisies and discourse in novel phrases of your complicated state of mind,/The meaning doesn't matter if it's only idle chatter of a transcendental kind.

WILLIAM S. GILBERT, *Patience*

Dare to err and to dream. Deep meaning often lies in childish plays.

JOHANN VON SCHILLER

> A voice in the wind I do not know;
> A meaning on the face of the high hills
> Whose utterance I cannot comprehend.
> A something is behind them: that is God.
>
> GEORGE MacDONALD

The Media

Journalism largely consists in saying "Lord Jones Dead" to people who never knew Lord Jones was alive.

G. K. CHESTERTON

Newspaper editors are men who separate the wheat from the chaff, and then print the chaff.

ADLAI STEVENSON

Journalism is literature in a hurry.

MATTHEW ARNOLD

Meditation, Memory

We're in the same position as a plumber laying a pipe. We're not responsible for what goes through the pipe.

DAVID SARNOFF

I keep reading between the lies.

GOODMAN ACE

Meditation

Contemplation is not in itself "more spiritual" than recording a vote or managing a business.

F. R. BARRY, *Christian Ethics and Secular Society*

The longest journey is the journey inward. . . . The road of holiness necessarily passes through the world of action.

DAG HAMMARSKJöld

If we have not quiet in our minds, outward comfort will do no more for us than a golden slipper on a gouty foot.

JOHN BUNYAN

A man of meditation is happy, not for an hour or a day, but quite round the circle of all his years.

ISAAC TAYLOR

Memory

A man's real possession is his memory. In nothing else is he rich, in nothing else is he poor.

ALEXANDER SMITH

A retentive memory is a good thing, but the ability to forget is the true token of greatness.

ELBERT HUBBARD

Own only what you can always carry with you: know languages, know countries, know people. Let your memory be your travel bag.

ALEKSANDR SOLZHENITSYN

When I was younger I could remember anything, whether it had happened or not.

MARK TWAIN

The advantage of a bad memory is that one enjoys several times the same good things for the first time.

FRIEDRICH NIETZSCHE

A couple was sitting in the worship service when the wife suddenly remarked, "Oh, how awful! I forgot to turn off the electric iron before I left home!"

"Don't worry, dear," the husband said cheerfully. "It won't burn long. I just remembered I forgot to turn off the faucet in the bathtub."

G. S.

We have committed the Golden Rule to memory; now let us commit it to life.

EDWIN MARKHAM

When saving for old age, be sure to put away a few pleasant thoughts.

ANONYMOUS

Like a bird singing in the rain, let grateful memories survive in time of sorrow.

ROBERT LOUIS STEVENSON

There are few greater treasures to be acquired in youth than great poetry—and prose—stored in the memory. At the time one may resent the labor of storing. But they sleep in the memory and awake in later years, illuminated by life and illuminating it.

RICHARD W. LIVINGSTONE

Mind

The mind is like the stomach. It is not how much you put into it that counts, but how much it digests.

A. J. NOCK

Nothing relieves and ventilates the mind like a resolution.

JOHN BURROUGHS

Little minds are interested in the extraordinary; great minds in the commonplace.

ELBERT HUBBARD

The mind of man is like a clock that is always running down, and requires to be as constantly wound up.

WILLIAM HAZLITT

Mission

Every church should support two pastors—one for the thousands at home, the other for the millions abroad.

JACOB CHAMBERLAIN

Mission

All the world is my parish.

JOHN WESLEY

"I can't get interested in missions," remarked a young lady.

"No," was the reply given to her, "you can hardly expect to. It is just like getting interest at a bank: you have to put in a little something first and the more you put in—time or money or prayer—the more the interest grows."

ANONYMOUS

"I am going down into the pit; you hold the ropes," said Carey the pioneer missionary. They that hold the ropes, and the daring miner that swings away down in the darkness, are one in work, may be one in the motive, and, if they are, shall be one in the reward.

ALEXANDER MACLAREN

The Spirit of Christ is the spirit of missions, and the nearer we get to Him the more intensely missionary we must become.

HENRY MARTYN

I look upon foreign missionaries as the scaffolding around a rising building. The sooner it can be dispensed with, the better; or rather, the sooner it can be transferred to other places, to serve the same temporary use, the better.

HUDSON TAYLOR

In 1956 *Life* magazine told of the shocking death of five missionaries in the jungles of Ecuador. For several months these men had tried to make contact with the primitive Auca Indians. On their first attempt to establish a camp, they were brutally murdered!

Today these same Auca tribesmen are all Christians. They are leaders of a small congregation that worship near the spot where the missionaries died. Many educators and government leaders have expressed astonishment at the miraculous change in these Indians. How did it happen? The answer lies in the love of God expressed to these people by the sister of Nate Saint and the wife of Jim Elliot, two of the martyred missionaries. Led by God who is love and not vengeance, these women were able to break down the walls of distrust. In time they were able to share the gospel with these tribesmen and see the love of Christ transform their lives.

G. S.

Attempt great things FOR God and expect great things FROM God.

WILLIAM CAREY

John Currier, a man who could not read or write, was found guilty of murder and sentenced to prison for life in 1949. Later he was transferred from prison and paroled to work for a wealthy farmer near Nashville, Tennessee.

In 1968, however, his sentence was terminated. State Correction Department records show that a letter was written to the convict and the farmer for whom he worked. The letter said he was free.

But Currier never saw the letter or even knew it had been written. One year went by . . . then two . . . then five, and finally, ten; and still he did not know that he was free.

By this time, the farmer to whom he had been paroled was dead, but Currier kept working, serving out his sentence. He was given a little money for personal needs—five dollars a week at first, then a little more, and finally twenty dollars weekly.

But life was hard and filled with labor. He slept in a drafty trailer, taking baths in a horse trough with a garden hose. Life held very little joy and no promise.

This went on till just a few years ago. Then a state parole officer learned of his plight and told him of the missing letter, according to the *Chicago Tribune,* February 7, 1979.

Would it matter to you if someone sent you an important message—the most important of your life, but year after year the urgent message was never delivered?

G. S.

I have four sons whom I love dearly. Suppose our lawn needed to be cut. I could say, "Boys, can you see the need? The grass is high. It's above my knees. Soon I will not be able to get to the garage. Don't you see the desperate need?" But in the final analysis, they get out the mower because their father says, "Mow the grass!" World evangelization is an imperative because Jesus said so.

G. S.

The story is told that during the reign of Oliver Cromwell, there was a shortage of currency in the British Empire. Representatives carefully searched the nation in hope of finding silver to meet the emergency.

After one month, the committee returned with its findings. "We have searched the empire in vain seeking to find silver," it reported. "To our dismay, we found none anywhere except in the cathedrals where the saints are carved from choice silver."

To this, Oliver Cromwell eloquently answered, "Let's melt down the saints and put them into circulation." Why not ask the Lord to melt us down for greater spiritual circulation?

G. S.

Mistakes

The man who is incapable of making a mistake is incapable of anything.

ABRAHAM LINCOLN

The man who makes no mistakes does not usually make anything.

EDWARD JOHN PHELPS

I may have my faults, but being wrong ain't one of them.

JAMES RIDDLE HOFFA

When Henry Ward Beecher was preaching in Brooklyn, he carried a handful of flowers into the pulpit one Lord's Day and placed them in a vase that they might adorn the stand from which he spoke. The newspapers, the next day, carried lengthy articles condemning Beecher for desecrating the pulpit with flowers.

And when Morse was trying to get money from Congress for a telegraph line from Baltimore to Washington, he had to endure the adverse criticisms of the press for eleven years.

And when, in 1845, Mr. Adam Thompson got up the first bathtub in America, the newspapers said he was "going to spoil the democratic simplicity of the republic."

And when Cyrus Field was trying to lay the Atlantic cable, the newspapers denounced his cable as "a mad freak of stubborn ignorance."

ROBERT G. LEE

Sometimes we may learn more from a man's errors than from his virtues.

HENRY WADSWORTH LONGFELLOW

The sages do not consider that making no mistakes is a blessing. They believe, rather, that the great virtue of man lies in his ability to correct his mistakes and continually to make a new man of himself.

WANG YANG-MING

Modern Culture

We live in the kind of world in which the only constant factor is change, and some of the changes are unhappy ones. . . . What do we do when the roof falls in?

EILEEN GUDER

We are living in a culture that is secular. Religion does not play the role that it used to play. This is particularly true for people under forty years of age in this society. When a strong religious bond is missing, there are few things that can hold the culture together.

RICHARD HOFSTADTER

Ours is an age without heroes . . . today no one bestrides our narrow world like a colossus.

ARTHUR M. SCHLESINGER, JR.

We ourselves were sure that at long last a generation had arisen keen and eager, to put this disorderly earth to right . . . and fit to do it . . . we meant so well, we tried so hard, and look what we have made of it. We can only muddle in the muddle. What is required is a new kind of man.

WALTER LIPPMANN

The greatest difficulty with the world is not its ability to produce, but its unwillingness to share.

ROY L. SMITH

We face the twin enemies of crime and Communism. Crime and moral decay are eating at us from within. And Communism stands ready to pick up the pieces.

J. EDGAR HOOVER

The greatest question of our time is not communism versus individualism, not Europe versus America, not even the East versus the West; it is whether men can bear to live without God. Can civilization hold together if man abandons his faith in God?

WILL DURANT

It is scarcely possible in most places to get anyone to attend a meeting where the only attraction is God.

A. W. TOZER

What on earth will today's younger generation be able to tell their children they had to do without?

Chicago Daily News

The midnight oil that modern students burn is gasoline.

ANONYMOUS

One of our great historians, Arnold Toynbee, writes of nineteen major civilizations that have existed since man began to structure governments. Of the nineteen, no more than five remain. Our Western civilization is among them. Today we are asking with growing concern, "Will it survive?"

G. S.

Whoever marries the spirit of this age will find himself a widower in the next.

WILLIAM R. INGE

Money

Secularism has this age by the throat.

WALTER LOWRIE

Money

fair

That money talks/I'll not deny,/I heard it once:/It said, "Goodbye."

RICHARD ARMOUR

fair

[Money is] an article which may be used as a universal passport to everywhere except Heaven, and as a universal provider of everything except happiness.

Wall Street Journal

Good

1-28-90 Money is a terrible master but an excellent servant.

P. T. BARNUM

fair

To be clever enough to get a great deal of money, one must be stupid enough to want it.

G. K. CHESTERTON

fair

Money reveals where our interests lie; it can direct our attitudes; it ever exposes us to the danger of worshipping it; and it represents value. Money not only talks; it screams.

LESLIE B. FLYNN

fair

The Bible is very clear on the point that if we have money enough to live well, and do not share with others in need, it is questionable whether God's love is in us at all.

G. S.

Good

1/28/90 A man's treatment of money is the most decisive test of his character—how he makes it and how he spends it.

JAMES MOFFATT

fair

Writer Bert Bacharach tells us that the highest income made in any year was Al Capone's "take" in 1927—reputed to have been one hundred and five *million* dollars. But his *"take"* when he died was nothing—*zero*. No money was in his shroud—his hands were empty—even as the hands of all the poor and all the rich are empty when burial is accomplished.

ROBERT G. LEE

Good

1-28-90 How we use our money demonstrates the reality of our love for God. In some ways it proves our love more conclusively than depth or

188

knowledge, length of prayers or prominence of service. These things can be feigned, but the use of our possessions shows us up for what we actually are.

CHARLES CALDWELL RYRIE, *Balancing the Christian Life*

Material wealth is either a window through which we see God or a mirror in which we see ourselves.

WARREN WIERSBE, *Live Like a King*

In seventeen of His thirty-seven parables, Jesus dealt with property and man's responsibility for using it wisely.

G. S.

Music

He did not see any good reasons why the devil should have all the good tunes.

ROWLAND HILL

Christianity is the only religion that abounds in song. Atheism is songless; agnosticism has nothing to sing about; the various forms of idolatry are not tuneful; but Judaism said, "O come, let us sing unto the Lord"; and when Christ came, the angels greeted His birth with praise, and since then Christian song has gained in fullness and strength of voice with each century.

ANONYMOUS

Music is the only language in which you cannot say a mean or sarcastic thing.

JOHN ERSKINE

Bach almost persuaded me to be a Christian.

ROGER FRY

I know that the twelve notes in each octave and the varieties of rhythm offer me opportunities that all of human genius will never exhaust.

IGOR STRAVINSKY

Without music life would be a mistake.

FRIEDRICH NIETZSCHE

There will be no song on our lips if there be no anguish in our hearts.

KARL BARTH

A friend once asked the great composer Haydn why his church music was always so full of gladness. He answered: "I cannot make it otherwise.

I write according to the thoughts I feel. When I think upon my God, my heart is so full of joy that the notes dance and leap from my pen; and since God has given me a cheerful heart, it will be pardoned me that I serve Him with a cheerful spirit."

HENRY VAN DYKE

← N →

Nation

National honor is national property of the highest value.

JAMES MONROE

It is not desirable to cultivate a respect for the law, so much as for the right.

HENRY THOREAU

The test of a nation is the growth of its people intellectually and spiritually. Money and so-called prosperity are of very little account! Babylon, Persia, Greece, Rome, Spain and France all had their turn in being the richest in the world. And instead of saving them, their so-called prosperity proved to be the ruin of them. Our nation is now the richest, but it could easily become a second-class nation and head downward. Money will not save us. Only a sane, spiritual revival which changes the desires of our people will save us.

ROGER BABSON

America! America!
God shed His grace on thee
And crown thy good with brotherhood
From sea to shining sea!

KATHERINE LEE BATES

When any nation has become overly pleasure-seeking, history has already begun its epitaph.

HOWARD WHITMAN

No nation has ever failed to prosper when its people put God first and their country second.

HAROLD LINDSELL, *The World, the Flesh and the Devil*

Nature

Nature is the art of God.

SIR THOMAS BROWNE

The art of seeing nature is a thing almost as much to be acquired as the art of reading the Egyptian hieroglyphics.

JOHN CONSTABLE

One touch of nature makes the whole world kin.

WILLIAM SHAKESPEARE, *Troilus and Cressida*

Nature's laws affirm instead of prohibit. If you violate her laws you are your own prosecuting attorney, judge, jury, and hangman.

LUTHER BURBANK

Nothing is more beautiful than the loveliness of the woods before sunrise.

GEORGE WASHINGTON CARVER

The man who has seen the rising moon break out of the clouds at midnight has been present like an archangel at the creation of light and of the world.

RALPH WALDO EMERSON

No sight is more provocative of awe than is the night sky.

LLEWELYN POWYS

Doth not all nature around me praise God? If I were silent, I should be an exception to the universe. Doth not the thunder praise Him as it rolls like drums in the march of the God of armies? Do not the mountains praise Him when the woods upon their summits wave in adoration? Doth not the lightning write His name in letters of fire? Hath not the whole earth a voice? And shall I, can I, silent be?

CHARLES H. SPURGEON

Neglect

When I was in the hospital in Hawaii, I read again of the shocking events which led up to the destruction of the United States fleet at Pearl Harbor. On that fateful day of December 7, 1941, the Japanese attacked. We know now that the attack was invited by our failure to be always vigilant. The result was the destruction of our fleet—the cause was tragic indifference. When comfort and ease and pleasure are put ahead of duty and conviction, progress is always set back. What makes us Christians shrug our shoulders when we ought to be flexing our muscles? What makes us apathetic in a day when there are loads to lift, a world to be won, and captives to be set free? Why are so many bored, when the times demand action? Christ told us that in the last days there would be an insipid attitude toward life.

BILLY GRAHAM

All that is necessary for the forces of evil to win in the world is for enough good men to do nothing.

EDMUND BURKE

Some of us are as dead to the perception of God's gracious call, just because it has been sounded on uninterruptedly, as are the dwellers by a waterfall to its unremitting voice.

ALEXANDER MacLAREN

The untended garden will soon be overrun with weeds; the heart that fails to cultivate truth and root our error will shortly be a theological wilderness.

A. W. TOZER

Neighbors

Good fences make good neighbors.

ROBERT FROST

No one is rich enough to do without a neighbor.

DANISH PROVERB

Because we cannot see Christ we cannot express our love to him; but our neighbors we can always see, and we can do to them what, if we saw him, we would like to do to Christ.

MOTHER TERESA

The Bible tells us to love our neighbors, and also to love our enemies; probably because generally they are the same people.

G. K. CHESTERTON

> To love the whole world
> For me is no chore;
> My only real problem's
> My neighbor next door.

C. W. VANDERBERGH

New Birth

The Reverend George Whitefield, having occasion to write to Dr. Franklin, in a letter, dated August 17, 1752, said, "I find you grow more and more famous in the learned world. As you have made a pretty considerable progress in the mysteries of electricity, I would now humbly recommend to your diligent, unprejudiced pursuit and study, the mystery of the new birth. It is a most important, interesting study; and, when mastered, will richly answer and repay you for all your pains. One, at whose bar we are shortly to appear, hath solemnly declared, without it we cannot enter the kingdom of heaven. You will excuse this freedom. I must have something of Christ in all my letters."

G. S.

. . . man's efforts to make himself personally and collectively happy in earthly terms are doomed to failure. He must indeed, as Christ said, be born again, be a new man, or he's nothing. So at least I have concluded, having failed to find . . . any alternative proposition. As far as I am concerned, it is Christ or nothing.

MALCOLM MUGGERIDGE

The sense of newness is simply delicious. It makes new the Bible, and friends, and all mankind, and love, and spiritual things, and Sunday, and church, and God Himself. So I've found.

TEMPLE GARDNER OF CAIRO

Every story of conversion is the story of a blessed defeat.

C. S. LEWIS

O Lord, convert the world—and begin with me.

A CHINESE STUDENT'S PRAYER

On January 12, 1723, I made a solemn dedication of myself to God, and wrote it down; giving up myself, and all that I had to God; to be for the future, in no respect, my own; to act as one that had no right to be himself, in any respect. And solemnly vowed to take God for my whole portion and felicity; looking on nothing else, as any part of my happiness, nor acting as if it were; and his law for the constant rule of my obedience: engaging to fight against the world, the flesh and the devil, to the end of my life.

JONATHAN EDWARDS, *Personal Narrative*

When by the Spirit of God, I understood these words, "The just shall live by faith," I felt born again like a new man: I entered through the open doors into the very Paradise of God!

MARTIN LUTHER

Someone else, describing his new life in Christ, said, "Everything seems new—the Bible, my friends, my love for others, even Sunday itself. I have a new desire for spiritual things, a desire to know more about God and His church."

Opinions

We must begin by acknowledging that we need God's help, God's power, and God's life. Dead things cannot grow; and without Christ, we are spiritually dead. We are powerless and defeated.

G. S.

Napoleon believed that the fate of every battle was decided in the space of five minutes. All his maneuvering and planning led to that strategic moment of crisis, the moment of action and decision.

So with you, my friend. Your future, your eternal welfare is decided in but a few moments of decision. . . .

G. S.

← O →

Opinions

As for the differences of opinion upon speculative questions, if we wait till they are reconciled, the action of human affairs must be suspended forever. But neither are we to look for perfection in any one man, nor for agreement among many.

JUNIUS

Opinions cannot survive if one has no chance to fight for them.

THOMAS MANN

We hardly find any persons of good sense save those who agree with us.

FRANÇOIS, DUC DE LA ROCHEFOUCAULD

Some praise at morning what they blame at night,/But always think the last opinion right.

ALEXANDER POPE

"That was excellently observed," say I when I read a passage in another where his opinion agrees with mine. When we differ, then I pronounce him to be mistaken.

JONATHAN SWIFT

194

Opportunity

> There is a tide in the affairs of men
> Which, taken at the flood, leads on to fortune;
> Omitted, all the voyage of their life
> Is bound in shallows and in miseries.
> On such a full sea are we now afloat,
> And we must take the current when it serves,
> Or lose our ventures.

> WILLIAM SHAKESPEARE, BRUTUS IN *Julius Caesar*

Small opportunities are often the beginning of great enterprises.

> DEMOSTHENES

Opportunities multiply as they are seized; they die when neglected.

> ANONYMOUS

A pessimist is one who makes difficulties of his opportunities; an optimist is one who makes opportunities of his difficulties.

> REGINALD B. MANSELL

> To each is given a bag of tools,
> A shapeless mass, and a book of rules,
> And each must make, ere life is flown,
> A stumbling-block or a stepping-stone.

> ANONYMOUS

The reason so many people never get anywhere in life is because, when opportunity knocks, they are out in the backyard looking for four-leaf clovers.

> WALTER P. CHRYSLER

When one door closes, another opens; but we often look so long and so regretfully upon the closed door that we do not see the one which has opened for us.

> ALEXANDER GRAHAM BELL

Wherever there is danger, there lurks opportunity; whenever there is opportunity, there lurks danger. The two are inseparable; they go together.

> EARL NIGHTINGALE

A man must make his opportunity as oft as find it.

> FRANCIS BACON

195

Four things come not back—the spoken word, the sped arrow, the past life, and the neglected opportunity.

ARABIAN PROVERB

The morning hour has gold in its mouth.

BENJAMIN FRANKLIN

When written in Chinese, the word "crisis" is composed of two characters—one represents danger and the other represents opportunity.

JOHN F. KENNEDY

← **P** →

Pastors

Senator Robert S. Kerr of Oklahoma was a member of the First Baptist Church of Oklahoma City. He was a long-time Sunday school teacher and Christian philanthropist. He gave more than one million dollars to Baptist institutions in Oklahoma.

His pastor, Dr. H. H. Hobbs, in his tribute to his friend at the memorial service in the church, quoted a prayer the senator had published many years before called "A Prayer for My Pastor":

"Our Father, let me be a pillar of strength to help hold him up and not a thorn in his back to pull him down. Let me support him without striving to possess him. Let me lift his hands without placing shackles around them. Let me give him help that he may devote more time in working for the salvation of others and less time in gratifying my vanity. Let me work for him as the pastor of all the members and not compel him to spend precious time in bragging on me. Let me be unselfish in what I do for him and not selfish in demanding that he do more for me. Let me strive to serve him and the church much and be happy as he serves me less and the church and others more."

ROBERT G. LEE

The one thing no church can stand is a pastor who really wants to be something else. The men who really want out ought to be helped out, for the Christian ministry is no place for a man who wants to be something else. It is a place for men who can give counsel, not the place for men who need counsel.

DUKE K. McCALL

196

Patience

Patience overcomes everything. The world is his who has patience.

PROVERB

Patience often gets the credit that belongs to fatigue.

ANONYMOUS

John Wesley, the founder of Methodism, used to recall that as a youth his behavior often displeased his father. His mother was more forbearing. "How can you have the patience," exploded the elder Wesley, "to tell that blockhead John the same thing twenty times over?"

"Why," replied Mrs. Wesley, "if I had told him but nineteen times I had wasted my breath!"

G. S.

The faith of Christ offers no buttons to push for quick service. The new order must wait the Lord's own time, and that is too much for the man in a hurry. He just gives up and becomes interested in something else.

A. W. TOZER

A doctor was once asked by a patient who had met with a serious accident, "Doctor, how long shall I have to lie here?"

"Only a day at a time," was his answer.

This taught the patient a valuable lesson. It was the same lesson God had recorded for His people for all ages. If we are faithful a day at a time, the long years will take care of themselves.

ANDREW MURRAY

The most useful virtue is patience.

JOHN DEWEY

He that can have patience can have what he will.

BENJAMIN FRANKLIN

Prayer of the modern American: "Dear God, I pray for patience. And I want it right now!"

OREN ARNOLD

New England preacher Phillips Brooks was known for his calmness and poise. His intimate friends, however, knew that he, too, suffered moments of frustration and irritability. One day a friend saw him pacing the floor like a caged lion. "What is the trouble, Dr. Brooks?" asked the friend. "The trouble is," replied Brooks, "that I'm in a hurry, but God isn't." Have you ever felt that way?

G. S.

> Did the leaves of the trees say something to you
>   as you passed them today?
> They were not created this spring, but months ago.
>   (And right now others are being fashioned
>   for another year.)
> At the bottom of every leaf is a cradle, and in it
>   is an infant germ:
> The winds will rock it and the birds will sing to it
>   all summer long and next spring it will unfold.

ANONYMOUS

Patriotism

I should like to be able to love my country and to love justice.

ALBERT CAMUS

I venture to suggest that patriotism is not a short and frenzied outburst of emotion but the tranquil and steady dedication of a lifetime.

ADLAI STEVENSON

If I added to their pride of America, I am happy.

CARL SANDBURG

Abandon your animosities and make your sons Americans!

ROBERT E. LEE

My country right or wrong, is a thing no patriot would think of saying except in a desperate case. It is like saying, "My mother, drunk or sober!"

G. K. CHESTERTON

Peace

> Drop Thy still dews of quietness,
>   Till all our strivings cease;
> Take from our souls the strain and stress,
> And let our ordered lives confess,
>   The beauty of Thy peace.

JOHN GREENLEAF WHITTIER

When each earthly prop gives under,
And life seems a restless sea,
Are you then a God-kept wonder,
Satisfied and calm and free?

ANONYMOUS

The winter's day has had its melancholy grey sky, with many a bitter dash of snow and rain—but it has stormed itself out, and at eventide a rent in the clouds reveals the sun, and it closes in peaceful clearness of night.

ALEXANDER MACLAREN

Peace, perfect peace, in this dark world of sin?/The blood of Jesus whispers peace within.

EDWARD HENRY BICKERSTETH

The sea was beating against the rocks in huge, dashing waves. The lightning was flashing, the thunder was roaring, the wind was blowing; but the little bird was asleep in the crevice of the rock, its head serenely under its wing, sound asleep. That is peace—to be able to sleep in the storm! In Christ, we are relaxed and at peace in the midst of the confusions, bewilderments, and perplexities of this life. The storm rages, but our hearts are at rest. We have found peace—at last!

BILLY GRAHAM

There is an end to all "the weary oar, the weary, wandering fields of barren foam." On the shore stands the Christ; and there is rest *there.*

ALEXANDER MACLAREN

People

The pressure of public opinion is like the pressure of the atmosphere; you can't see it—but, all the same, it is sixteen pounds to the square inch.

JAMES RUSSELL LOWELL

All the world is queer save thee and me, and even thou art a little queer.

ROBERT OWEN

People do not lack strength; they lack will.

VICTOR HUGO

Perseverance, Persistence

Perseverance is the most overrated of traits if it is unaccompanied by talent; beating your head against a wall is more likely to produce a concussion in the head than a hole in the wall.

SYDNEY HARRIS

Perseverance, Persistence

It was among the Parthians the custom that none were to give their children any meat in the morning before they saw the sweat on their faces. . . . You shall find this to be God's usual course: not to give His children the taste of His delights till they begin to sweat in seeking after them.

RICHARD BAXTER

Oh, the little more, and how much it is!/And the little less, and what worlds away!

ROBERT BROWNING

Feather by feather the goose is plucked.

JOHN RAY

The difference between perseverance and obstinacy is, that one often comes from a strong will, and the other from a strong won't.

HENRY WARD BEECHER

The Man Who Quits

The man who quits has a brain and hand
As good as the next, but lacks the sand
That would make him stick, with a courage stout,
To whatever he tackles, and fight it out.

He starts with a rush, and a solemn vow
That he'll soon be showing the other how;
Then something new strikes his roving eye,
And his task is left for the bye-and-bye.

It's up to each man what becomes of him;
He must find in himself the grit and vim
That brings success; he can get the skill
If he brings to the task a steadfast will.

No man is beaten till he gives in;
Hard luck can't stand for a cheerful grin;
The man who fails needs a better excuse,
Than the quitter's whining, "What's the use?"

For the man who quits lets his chances slip,
Just because he's too lazy to keep his grip.
The man who sticks goes ahead with a shout,
While the man who quits joins the "Down and out."

ANONYMOUS

The great composer does not set to work because he is inspired, but becomes inspired because he is working. Beethoven, Wagner, Bach and Mozart settled down day after day to the job in hand with as much

200

regularity as an accountant settles down each day to his figures. They didn't waste time waiting for an inspiration.

ERNEST NEWMAN

Perseverance: a lowly virtue whereby mediocrity achieves an inglorious success.

AMBROSE BIERCE

Mon centre cède, ma droite recule, situation excellente, j'attaque—My center is giving way, my right is retreating. Situation excellent. I shall attack.

FIELD MARSHAL FERDINAND FOCH

Nothing in the world can take the place of persistence. Talent will not; nothing is more common than unsuccessful men with talent. Genius will not; unrewarded genius is almost a proverb. Education will not; the world is full of educated derelicts. Persistence and determination alone are omnipotent.

CALVIN COOLIDGE

We have all a few moments in life of hard, glorious running; but we have days and years of walking—the uneventful discharge of small duties.

ALEXANDER MACLAREN

For all your days prepare,
And meet them ever alike:
When you are the anvil, bear—
When you are the hammer, strike.

EDWIN MARKHAM

Inspiration without perspiration leads to frustration and stagnation.

BILL BRIGHT

It is more important to gird ourselves for the grind of life than it is to throw ourselves into high gear only for the grandiose affairs of life.

CHARLES CALDWELL RYRIE

Pleasure

America rocks from a pleasure explosion. Every week, twelve million golfers vie for tee-off times, nine million tennis players compete across the nets; while four million skiers spend millions of dollars on equipment and resorts. Each year twenty-three million fishermen and hunters search for game in the woodlands of our nation.

G. S.

But pleasures are like poppies spread—
You seize the flow'r, its bloom is shed;
Or like the snow falls in the river—
A moment white, then melts forever.

ROBERT BURNS

Human nature is indeed in the grip of an overwhelming army of occupation. Its natural aim, it can truthfully be said, is pleasure; and when we consider the amount of time, energy, money, interest and enthusiasm that men and women give to the satisfaction of this aim we can appreciate the accuracy of James' diagnosis; and Christians can use it as a reliable yardstick by which to measure the sincerity of their religion. Is God or pleasure the dominant concern of their life?

R. V. G. TASKER

Here are two tests to evaluate our pleasure:
First, do these pleasures encourage Christian development? "All things are lawful unto me, but all things are not expedient" (1 Corinthians 6:12). "Expedient" means profitable. Many activities may be legitimate, but do they help me to glorify my Lord and Savior Jesus Christ?
Second, do these pleasures endanger Christian maturity? "All things are lawful for me," said Paul, "but I will not be brought under the power of any" (1 Corinthians 6:12*b*). Seemingly innocent pleasures can choke out our spiritual lives.
God's Word talks about another kind of pleasure: eternal pleasure, lasting pleasure, pleasures forevermore. David said, "Thou wilt shew me the path of life: in thy presence is fulness of joy; at thy right hand there are pleasures for evermore" (Psalm 16:11).

G. S.

Satan is not such a fool as to fish without bait.

ANONYMOUS

Politics

I tell you, Folks, all Politics is Apple Sauce.

WILL ROGERS

Whenever a man has cast a longing eye on offices, a rottenness begins in his conduct.

THOMAS JEFFERSON

He serves his party best who serves the country best.

RUTHERFORD B. HAYES

But the future lies with those wise political leaders who realize that the great public is interested more in government than in politics.

FRANKLIN D. ROOSEVELT

Politics has got so expensive that it takes lots of money to even get beat with.

WILL ROGERS

Politics are almost as exciting as war, and quite as dangerous. In war you can only be killed once, but in politics many times.

WINSTON CHURCHILL

Politics is the art of the possible, not the art of the ideal.

RUSSELL KIRK

Poverty

Poverty is not dishonorable in itself, but only when it comes from idleness, intemperance, extravagance, and folly.

PLUTARCH

For every talent that poverty has stimulated it has blighted a hundred.

JOHN W. GARDNER

Not he who has little, but he who wishes more, is poor.

SENECA

This Administration here and now declares unconditional war on poverty in America.

LYNDON B. JOHNSON

If you spend all your time collecting money for fear of poverty, you are practicing poverty already.

ANONYMOUS

You don't have to look for distress; it is screaming at you!

SAMUEL BECKETT

No society can surely be flourishing and happy, of which the far greater part of the members are poor and miserable.

ADAM SMITH

Power

Responsibility gravitates toward him who gets ready for it, and power flows to him and through him who can use it.

GEORGE WALTER FISKE

Praise (See Nature), Prayer

Self-reverence, self-knowledge, self-control/These three alone lead life
to sovereign power.

ALFRED, LORD TENNYSON

It is the magician's bargain: give up our souls, get power in return.
But once our souls, that is, our selves, have been given up, the power
thus conferred will not belong to us. We shall in fact be the slaves
and puppets of that to which we have given our souls.

C. S. LEWIS

Meekness is power under control.

WARREN WIERSBE, *Live Like a King*

Praise (See Nature)

F

Prayer

The moment you wake up each morning, all your wishes and hopes
for the day rush at you like wild animals. And the first job each morning
consists in shoving it all back; in listening to that other voice, taking
that other point of view, letting that other, larger, stronger, quieter
life come flowing in.

C. S. LEWIS

G

2-6-00 To be a Christian without prayer is no more possible than to be alive
without breathing.

MARTIN LUTHER

F

The principal cause of my leanness and unfruitfulness is owing to an
unaccountable backwardness to pray. I can write or read or converse
or hear with a ready heart; but prayer is more spiritual and inward
than any of these, and the more spiritual any duty is the more my
carnal heart is apt to start from it.

RICHARD NEWTON

F

Prayer is not something to be added after other approaches in our
search for the will of God have been tried and have failed. No, we
should pray as we use the personal resources God has given us.

T. B. MASTON

F

Hurry is the death of prayer.

SAMUEL CHADWICK

G

Do not pray for tasks equal to your powers. Pray for powers equal
to your tasks.

PHILLIPS BROOKS

204

If you pray for bread and bring no basket to carry it, you prove the doubting spirit which may be the only hindrance to the gift you ask.

D. L. MOODY

Prayer is the preface to the book of Christian living, the text of the new life sermon, the girding on of the armor for battle, the pilgrim's preparation for his journey; and it must be supplemented by action or it amounts to nothing.

ANONYMOUS

Nothing lies beyond the reach of prayer except that which lies outside the will of God.

ANONYMOUS

[About Praying (John) Hyde] He prayed as if God were at his elbow.

ANONYMOUS

Prayer is the key of the morning and the bolt of the evening.

MATTHEW HENRY

Pray for great things, expect great things, work for great things, but above all, pray.

R. A. TORREY

Prayer is not overcoming God's reluctance: it is laying hold of His highest willingness.

RICHARD CHENEVIX, ARCHBISHOP TRENCH

Work as if everything depended upon your work, and pray as if everything depended upon your prayer.

GENERAL WILLIAM BOOTH

More things are wrought by prayer than this world dreams of.

ALFRED, LORD TENNYSON

And Satan trembles when he sees/The weakest saint upon his knees.

ANONYMOUS

I judge that my prayer is more than the devil himself. If it were otherwise I would have fared differently long before this. Yet men will not see and acknowledge the great wonders or miracles God works in my behalf. If I should neglect prayer but a single day, I should lose a great deal of the fire of faith.

MARTIN LUTHER

Prayer

F

By one hour's intimate access to the throne of grace, where the Lord causes His glory to pass before the soul that seeks Him you may acquire more true spiritual knowledge and comfort than by a day's or a week's converse with the best of men, or the most studious perusal of many folios.

JOHN NEWTON

G

I have been driven many times to my knees by the overwhelming conviction that I had nowhere else to go. My own wisdom, and that of all about me seemed insufficient for the day.

ABRAHAM LINCOLN

G

Trouble and perplexity drive us to prayer, and prayer driveth away trouble and perplexity.

PHILIPP MELANCTHON

F

Did any of you, parents, ever hear your child wake from sleep with some panic fear and shriek the mother's name through the darkness? Was not that a more powerful appeal than all words? And, depend upon it, that the soul which cries aloud on God, "the God and Father of our Lord Jesus Christ," though it have "no language but a cry," will never call in vain.

ALEXANDER MACLAREN

F

Let us advance upon our knees.

JOHN HARDY NEESIMA

F

When we become too glib in prayer we are most surely talking to ourselves.

A. W. TOZER

F

When God inclines the heart to pray,
He hath an ear to hear;
To him there's music in a groan,
And beauty in a tear.

ANONYMOUS

F

Since the Holy Spirit makes intercession for the infirmed saints according to God's will, who are we to pray any other way? (Rom. 8:22–27).

G. S.

F

In my thinking, the "prayer of faith" cannot be prayed simply at will. It is given of God in certain cases to serve His purpose and to accomplish His sovereign will.

G. S.

206

Prayer will make a man cease from sin, or sin will entice a man to cease from prayer.

JOHN BUNYAN

> We, ignorant of ourselves,
> Beg often our own harms, which the wise powers
> Deny us for our good; so find we profit
> By losing of our prayers.

WILLIAM SHAKESPEARE, *Antony and Cleopatra*

Prayer without work is like an empty wagon—lots of noise but no load.

ANONYMOUS

Good prayers never come creeping home. I am sure I shall receive either what I ask or what I should ask.

JOSEPH HALL

Will petitions that do not move the heart of the suppliant, move the heart of Omnipotence?

ANONYMOUS

Is there any place in any of our rooms where there is a little bit of carpet worn white by our knees?

ALEXANDER MACLAREN

Prayer is the gymnasium of the soul.

SAMUEL M. ZWEMER

Dwight L. Moody had a practical mind that never let a meeting get out of hand. Long public prayers particularly irritated him. Once he told his song leader, Sankey, "Lead us in a hymn while our brother is finishing his prayer."

G. S.

The life of prayer shapes the unity of Christian morality.

CARL F. H. HENRY, *Christian Personal Ethics*

Whoever only speaks *of* God, but never or seldom *to* God, easily leases body and soul to idols. The Christian thus places his whole future in jeopardy by a stunted prayer life.

CARL F. H. HENRY

The very breath of prayer sustains the Christian life.

CARL F. H. HENRY

Preaching

F

Yes, there is only one thing that will save us in this hour of desperation, and that is prayer.

STEPHEN OLFORD, *Heart Cry for Revival*

F

There are great drynesses even in the way of meditation; the bread of prayer is often without taste.

FRANCOIS MALAVAL, *A Simple Method of Raising the Soul to Contemplation*

G

The function of prayer is to set God at the center of attention.

ALBERT EDWARD DAY

F

We must alter our lives in order to alter our hearts, for it is impossible to live one way and pray another.

WILLIAM LAW

F

Prayer is the world in tune.

HENRY VAUGHAN

G

Humanity is never so beautiful as when praying for forgiveness or else forgiving another.

JEAN PAUL RICHTER

F

Prayer begins where human capacity ends.

NORMAN VINCENT PEALE

F

Prayer moves the Hand which moves the world.

JOHN A. WALLACE

Preaching

. . . faith comes from hearing the message, and the message is heard through the word of Christ.

ROMANS 10:17, NIV

I am certain that when I enter the pulpit or stand at the lectern to read, it is not my word, but my tongue is the pen of a ready writer.

MARTIN LUTHER

God . . . deigns to consecrate to himself the mouths and tongues of men in order that his voice may resound in them.

JOHN CALVIN

With preaching Christianity stands or falls because it is the declaration of a Gospel. Nay, more—far more—it is the Gospel prolonging and declaring itself.

P. T. FORSYTH

The preaching that kills may be, and often is, orthodox—dogmatically, inviolably orthodox. In the Christian system, unction is the anointing of the Holy Ghost, separating a person unto God's work and preparing him for it. This unction is the one divine enablement by which the preacher accomplishes the peculiar and saving ends of preaching. Without this unction there are no true spiritual results accomplished. The results and forces in preaching do not rise above the results of unsanctified speech. Without unction the former is as potent as the pulpit . . . without it the gospel has no more power to propagate itself than any other system of truth. This is the seal of its divinity. Unction in the preacher puts God in the gospel.

CHARLES H. SPURGEON

. . . until we have wrestled with God till the break of day, like Jacob: that is, until we have struggled to the utmost limits of our strength, and have known the despair of defeat. . . . [until] we have really understood the actual plight or our contemporaries, when we have heard their cry of anguish, [until] we have shared their suffering, both physical and spiritual, and their despair and desolation . . . then we shall be able to proclaim the word of God—but not till then!

JACQUES ELLUL

Richard Baxter praised those preachers who "preached as never sure to preach again . . . as a dying man to dying men."

G. S.

We preachers ought to think like great men, but speak like common people.

ROGER ASCHAM

The hearer's life is the preacher's best commendation.

ANONYMOUS

Prejudice

Prejudice is the ink with which all history is written.

MARK TWAIN

[Prejudice is] the mistreatment of people without their having done anything to merit such mistreatment. It has been a source of human unhappiness and misunderstanding wherever and whenever it has arisen.

ARNOLD ROSE, *The Roots of Prejudice*

To label people as worthy and unworthy, as good and bad, as acceptable and repulsive, is contrary to God's law and thoroughly anti-Christian.

G. S.

209

Pride

The mind of the bigot is like the pupil of the eye; the more light you pour upon it, the more it will contract.

OLIVER WENDELL HOLMES, JR.

I am free of all prejudices. I hate every one equally.

W. C. FIELDS

All looks yellow to a jaundiced eye.

ALEXANDER POPE

Nothing is so firmly believed as that which is least known.

MICHEL DE MONTAIGNE

A man convinced against his will/Is of the same opinion still.

SAMUEL BUTLER

No man has a right in America to treat any other man tolerantly, for tolerance is the assumption of superiority.

WENDELL WILLKIE

The real democratic American idea is, not that every man shall be on a level with every other man, but that every man shall have liberty to be what God made him, without hindrance.

HENRY WARD BEECHER

Pride

The animals were arguing about who had the biggest litters. Some talked big about their twins or triplets, some bragged of a dozen.

Finally they asked the lioness, who rather quietly replied, "Only one—but that one is a lion."

Aesop's Fables, adaptation

But too many people now climb onto the cross merely to be seen from a greater distance, even if they have to trample somewhat on the one who has been there so long.

ALBERT CAMUS

He that is proud eats up himself; pride is his own glass, his own trumpet, his own chronicle!

WILLIAM SHAKESPEARE, *Troilus and Cressida*

If you feel or imagine that you are right and suppose that your book, teaching or writing is a great achievement. . . . then, my dear man, feel your ears. If you are doing so properly, you will find that you have a splendid pair of big, long shaggy asses' ears.

MARTIN LUTHER

God made us, and God is able to empower us to do whatever He calls us to do. Denying that we can accomplish God's work is not humility; it is the worst kind of pride! . . . The proud man is possessed by things; the humble man possesses things and uses them for the good of others and the glory of God.

WARREN WIERSBE, *Live Like a King*

A proud man is always looking down on things and people; and, of course, as long as you're looking down, you can't see something that's above you.

C. S. LEWIS

Lord . . . where we are wrong, make us willing to change, and where we are right, make us easy to live with.

PETER MARSHALL

The wonderful thing about cockiness is that it can be overcome by a little maturity.

D. ELTON TRUEBLOOD

Progress

Restlessness and discontent are the first necessities of progress.

THOMAS A. EDISON

You can't hold a man down without staying down with him.

BOOKER T. WASHINGTON

> How does the soul grow? Not all in a minute!
> Now it may lose ground, and now it may win it;
> Now it resolves, and again the will faileth;
> Now it rejoiceth, and now it bewaileth;
> Now its hopes fructify, then they are blighted;
> Now it walks sullenly, now gropes benighted;
> Fed by discouragements, taught by disaster;
> So it goes forward, now slower, now faster,
> Till all the pain is past, and failure made whole,
> It is full grown, and the Lord rules the soul.

SUSAN COOLIDGE

Purpose of Man

Man was made to grow, not stop.

ROBERT BROWNING

Purpose of Man

To look up and not down,
To look forward and not back,
To look out and not in, and
To lend a hand.

EDWARD E. HALE

Thou hast made us for Thyself, and the heart of man is restless until it finds its rest in Thee.

SAINT AUGUSTINE

Life is a mission. Every other definition is false, and leads all who accept it astray.

GUISEPPE MAZZINI

When God wanted sponges and oysters He made them and put one on a rock and the other in the mud. When He made man He did not make him to be a sponge or an oyster; He made him with feet and hands, and head and heart, and vital blood, and a place to use them and He said to him, "Go work."

HENRY WARD BEECHER

Lives of great men all remind us
We can make our lives sublime,
And, departing, leave behind us
Footprints on the sands of time.

HENRY WADSWORTH LONGFELLOW

I see no business in life but the work of Christ.

HENRY MARTYN

In the spring of 1871, a young man picked up a book and read twenty-one words that had a profound effect on his future. A medical student at the Montreal General Hospital, he was worried about passing the final examination, worried about what to do, where to go, how to build up a practice, how to make a living.

The twenty-one words that this young medical student read in 1871 helped him to become the most famous physician of his generation. He organized the world-famous Johns Hopkins School of Medicine. He became Regius Professor of Medicine at Oxford—the highest honor that can be bestowed upon any medical man in the British Empire. He was knighted by the King of England. When he died, two huge volumes containing 1466 pages were required to tell the story of his life.

His name was Sir William Osler. Here are the twenty-one words that he read in the spring of 1871—twenty-one words from Thomas Carlyle that helped him lead a life free from worry: *"Our main business is not to see what lies dimly at a distance, but to do what lies clearly at hand."*

DALE CARNEGIE, *How to Stop Worrying and Start Living*

Fear God and work hard.

DAVID LIVINGSTONE

[Morning prayer]: Good morning, God, I love You! What are You up to today? I want to be a part of it.

NORMAN GRUBB

I have loved to hear my Lord spoken of; and wherever I have seen the print of his shoe in the earth, there I have coveted to set my foot too. His name has been to me as a civet-box; yea, sweeter than all perfumes. . . . And his countenance I have more desired than they that have most desired the light of the sun.

JOHN BUNYAN

← **R** →

Race

Jesus has a family in an interracial neighborhood called heaven.

Decision

In teaching race pride, it will be disastrous if we teach a false distinction and a false superiority. We do not correct white racism by erecting black racism.

ROY WILKINS

There are no "white" or "colored" signs on the foxholes or graveyards of battle.

JOHN F. KENNEDY

God is color-blind to skin.

G. S.

Race prejudice is not only a shadow over the colored—it is a shadow over all of us, and the shadow is darkest over those who feel it least and allow its evil effects to go on.

PEARL S. BUCK

For I am my mother's daughter, and the drums of Africa still beat in my heart. They will not let me rest while there is a single Negro boy or girl without a chance to prove his worth.

MARY McLEOD BETHUNE

All colors will agree in the dark.

FRANCIS BACON

Redemption

Two small boys were comparing progress in study for the Saturday catechism lesson.

"I've gotten as far as redemption," said one. "How far you got?"

"Oh, I'm way beyond redemption," said the other proudly.

ANONYMOUS

To deliver us from evil is not merely to take us out of hell, it is to take us into heaven.

P. T. FORSYTH, *The Work of Christ*

We are God's very own, being redeemed by Him. Every Christian therefore should wear a sign in his heart, "Not for sale!"

ANONYMOUS

But God will redeem my soul from the power of the grave: for he shall receive me.

PSALM 49:15

Let Israel hope in the Lord: for with the Lord there is mercy, and with him is plenteous redemption.

PSALM 130:7

He will swallow up death in victory; and the Lord God will wipe away tears from off all faces; and the rebuke of his people shall he take away from off all the earth: for the Lord hath spoken it.

ISAIAH 25:8

For ye are bought with a price: therefore glorify God in your body, and in your spirit, which are God's.

1 CORINTHIANS 6:20

Religion

Men will wrangle for religion; write for it; fight for it; anything but—live for it.

CHARLES CALEB COLTON

Religion . . . is the opium of the people.

KARL MARX

We have just enough religion to make us hate, but not enough to make us love one another.

JONATHAN SWIFT

Most men, indeed, play at religion as they play at games, religion itself being of all games the one most universally played.

A. W. TOZER

Going to church doesn't make you a Christian any more than going to a garage makes you an automobile.

BILLY SUNDAY

I have treated many hundreds of patients. Among those over 35, there has not been one whose problem in the last resort was not that of finding a religious outlook on life.

CARL JUNG

This I know—men without religion are moral cowards. The cause of Europe's miseries was its lack of religion.

GEORGE BERNARD SHAW

Our great-grandfathers called it the holy Sabbath; our grandfathers, the Sabbath; our fathers, Sunday, but today we call it the weekend. We have substituted a holiday for the holy day.

Wesleyan Methodist

Repentance

Man is born with his back toward God. When he truly repents, he turns right around and faces God. Repentance is a change of mind. . . . Repentance is the tear in the eye of faith.

D. L. MOODY

There is one case of death-bed repentance recorded—the penitent thief— that no one should despair; and only one, that no one should presume.

SAINT AUGUSTINE

He that hath promised pardon on our repentance hath not promised life till we repent.

FRANCIS QUARLES

True repentance has a double aspect; it looks upon things past with a weeping eye, and upon the future with a watchful eye.

ROBERT SMITH

215

Jesus said, "I came not to call the righteous, but sinners to repentance."
LUKE 5:32, KJV

Reputation

> Who steals my purse steals trash . . .
> But he that filches from me my good name,
> Robs me of that which not enriches him,
> And makes me poor indeed.
>
> WILLIAM SHAKESPEARE, *Othello*

It is a maxim with me that no man was ever written out of reputation but by himself.

RICHARD BENTLEY

To disregard what the world thinks of us is not only arrogant but utterly shameless.

CICERO

Reputations, like beavers and cloaks, shall last some people twice the time of others.

DOUGLAS JERROLD

A man's virtue is his monument, but forgotten is the man of evil repute.
EGYPTIAN TOMBSTONE INSCRIPTION (2100 B.C.)

Responsibility

If people concentrated on their responsibilities, others would have their rights.

STUART BRISCOE, *What Works*

Life always gets harder toward the summit—the cold increases, responsibility increases.

FRIEDRICH NIETZSCHE

You can't escape the responsibility of tomorrow by evading it today.
ABRAHAM LINCOLN

Ask not what your country can do for you; ask what can you do for your country.

JOHN F. KENNEDY

When they told me yesterday what had happened, I felt like the moon, the stars and all the planets had fallen on me. If you fellows ever pray, pray for me.
HARRY S. TRUMAN, After his accession to the Presidency, 13 April 1945

If you can't stand the heat, stay out of the kitchen.

HARRY S. TRUMAN

I believe that every right implies a responsibility; every opportunity, an obligation; every possession, a duty.

JOHN D. ROCKEFELLER, JR.

The ability to accept responsibility is the measure of the man.

ROY L. SMITH

Resurrection

In the early 1920s, Nikolai Bukharin was sent from Moscow to Kiev to address a vast anti-God rally. For an hour he abused and ridiculed the Christian faith until it seemed as if the whole structure of belief was in ruins. Questions were invited. A priest of the Orthodox church rose and asked leave to speak. He faced the people and gave them the ancient Easter greeting, "Christ is risen." Instantly the whole vast assembly rose to its feet, and the reply came back like a crash of breakers against the cliff, "He is risen indeed."

G. S.

Germany's Count Bismarck is said to have remarked, "Without the hope of eternal life, this life is not worth the effort of getting dressed in the morning." There is a great deal of truth in that statement. "For what is your life?" asks James, "It is even a vapour, that appeareth for a little time, and then vanisheth away" (James 4:14).

Job knew something of the brevity and futility of life. "My days are swifter than a weaver's shuttle," he said, "and are spent without hope" (Job 7:6). "Man that is born of a woman is of few days, and full of trouble. He cometh forth like a flower, and is cut down: he fleeth also as a shadow, and continueth not" (Job 14:1–2).

Isaiah wrote, "All flesh is grass, and all the goodliness thereof is as the flower of the field: the grass withereth, the flower fadeth" (Isaiah 40:6–7).

Yes, this life is brief and full of sorrows. And if our existence ends with the grave, what is the use? That is what Paul meant when he wrote in 1 Corinthians 15:19, "If in this life only we have hope in Christ, we are of all men most miserable." But the hope that Jesus gives goes beyond the grave, and His resurrection is the proof of it.

Paul goes on to say, "But now is Christ risen from the dead, and become the firstfruits of them that slept" (v. 20). He is the firstfruits. The harvest is yet to come. All who put their trust in Him will be a part of that great harvest of souls that will rise from the dead.

G. S.

Retirement

In Glendale, California, at Forest Lawn Cemetery hundreds of people each year stand before two huge paintings. One pictures the crucifixion of Christ. The other depicts His resurrection. In the second painting the artist has pictured an empty tomb with an angel near the entrance. In the foreground stands the figure of the risen Christ. But the striking feature of that huge canvas is a vast throng of people, back in the misty background, stretching into the distance and out of sight, suggesting the multitude who will be raised from the dead because Jesus first died and rose for them.

G. S.

The Result of the Resurrection

1. It guarantees the deity of the Lord Jesus. He is "declared to be the Son of God with power, according to the Spirit of holiness, by the resurrection from the dead" (Rom. 1:4).

2. It is essential to our justification. (See Rom. 4:25; 8:34.) Because Jesus rose from the dead all who believe in Him are justified "from all things, from which ye could not be justified by the law of Moses" (Acts 13:39).

3. It makes possible the forgiveness of sins. (See 1 Cor. 15:17.)

4. It makes certain a final judgment "because he hath appointed a day, in the which he will judge the world in righteousness by that man whom he hath ordained; whereof he hath given assurance unto all men, in that he hath raised him from the dead" (Acts 17:31).

5. It furnishes every believer with a deathless hope. "But now is Christ risen from the dead, and become the first-fruits of them that slept" (1 Cor. 15:20). As He rose from the dead and liveth forever, so will the bodies of believers be raised from the tomb. This is the unshakable confidence of the saints.

HAROLD LINDSELL and CHARLES WOODBRIDGE

4-23-00 Our Lord has written the promise of the resurrection, not in books alone, but in every leaf in springtime.

MARTIN LUTHER

Retirement

When some people retire, it's going to be mighty hard to be able to tell the difference.

VIRGINIA GRAHAM

I'm against mandatory retirement. It ought to be left to individuals. It is a shame to assume that all fools are old fools. I've found that there are more young fools than old fools. Nature has a way of getting rid of old fools.

SAM ERVIN

Revival

The best way to revive a church, is to build a fire in the pulpit.

D. L. MOODY

. . . times of refreshing from the Lord.   10-8-00

J. EDWIN ORR

[Revival is a] new beginning of obedience to God. . . . Just as in the case of a converted sinner, the first step is a deep repentance, a breaking down of heart, a getting down in the dust before God, with deep humility and a forsaking of sin.

CHARLES FINNEY

The greatest obstacle to the conversion of Nineveh was not to be found in Nineveh. It was not the sin and corruption of the Ninevites, although those were great. It was not the graft-ridden police force or corrupt politicians. It was not the false cults and religions. The biggest obstacle to the salvation of Nineveh was found in the heart of a pious, prejudiced man named Jonah. There was no deceitfulness in all of Nineveh like the deceitfulness in Jonah's heart.

Jonah was the key to the salvation of Nineveh. God's people are the *key* to the spiritual climate of our nation and the world.

G. S.

I can give a prescription that will bring revival . . . revival to any church, or community, or any city on earth.

First: Let a few Christians get thoroughly right with God. If this is not done, the rest will come to nothing.

Second: Let them bind themselves together to pray for revival until God opens the windows of heaven and comes down.

Third: Let them put themselves at the disposal of God for His use as He sees fit in winning others to Christ. That is all. I have given this prescription around the world . . . and in no instance has it failed. It cannot fail.

R. A. TORREY

Revival is absolutely essential to restrain the righteous anger of God, 10-8-00 to restore the conscious awareness of God, and to reveal the gracious activity of God.

STEPHEN OLFORD, *Heart Cry*

O that God would teach us that it is just as important to be spiritual as to be sound in our approach to the Bible, just as vital to be obedient

219

as to be orthodox, and that the purpose of revelation is nothing less than transformation of human lives!

STEPHEN OLFORD, *Heart Cry*

Seven steps to revival.

1. *Develop the desire to know Jesus Christ better.* Develop a holy dissatisfaction. The contented Christian is the sterile Christian. Paul said in substance, "Jesus arrested me on the Damascus road. Now I want to lay hold of all that for which I was arrested by God." Be thoroughly dissatisfied with your spiritual posture.

2. *Pray for a revolutionary change in your life.* I think of Jacob wrestling with God. He wanted blessing. He wouldn't be denied. Throw your entire life into the will of God. Seek God's very best.

3. *Do what you know to do.* If we pray for revival and neglect prayer, that's hypocrisy. To pray for growth and neglect the local church is absolute foolishness. To pray that you'll mature and neglect the Word of God is incongruous. Put yourself in the way of blessing.

4. *Totally repent.* "Create in me a clean heart!" David sobbed. For a whole year David was out of fellowship. But he confessed his sin; he turned from that sin, and then he could sing again; he could write again; he could pray again.

5. *Make the crooked straight.* If you owe a debt, pay it. Or have an understanding with the people you owe. Zacchaeus said, "Lord, the half of my goods I give to the poor; and if I have taken anything from any man by false accusation, I restore him fourfold" (Lk 19:8). As much as possible, make the crooked straight.

6. *Develop a seriousness of purpose.* Keep off the detours. Let nothing deflect the magnetic needle of your calling. If there is anything that is a Trojan horse in our day, it is the television set. Beware lest it rob you of your passion and your purpose.

7. *Major in majors.* The Christian life requires specialists. Jesus said in effect, "Be a one-eyed man" (cf. Lk 11:34–36). Paul said, "This one thing I do." Too many of us burn up too much energy without engaging in things that bring us nearer to God.

Refuse to rust out. Start sharing your faith. Make yourself available. Back your decision with your time and talent and dollars. Finally, ask God for great faith in Him. Begin to expect great things.

G. S.

Righteousness

You can always tell when you are on the road of righteousness—it's uphill.

ERNEST BLEVINS

I greatly longed to understand Paul's Epistle to the Romans, and nothing stood in the way but that one expression, "the righteousness of God," because I took it to mean that righteousness whereby God is righteous and deals righteously in punishing the unrighteous. . . . Night and day I pondered until . . . I grasped the truth that the righteousness of God is that righteousness whereby, through grace and sheer mercy, he justifies us by faith. Thereupon I felt myself to be reborn and to have gone through open doors into paradise. The whole of Scripture took on a new meaning, and whereas before "the righteousness of God" had filled me with hate, now it became to me inexpressibly sweet in greater love. This passage of Paul became to me a gateway to heaven.

MARTIN LUTHER

← S →

Saints

A humble saint looks most like a citizen of heaven.

D. L. MOODY

Why, why will we most gladly set days aside to honor the fathers of our nation—Washington, Lincoln, Jefferson—but draw back in dismay from giving honor to the Fathers of our Faith?

THOMAS HOWARD, *Evangelical Is Not Enough*

The saints are the sinners who keep on going.

ROBERT LOUIS STEVENSON

He that falls into sin is a man; that grieves at it is a saint; that boasteth of it, is a devil.

THOMAS FULLER

Salvation

It is the rightful heritage of every believer, even the newest in the family of faith, to be absolutely certain that eternal life is his present possession. To look to self is to tremble. To look to Calvary's finished work is to triumph.

LARRY McGUILL

If I can get a man to think for five minutes about his soul, he is almost certain to be converted.

D. L. MOODY

Salvation

I've never gotten over the wonder of it all.

GIPSY SMITH

The elect are the "whosoever wills"; the non-elect are the "whosoever won'ts."

D. L. MOODY

One might better try to sail the Atlantic in a paper boat than to get to heaven in good works.

CHARLES H. SPURGEON

> My father is rich in houses and lands,
> He holds the wealth of the world in His hands.
> Of rubies and diamonds, of silver and gold,
> His coffers are full,
> He has riches untold. . . .
> I'm a child of the King, a child of the King
> With Jesus my Saviour, I'm a child of the King.

HARRIET E. BUELL

Diverse are the ways by which men come to Christ. And great is the temptation to judge others if they do not have mud put on their eyes and go to Siloam exactly as we did.

VANCE HAVNER

No one can make you again but He who made you the first time.

W. Y. FULLERTON

When Bishop John Taylor Smith, former Chaplain General of the British Army, was in this country at the time of the D. L. Moody Centenary meetings, it was my privilege to hear him one noon hour in Christ Church, Indianapolis. The sanctuary was crowded with eager listeners, to whom the Bishop spoke most solemnly, yet tenderly, upon the necessity of the new birth, using the text quoted above (John 3:7; "Ye must be born again"). As a telling illustration, he related the following incident:

On one occasion, he told us, he was preaching in a large cathedral on this same text. In order to drive it home, he said: "My dear people, do not substitute anything for the new birth. You may be a member of a church, even the great church of which I am a member, the historic Church of England, but church membership is not new birth and 'except a man be born again he cannot see the kingdom of God.' The rector was sitting at my left. Pointing to him, I said, You might be a clergyman like my friend the rector here and not be born again, and 'except a

222

man be born again he cannot see the kingdom of God.' On my left sat the archdeacon in his stall. Pointing directly at him, I said, You might even be an archdeacon like my friend in his stall and not be born again and 'except a man be born again he cannot see the kingdom of God.' You might even be a bishop, like myself, and not be born again and 'except a man be born again he cannot see the kingdom of God.' "

Then he went on to tell us that a day or so later he received a letter from the archdeacon, in which he wrote: "My dear Bishop: You have found me out. I have been a clergyman for over thirty years, but I had never known anything of the joy that Christians speak of. I never could understand it. Mine has been hard, legal service. I did not know what was the matter with me, but when you pointed directly to me and said, You might even be an archdeacon and not be born again, I realized in a moment what the trouble was. I had never known anything of the new birth."

He went on to say that he was wretched and miserable, had been unable to sleep all night, and begged for a conference, if the bishop could spare the time to talk with him.

"Of course, I could spare the time," said Bishop Smith, "and the next day we got together over the Word of God and after some hours we were both on our knees, the archdeacon taking his place before God as a poor, lost sinner and telling the Lord Jesus he would trust Him as his Saviour. From that time on everything has been different."

H. A. IRONSIDE

As a man writes his name upon the fly-leaf of his books, or stamps his initials on his valuables, so Christ gives His name in token of proprietorship, and builds on the fact at once the assurance of protection and the demand for service.

ALEXANDER MACLAREN

Thank God for that "fine linen, clean and white, the righteousness" with which Christ covers our wounded nakedness. It becomes ours, though no thread of it was wrought in our looms.

ALEXANDER MACLAREN

The recognition of sin is the beginning of salvation.

ANONYMOUS

Sanctification
Lord, make me more like Yourself, less like myself.

ANONYMOUS

223

Science, Search for Meaning

Next to the might of God, the serene beauty of a holy life is the most powerful influence for good in all the world.

D. L. MOODY

Thoughtfulness is the beginning of great sanctity. If you learn this art of being thoughtful, you will become more and more Christlike, for His heart was meek and He always thought of others.

MOTHER TERESA

God never gave a man a thing to do concerning which it were irreverent to ponder how the Son of God would have done it.

GEORGE MacDONALD

Take up the cross if thou the crown would'st gain.

PAULINUS, BISHOP OF NOLA

Science

Science without religion is lame; religion without science is blind.

ALBERT EINSTEIN

Science increases our power in proportion as it lowers our pride.

CLAUDE BERNARD

Science is a first-rate piece of furniture for a man's upper chamber if he has common sense on the ground floor.

OLIVER WENDELL HOLMES, SR.

Search for Meaning

There are no more worlds to conquer.

ALEXANDER THE GREAT

As I see him, the unutterably infinitesimal individual weaves among the mysteries a floss-like and wholly meaningless course—if course it be. In short, I catch on meaning from all I have seen and pass quite as I came, confused and dismayed.

THEODORE DREISER, *What I Believe*

Youth is a blunder; manhood a struggle; old age a regret.

BENJAMIN DISRAELI

> Alas how scant the sheaves for all the trouble,
> The toil, the pain and the resolve sublime—
> A few full ears; the rest but weeds and stubble,
> And withered wildflowers plucked before their time.

A. B. BRAGDON

. . . . Out, out, brief candle!
Life's but a walking shadow, a poor player
That struts and frets his hour upon the stage,
And then is heard no more; it is a tale
Told by an idiot, full of sound and fury,
Signifying nothing.

WILLIAM SHAKESPEARE, *Macbeth*

Man is an inhabitant of a thin rind on a negligible blob of matter, belonging to one of the millions of stars, in one among millions of island universes.

H. G. WELLS

[Life] bubbles on the rapid stream of time.

EDWARD YOUNG

The Juke-Box
Exiles from themselves,
    And with the wrong address,
They drain the raucous songs
    To fill their emptiness.

Louder the juke-box cries
    To each poor, wandered ghost:
He wonders why he's here
    And fears the silence most.

LOUIS GINSBERG

. . . what shadows we are, and what shadows we pursue!

EDMUND BURKE

My Quest
We search the world for truth, we cull
The good, the pure, the beautiful,
From graven stone and written scroll,
From the old flower-fields of the soul,
And, weary seekers for the best,
We come back laden from our quest,
To find that all the sages said
Is in the Book our mothers read.

JOHN GREENLEAF WHITTIER

Second Coming

The great Dwight L. Moody used to say, "I never preach a sermon without thinking that possibly the Lord may come before I preach

225

another." Dr. G. Campbell Morgan, the distinguished British clergyman, said, "I never begin my work in the morning without thinking that perhaps He may interrupt my work and begin His own. I am not looking for death, I am looking for Him." That is the way a Christian should live his life—in the constant anticipation of the return of Jesus Christ! If we could live every day as though it might be the very last one before the final judgment, what a difference it would make here on earth! But we don't like to think that way. We don't like to think that our carefully made plans, our long-range schemes may be interrupted by the trumpet of God. Too many people would rather say, "Oh well, the end of the world hasn't come yet, so why think about it—it's probably a thousand years away."

BILLY GRAHAM

The bloom of beauty of Apostolic Christianity was created by the upward look.

JAMES DENNEY

More than a fourth of the Bible is predictive prophecy. Approximately one-third of it has yet to be fulfilled. Both the Old and New Testaments are full of promises about the return of Jesus Christ. Over 1,800 references appear in the Old Testament, and seventeen Old Testament books give prominence to this theme. Of the 260 chapters in the New Testament, there are more than 300 references to the Lord's return—one out of every thirty verses. Twenty-three of the twenty-seven New Testament books refer to this great event. Three of the four other books are single-chapter letters written to individuals concerning a particular subject, and the fourth is Galatians, which does imply Christ's coming again. For every prophecy on the first coming of Christ, there are eight on Christ's second coming.

G. S.

Dr. Reuben A. Torrey, second president of the Moody Bible Institute, stated: "The latter truth [the second coming of Christ] transformed my whole idea of life; it broke the power of the world and its ambition over me, and filled my life with the most radiant optimism even under the most discouraging circumstances." Dr. Torrey was asked, "Is not the doctrine of Christ's personal and near coming one of practical power and helpfulness?" He replied, "It is transforming the lives of more men and women than almost any doctrine I know of."

G. S.

If Christ were coming again tomorrow, I would plant a tree today.

MARTIN LUTHER

The truth of the catching away of the church was important to my father. I remember him calling it to our attention as children. On one occasion after reading 1 Thessalonians chapter four, he quietly and methodically faced each of his six children with the question, "If Jesus returned tonight, would you be ready?" It was moving to hear each child answer, "Yes, I'm ready." Father then led us in singing the hymn "Will the Circle Be Unbroken When He Comes?" That is a question each individual must answer.

G. S.

Pastor Horatius Bonar lived in the glow of Christ's coming. As he would conclude his day's ministry, he would draw the curtains of his window and utter as he looked upward, "Perhaps tonight, Lord!" In the morning, as he awoke and looked out on the dawn of a new day, he would pray, looking up into the sky, "Perhaps today, Lord!"

G. S.

The doctrine of the second coming has failed, so far as we are concerned, if it does not make us realize that at every moment of every year in our lives Donne's question, "What if this present were the world's last night?" is equally relevant.

C. S. Lewis

This is the Voice of Freedom, General MacArthur speaking. People of the Philippines: I have returned. By the grace of Almighty God, our forces stand again on Philippine soil. . . . The hour of your redemption is here. . . . Rally to me.

Douglas MacArthur, On landing at Leyte Island
in the Philippines, 20 October 1944

Selfishness

Whenever you are too selfishly looking out for your own interest, you have only one person working for you—yourself. When you help a dozen other people with their problems, you have a dozen people working with you.

William B. Given, Jr.

He who lives to benefit himself confers on the world a benefit when he dies.

Tertullian

> . . . he who seeks all things, wherever he goes,
> Only reaps from the hopes which around him he sows
> A harvest of barren regrets.

Owen Meredith (Lord Lytton)

Self-Knowledge

From the morning to the evening, careless of the sun or of the rain, the spectators, who sometimes numbered 400,000 remained at eager attention . . . The happiness of Rome seemed to hang on the event of a race.

EDWARD GIBBON

Recipe for a Miserable Life:
Think about yourself.
Talk about yourself.
Use I as often as possible.
Mirror yourself continually in the opinion of others.
Listen greedily to what people say about you.
Expect to be appreciated.
Be suspicious.
Be jealous and envious.
Be sensitive to slights.
Never forgive a criticism.
Trust nobody but yourself.
Insist on consideration and respect.
Demand agreement with your own views on everything.
Sulk if people are not grateful to you for favors shown them.
Never forget a service you may have rendered.
Be on the lookout for a good time for yourself.
Shirk your duties if you can.
Do as little as possible for others.
Love yourself supremely.
Be selfish.

ANONYMOUS

Salvianus . . . assures us that Christians were indulging in the madness of the theatre, when the arms of the Vandals were ringing round the walls, and that the applause of the spectators was mingled with the groans of the dying and the battle cries of the attackers.

SAMUEL DILL, *Roman Society in the Last Century of the Western Empire*

Self-Knowledge

Search thy own heart; what paineth thee in others in thyself may be.

JOHN GREENLEAF WHITTIER

Do you want to know the man against whom you have most reason to guard yourself? Your looking-glass will give a very fair likeness of his face.

RICHARD WHATELY

We are so accustomed to wearing a disguise before others that eventually we are unable to recognize ourselves.

FRANÇOIS, DUC DE LA ROCHEFOUCAULD

It is not only the most difficult thing to know oneself, but the most inconvenient one, too.

H. W. SHAW

The more faithfully you listen to the voice within you, the better you will hear what is sounding outside. And only he who listens can speak.

DAG HAMMARSKJÖLD

In proportion as our inward life fails, we go more constantly and desperately to the post-office. You may depend on it, that poor fellow who walks away with the greatest number of letters, proud of his extensive correspondence, has not heard from himself this long while.

HENRY THOREAU

Self-Pity

Milton the blind, who looked on Paradise!
Beethoven, deaf, who heard vast harmonies!
Byron, the lame, who climbed toward Alpine skies!
Who pleads a handicap, remembering these?

VIOLET A. STOREY, *Tea in an Old House*

Never allow your own sorrow to absorb you, but seek out another to console, and you will find consolation.

J. C. MACAULAY

Who lets his feelings run
In soft luxurious flow,
Shrinks when hard service must be done,
And faints at every woe.

JOHN HENRY NEWMAN

Great souls suffer in silence.

JOHANN VON SCHILLER

Never give way to melancholy; resist it steadily, for the habit will encroach.

SYDNEY SMITH

Sermons

All preachers should keep in mind the maxim: The mind cannot retain what the seat cannot endure.

ANONYMOUS

A church attender commended her pastor for his sermon and said, "You'll never know what your sermon meant to me. It was like water to a drowning man."

G. S.

What too many orators want in depth they give you in length.

BARON DE MONTESQUIEU

The minister of a local congregation approached the desk of the city editor. "I just dropped by," he said, "to thank you for the very generous report on my sermon in your morning edition, and also to register a mild protest. In your article you referred to me as 'the reverend' but you spelled it 'neverend.' "

ANONYMOUS

The sermon is the house; the illustrations are the windows that let in the light.

CHARLES H. SPURGEON

Service

The service we render to others is really the rent we pay for our room on this earth. It is obvious that man is himself a traveller; that the purpose of this world is not "to have and to hold" but "to give and to serve." There can be no other meaning.

WILFRED T. GRENFELL

The greatest pleasure I know is to do a good action by stealth and have it found out by accident.

CHARLES LAMB

> The quality of mercy is not strain'd,
> It droppeth as the gentle rain from heaven
> Upon the place beneath. It is twice bless'd:
> It blesseth him that gives and him that takes.
>
> WILLIAM SHAKESPEARE

It is high time that the ideal of success should be replaced by the ideal of service.

ALBERT EINSTEIN

Our opportunities to do good are our talents.

COTTON MATHER

Be an opener of doors for such as come after thee, and do not try to make the universe a blind alley.

RALPH WALDO EMERSON

No man or woman of the humblest sort can really be strong, gentle, pure, and good without the world being better for it, without somebody being helped and comforted by the very existence of that goodness.

PHILLIPS BROOKS

Try to forget yourself in the service of others. For when we think too much of ourselves and our own interests, we easily become despondent. But when we work for others, our efforts return to bless us.

SIDNEY POWELL

Service to a just cause rewards the worker with more real happiness and satisfaction than any other venture in life.

CARRIE CHAPMAN CATT

To give real service you must add something which cannot be bought or measured with money, and that is sincerity and integrity.

DONALD A. ADAMS

Only a burdened heart can lead to fruitful service.

ALAN REDPATH

Service can never become slavery to one who loves.

J. L. MASSE

Silence

The best time for you to hold your tongue is the time you feel you must say something or bust.

JOSH BILLINGS

Many a time I have wanted to stop talking and find out what I really believed.

WALTER LIPPMANN

Besser stumm als dumm—Better silent than stupid.

GERMAN PROVERB

If you don't say anything, you won't be called on to repeat it.

CALVIN COOLIDGE

When Calvin Coolidge was Vice-President, Channing N. Cox, who had succeeded him as Governor of Massachusetts, came to Washington and called on his predecessor. Cox noted that Coolidge was able to see long lists of callers daily and finish his work at five o'clock, while Cox found himself held at his desk as late as nine P.M.

"How come the difference?" he asked.

"You talk back," Coolidge explained.

WALTER TROHAN

The most difficult thing in the world is to know how to do a thing and to watch somebody else doing it wrong, without comment.

T. H. WHITE

In times like the present, men should utter nothing for which they would not willingly be responsible through time and eternity.

ABRAHAM LINCOLN

Sign in an office at a Southern Air base: *Caution:* Be Sure Brain Is Engaged Before Putting Mouth in Gear.

ANONYMOUS

He who knows does not talk; he who talks does not know.

LAO-TZU

Sin

The Son of Man came to seek and to save what was lost.

LUKE 19:10, NIV

[Sin is] cosmic treason.

R. C. SPROUL

They can gas me, but I am famous. I have achieved in one day what it took Robert Kennedy all his life to do.

SIRHAN SIRHAN, Shortly after shooting Kennedy, June 1968

We have all sinned, some more, some less.

SENECA

One reason sin flourishes is that it is treated like a cream puff instead of a rattlesnake.

BILLY SUNDAY

Looking at the wound of sin will never save anyone. What you must do is look at the remedy.

D. L. MOODY

The instances are exceedingly rare of men immediately passing over a clear marked line from virtue into declared vice and corruption. There are middle tints and shades between the two extremes; there is something uncertain on the confines of the two empires which they must pass through, and which renders the change easy and imperceptible.

EDMUND BURKE

The voice of sin may be loud, but the voice of forgiveness is louder.

D. L. MOODY

There are certain diseases of which a constant symptom is unconsciousness that there is anything the matter. A deep-seated wound does not hurt much.

ALEXANDER MACLAREN

> Of Man's first disobedience, and the fruit
> Of that forbidden tree, whose mortal taste
> Brought death into the world, and all our woe,
> With loss of Eden, till one greater Man
> Restore us, and regain the blissful seat,
> Sing, Heavenly Muse.

JOHN MILTON, *Paradise Lost*

By nature I was too blind to know Him, too proud to trust Him, too obstinate to serve Him, too base-minded to love Him.

JOHN NEWTON

Many a ship has stood the tempest, and then has gone down in the harbour because its timbers have been gnawed to pieces by white ants and many a man can do what is wanted in the trying moments, and yet make shipwreck of his faith in uneventful times.

"Like ships that have gone down at sea,/When heaven was all tranquillity."

ALEXANDER MACLAREN, (VERSE BY THOMAS MOORE)

The chains of sin can be got off. Christ looses them by His blood. Like a drop of corrosive acid that blood, falling upon the fetters, dissolves them, and the prisoner goes free, emancipated by the Son.

ALEXANDER MACLAREN

What Is Sin? The Bible Answers . . .
1. Sin is transgression of the law—lawlessness (1 John 3:4).
2. A grievous malady, contaminating the whole of man's being (Isaiah 1:4, 5; Romans 3:10–18).
3. An obscuring cloud, which hides the face of God's blessing (Isaiah 59:2).

4. A binding cord, which holds man in its power (Proverbs 5:22).
5. A tyrannical owner, who embitters the lives of his slaves (Nehemiah 9:37).
6. A disturber of rest, which causes disorder and anxiety (Psalm 38:3).
7. A robber of blessing, which strips and starves the soul (Jeremiah 5:25).
8. A terrible devastation, which brings untold desolation (Micah 6:13).
9. A tripper-up, which continually overthrows the sinner to his hurt (Proverbs 13:6).
10. A record writer, which leaves its indelible mark upon the committer (Jeremiah 17:1).
11. A betraying presence, which "will out" no matter what pains are taken to hide it (Ezekiel 21:24).
12. A sure detective, which turns upon the sinner and finds him out (Numbers 32:23).
13. An accusing witness, which points its condemning finger at the prisoner in the bondage of sin (Isaiah 59:12).
14. A sum of addition which accumulates its weight to the condemnation of the sinner (Isaiah 30:1).

ROBERT G. LEE

I wander thro' each charter'd street,
Near where the charter'd Thames does flow,
And mark in every face I meet
Marks of weakness, marks of woe.

In every cry of every Man,
In every Infant's cry of fear,
In every voice, in every ban
The mind-forg'd manacles I hear . . .

WILLIAM BLAKE

Seven deadly sins: politics without principle, wealth without work, pleasure without conscience, knowledge without character, business without morality, science without humanity, and worship without sacrifice.

E. STANLEY JONES

A man who believes himself a sinner, who feels himself sinful, is already at the gates of the Kingdom of heaven.

FRANCOIS MAURIAC

Let us not forget that violence does not have its own separate existence and is, in fact, incapable of having it: it is invariably interwoven with the lie. They have the closest of kinship, the most profound natural tie: violence has nothing with which to cover itself except the lie, and the lie has nothing to stand on other than violence.

ALEKSANDER SOLZHENITSYN

I've been asked many times as Sheriff, "Do you think you will ever eliminate crime?" I'm not naive enough to think that crime can ever be eliminated. There were prostitutes and pickpockets in the days of Christ. There was gambling and debauchery in the days of the prophets. There will always be some who submit to the soft, glittery pleasures and it will always be for the spiritually strong to lead those back.

RICHARD OGILVIE

We are too Christian really to enjoy sinning, and too fond of sinning really to enjoy Christianity. Most of us know perfectly well what we ought to do; our trouble is that we do not want to do it.

PETER MARSHALL

To sin by silence when they should protest makes cowards of men.

ABRAHAM LINCOLN

Our nation was shocked some time ago by the mass murder of eight young student nurses in a Chicago hospital dormitory. Corazon Amurao, an exchange nurse from the Philippines, was the only one to escape. Through police photographs, she was able to identify Richard Speck as the killer. Literally thousands of police were mobilized in a massive manhunt to find this twenty-five-year-old man.

After three days on the run, Speck ended up in the Starr Hotel on West Madison Street. There, in cage 584, an eight-by-six-foot wire cubicle costing ninety cents a night, Speck was found.

Speck had drifted through the underbelly of this great city, reading papers, drinking heavily, and hiding out on skid row. The day before he was captured he had spent drinking, trying to find courage to end his life. At 12:30 A.M. Sunday morning, he was rushed to the Cook County Hospital, bleeding to death, an unknown drifter from skid row.

As Dr. LeRoy Smith washed the blood off his arm, he saw the tattoo, which read, "Born to raise hell." Immediately he realized this was the killer. Within minutes the police arrived, and the manhunt was over.

In a very real sense, modern man is in flight. He wants to live his own life, be his own judge, his own creator, and his own saviour. But the more he makes himself independent, the more lonely and frightened he becomes.

G. S.

Solitude

Unfortunately the world today does not seem to understand, in either man or woman, the need to be alone. Anything else will be accepted as a better excuse. If one sets time aside for a shopping expedition, that time is accepted as inviolable; but if one says, "I cannot come because it is my hour to be alone," one is considered rude, egotistical, or strange.

ANNE MORROW LINDBERGH

The power to stand alone is worth acquiring at the expense of much sorrowful solitude.

GEORGE BERNARD SHAW

Solitude, the safeguard of mediocrity, is to genius the stern friend.

RALPH WALDO EMERSON

I never found the companion that was so companionable as solitude.

HENRY THOREAU

Solitude is the nurse of enthusiasm, and enthusiasm is the true parent of genius. In all ages solitude has been called for—has been flown to.

ISAAC DISRAELI

Sorrow

Every heart hath its own ache.

THOMAS FULLER

Sorrow is like a precious treasure,
Shown only to friends.

AFRICAN PROVERB

O for the touch of a vanish'd hand,
And the sound of a voice that is still!

ALFRED, LORD TENNYSON

Christ is the answer to sorrow. When Harry Lauder, the great Scottish comedian, received word that his son had been killed in France, he said, "In a time like this, there are three courses open to man: He may give way to despair and become bitter. He may endeavor to drown his sorrow in drink or in a life of wickedness. Or he may turn to God." In your sorrow, turn to God. There are thousands of people who have turned to God, but you may be still carrying your burdens.

But God begs of you, "Cast all your care on me, for I care for you" (1 Peter 5:7). You who must go through the valley of the shadow of death, you who must say goodbye to those whom you have loved, you who suffer privation and misery, you who are unjustly persecuted for righteousness' sake—take heart, take courage. Our Christ is more than adequate for sorrow.

BILLY GRAHAM

Our sorrows are never so great that they hide our mercies. The sky is never covered with clouds so that neither sun nor stars appear for many days.

ALEXANDER MACLAREN

> I walked a mile with Pleasure,
> She chattered all the way;
> But left me none the wiser,
> For all she had to say.
>
> I walked a mile with Sorrow,
> And ne'er a word said she;
> But, oh, the things I learned from her
> When Sorrow walked with me!

ROBERT BROWNING HAMILTON

> Nothing begins, and nothing ends,
> That is not paid with moan;
> For we are born in others pain,
> And perish in our own.

FRANCIS THOMPSON

Of all the days of the war, there are two especially I can never forget. Those were the days following the news, in New York and Brooklyn, of that first Bull Run defeat, and the day of Abraham Lincoln's death. I was home in Brooklyn on both occasions. The day of the murder we heard the news very early in the morning. Mother prepared breakfast—and other meals afterward—as usual; but not a mouthful was eaten all day by either of us. We each drank half a cup of coffee; that was all. Little was said. We got every newspaper morning and evening, and the frequent extras of that period, and passed them silently to each other.

WALT WHITMAN

The sorrows of life do not *create* problems, they *reveal* them.

WARREN WIERSBE, *Live Like a King*

Believe me, every heart has its sorrows, which the world knows not; and oftentimes we call a man cold when he is only sad.

HENRY WADSWORTH LONGFELLOW

Speech

The Tongue Loosed

"And the string of his tongue was loosed, and he spake plain" (Mark 7:35).

Recalling this miracle wrought by Jesus, a Christian friend—"Sister Ida"—on the other side of the Atlantic has written the following prayer:

Loose Thou my tongue, so silent have I been, Lord,
In telling others of Thy love divine;
Loose Thou my tongue, and use it for Thy glory,
That straying lambs, back to Thy fold may come.

Loose Thou my tongue, that Thou canst always help me
To strengthen those by storm and tempest tossed;
Loose Thou my tongue, to guide the sad and lonely
To find in Thee, their refuge and their rock.

Loose Thou my tongue, for Thee, O blessed Master,
That I may speak Thy words of truth divine;
Loose Thou my tongue, that I may tell the story
Of all the wondrous things that Thou hast done.

Loose Thou my tongue, baptize with love and fire, Lord,
To teach Thy Cross and resurrection power;
Loose Thou my tongue, and fill me with Thy fullness
Till others, too, shall crown Thee Lord of all.

This prayer, if prayed from clean hearts and lives submissive to God's will, would put tongues of fire where there are now tongues draped in icicles—would melt the frozen fountains of testimony and start refreshing streams in dry gardens—would give us the plain language of truth where there is now evasive stammering and beclouding bombast.

ROBERT G. LEE

It is not sufficient to know what one ought to say, but one must also know how to say it.

ARISTOTLE

Dr. Wernher von Braun, the American space pioneer, made some startling predictions concerning mass communications. In an article appearing in the Astronautics and Aeronautics Journal, the NASA chief suggested that soon it will be possible to carry out so many different kinds of transactions within the home, that people will be able to live anywhere. Home communication centers will make office buildings, banks, and stores almost obsolete. Direct visual and audio communication will be possible with anyone at any time and anywhere.

G. S.

Take my lips, and let them be/ Filled with messages for Thee.

FRANCES RIDLEY HAVERGAL

A young man had cancer of the tongue. Before the operation the doctor told him that he would never speak again. The young man paused and then said, "Thank God for Jesus Christ." What beautiful last words.

G. S.

Silent Cal Coolidge was famous for his brevity of speech. One day Mrs. Coolidge surprised him with a presidential portrait hung in the library of the White House. Coolidge first saw it when he walked in with a senator. For a long moment the two men looked at the portrait without saying a word. At last Coolidge said, "I think so, too."

G. S.

Bernard of Clairvaux spoke, and thousands left all their earthly goods for the Second Crusade. Patrick Henry's immortal words, "Give me liberty, or give me death!" inspired a nation to fight furiously for liberty. Young William Jennings Bryan came to the 1896 Democratic National Convention simply as an alternate delegate. As he spoke to the great throng of delegates there, he lifted them out of their seats with his oratory and was acclaimed their nominee for the presidency of the United States. The tongue is powerful.

G. S.

One slogan used during World War II was, "a slip of the lip may sink a ship." I have a picture of a South Pacific battle scene in which Marines are storming a beachhead. They are dropping everywhere. One Marine is wounded and bleeding. The picture bears a two-word title: Somebody Talked. It may be that the tongue has slain more than have all the bullets and bombs of battle. The book of Proverbs tells us that "A soft tongue breaketh the bone" (Prov. 25:15b). And again we read, "He that keepeth his mouth keepeth his life" (Prov. 13:3).

G. S.

Edward Everett Hale in his story "The Man Without a Country" tells of the young naval officer, Philip Nolan, who with some others was on trial for being false to the service.

As the court session dragged on and the trial came to a close, Nolan was asked if he wished to say anything to show that he had always been faithful to the United States. In a fit of temper he cursed and said, "I wish that I may never hear of the United States again!"

The judge and the jury were shocked! In fifteen minutes they issued the verdict: "The Court decides, subject to the approval of the President, that you shall never hear the name of the United States again." Nolan laughed, but no one else laughed, and he became the man without a country.

G. S.

Stewardship

Every charitable act is a stepping-stone toward heaven.

HENRY WARD BEECHER

The problem with our giving is that we give the widow's mite, but not with the widow's spirit.

ANONYMOUS

> Where your pleasure is, there is your treasure.
> Where your treasure is, there is your heart.
> Where your heart is, there is your happiness.

SAINT AUGUSTINE

Stories

They say I tell a great many stories, I reckon I do, but I have found in the course of a long experience that common people, take them as they run, are more easily informed through the medium of a broad illustration than in any other way, and as to what the hypercritical few may think, I don't care.

ABRAHAM LINCOLN

Anecdotes are stories with points. They are tools—nail sinkers to drive home arguments firmly. They are the origin of all teaching.

EDMUND FULLER

> I love to tell the story
> Of unseen things above,
> Of Jesus and his glory,
> Of Jesus and his love.
>
> I love to tell the story,
> Because I know 'tis true;
> It satisfies my longings
> As nothing else would do.

KATHERINE HANKEY

[The art of the novel] does not simply consist in the author's telling a story about the adventures of some other person. . . . It happens because the storyteller's own experience of men and things, whether for good or ill . . . has moved him to an emotion so passionate that he can no longer keep it shut up in his heart.

MURASAKI SHIKIBU

Jesus spoke to them again in parables, saying. . . .

MATTHEW 22:1, NIV

Submission

Supreme authority in both church and home has been divinely vested in the male as the representative of Christ, who is the Head of the church. It is in willing submission rather than grudging capitulation that the woman in the church (whether married or single) and the wife in the home find their fulfillment.

ELISABETH ELLIOT

Contemporary society. . . . does not value personal submission. Rather, it teaches that the ideal, the highest position a human being can attain, is that of personal autonomy.

STEPHEN B. CLARK, *Man and Woman in Christ*

A Christian man is the most free lord of all, and subject to none; a Christian man is the most dutiful servant of all, and subject to everyone.

MARTIN LUTHER

The purpose of life is not to find your freedom, but your master.

P. T. FORSYTH

Make me a captive, Lord,
And then I shall be free;
Force me to render up my sword,
And I shall conqueror be.

I sink in life's alarms
When by myself I stand;
Imprison me within Thine arms,
And strong shall be my hand.

GEORGE MATHESON

As Thou wilt; what Thou wilt; when Thou wilt.

THOMAS À KEMPIS

Success

Our Lord died an apparent failure, discredited by the leaders of established religion, rejected by society and forsaken by his friends. It took the resurrection to demonstrate how gloriously Christ had triumphed. Yet today the professed church seems to have learned nothing. How much eager-beaver religious work is done out of a carnal desire to make good.

A. W. TOZER

Nothing *recedes* like success.

ANONYMOUS

Nothing is particularly hard if you divide it into small jobs.

HENRY FORD

Speaking of Frederick the Great, the historian said: "Frederick the Great won Rossbach by his miraculous marching on the lightest possible equipment."

Another historian, speaking of General Grant, said: "When Grant started out to capture Vicksburg, he took nothing with him but a gun coat and a toothpick."

What are the historians saying? That we must not give too much attention to baggage.

ROBERT G. LEE

Veni, vidi, vici—I came, I saw, I conquered.

JULIUS CAESAR

The common idea that success spoils people by making them vain, egotistic, and self-complacent is erroneous; on the contrary, it makes them, for the most part, humble, tolerant, and kind. Failure makes people cruel and bitter.

W. SOMERSET MAUGHAM

Success is counted sweetest/By those who ne'er succeed.

EMILY DICKINSON

If one advances confidently in the direction of his dreams, and endeavors to live the life which he has imagined, he will meet with a success unexpected in common hours. . . . Why should we be in such desperate haste to succeed, and in such desperate enterprises? If a man does not keep pace with his companions, perhaps it is because he hears a different drummer. Let him step to the music which he hears, however measured or far away.

HENRY THOREAU

Six essential qualities that are the key to success: Sincerity, personal integrity, humility, courtesy, wisdom, charity.

WILLIAM MENNINGER

Suffering

We are not at our best perched at the summit; we are climbers, at our best when the way is steep.

JOHN W. GARDNER

The real problem is not why some pious, humble, believing people suffer, but why some do not.

C. S. LEWIS

Suffering, although it is a burden, is a useful burden, like the splints used in orthopedic treatment.

SÖREN KIERKEGAARD

You must submit to supreme suffering in order to discover the completion of joy.

JOHN CALVIN

He who fears to suffer cannot be His who suffered.

TERTULLIAN

I do not believe that sheer suffering teaches. If suffering alone taught, then all the world would be wise, since everyone suffers. To suffering must be added mourning, understanding, patience, love, openness and the willingness to remain vulnerable.

ANNE MORROW LINDBERGH

← T →

Tact

Many people are so tactful that they never make contact with people.

ANONYMOUS

Do not use a hatchet to remove a fly from your friend's forehead.

CHINESE PROVERB

Cultivate tact, for it is the mark of culture . . . the lubricant of human relationships, softening contacts and minimizing friction.

BALTASAR GRACIÁN

Tact is like a girdle. It enables you to organize the awkward truth more attractively.

ANONYMOUS

Teaching

Tact comes as much from goodness of heart as from fineness of taste.

ENDYMION

Tact is the unsaid part of what you think; its opposite, the unthought part which you say.

HENRY VAN DYKE

Tact is the art of making a point without making an enemy.

HOWARD W. NEWTON

Tact consists in knowing how far to go too far.

JEAN COCTEAU

Tact is the ability to describe others as they see themselves.

ABRAHAM LINCOLN

Tact has been defined as the right touch rather than the wrong touch. We are instructed in Scripture to let our lights shine, but remember— not like a blow torch! J. Oswald Sanders defines tact as "an intuitive perception of what is proper or fitting; the mental ability of saying and doing the right thing at the right time, so as not to unnecessarily offend or anger. This qualification is sadly often conspicuous by its absence and the worker spoils the very work about which he is so concerned."

G. S.

Recently I was flying to Washington, D.C. The businessman sitting next to me offered me a drink of vodka. In a friendly, natural way I simply said, "No, thank you."

A few minutes later he noticed my Bible and said, "You seem to be religious, and I guess you think I'm ugly."

"No," I responded, "I think you're a very generous person." Immediately he was receptive, and I tactfully shared the gospel with him.

I could easily have answered, "No, thank you, I'm a Christian." In all likelihood he would have felt I was putting him down, and the door of opportunity would have been closed.

G. S.

Teaching

If the teacher be corrupt, the world will be corrupt.

PERSIAN PROVERB

To teach is to learn twice.

JOSEPH JOUBERT

244

Not only is there an art in knowing a thing, but also a certain art in teaching it.

CICERO

Instruction does not prevent waste of time or mistakes; and mistakes themselves are often the best teachers of all.

JAMES A. FROUDE

Television

Our broadcasts have not improved. If anything, their quality has declined. The tube has become a trip, a national opiate, a baby-sitter who charges nothing, something to iron by, and to shave to, and to doze over.

ROGER MUDD

I don't think that television has corrupted man. But I do think that man has invented it to flee from reality.

MALCOM MUGGERIDGE

A TV set is only a machine—glass, metal, wires, and little gadgets— until you place it in your home. . . . In some homes, TV becomes a baby-sitter, for babies of all ages. In other homes, TV is a narcotic, an escape from reality. Or it may be a thief, stealing time, thoughts, friendships, creativity, and opportunities for much-needed recreation and companionship. In too few homes, TV is a servant, providing information, insight, commentary on life, news, laughter, music, and worthwhile entertainment.

What TV becomes depends on you, the user. If you accept it as a tool, use it sparingly, wisely, and purposefully, it can become a servant. If you accept it as a friend, watch and listen continuously, it will become your master.

DAVID AUGSBURGER

Temptations

We prayed a lot . . . I'm a free man now . . . every once in a while I meet a youngster who knows I used to be a drug addict, as he is now. He asks what he can do to kick the habit. I tell him what I've learned: "Give God's temple, your body, back to Him. The alternative is death."

JOHNNY CASH

Temptations discover what we are.

THOMAS À KEMPIS

245

Thanks and Praise

The long, dull monotonous years of middle-aged prosperity or middle-aged adversity are excellent campaigning weather [for the devil].

C. S. LEWIS, *Screwtape Letters*

No one knows how bad he is until he has tried to be good. There is a silly idea about that good people don't know what temptation means.

C. S. LEWIS, *Screwtape Letters*

9-23-90

Oscar Wilde, the well-known British writer, summed up the attitude of millions of people when he said, "I can resist anything except temptation."

Unfortunately "resisting temptation" has gone out of style and "doing what comes naturally" has become the "in" thing.

Once Jesus told His disciples to "Watch and pray, that ye enter not into temptation" (Matt. 26:41).

G. S.

When Christians find themselves exposed to temptation they should pray to God to uphold them, and when they are tempted they should not be discouraged. It is not a sin to be tempted; the sin is to fall into temptation.

D. L. MOODY

The temptation once yielded to gains power. The crack in the embankment which lets a drop or two ooze through is soon a hole which lets out a flood.

ALEXANDER MACLAREN

9-23-90

If you would master temptation, you must first let Christ master you.

ANONYMOUS

Thanks and Praise

Let us, with a gladsome mind,
Praise the Lord, for he is kind:
For his mercies aye endure,
Ever faithful, ever sure.

JOHN MILTON, *Psalm 136*

Get Guiterman's wisdom:
Though right it is to *give* thanks,
True gratitude will *live* thanks!

ROBERT G. LEE

246

Thou who hast given so much to me, give one thing more—a grateful heart!

GEORGE HERBERT

The worst moment for the atheist is when he is really thankful and has nobody to thank.

DANTE GABRIEL ROSSETTI

Thanksgiving Proclamation
We have been a most favored people. We ought to be a most grateful people.

We have been most blessed people. We ought to be a most thankful people.

CALVIN COOLIDGE

O Lord, that lends me life,
Lend me a heart replete with thankfulness.

WILLIAM SHAKESPEARE

Thinking

9-25-88

Thinking is the talking of the soul with itself.

PLATO

Thinking is the hardest work there is, which is probably the reason why so few engage in it. 9-25-88

HENRY FORD

Few people think more than two or three times a year. I have made an international reputation by thinking once or twice a week.

GEORGE BERNARD SHAW

There's nothing either good or bad but thinking makes it so.

WILLIAM SHAKESPEARE

When my gasoline tank registers empty, I know it is full—that is, it is full of air. But the automobile was not built to run on air. To displace the air, I must fill it with gasoline.

God's cure for evil thinking is to fill our minds with that which is good. "Finally, brethren, whatsoever things are true, whatsoever things are honest, whatsoever things are just, whatsoever things are pure, whatsoever things are lovely, whatsoever things are of good report; if

247

there be any virtue, and if there be any praise, think on these things"
(Phil. 4:8).

G. S.

Thirst for God

If we care anything about Christ at all, our hearts will turn to Him
as naturally as, when the winter begins to pinch, the migrating birds
seek the sunny south, turning by an instinct that they do not themselves
understand.

ALEXANDER MACLAREN

Once a man is united to God how could he not live forever? Once a
man is separated from God, what can he do but wither and die?

C. S. LEWIS

Almost every day of my life I am praying that "a jubilant pining and
longing for God" might come back on the evangelical churches. We
don't need to have our doctrine straightened out; we are as orthodox
as the Pharisees of old. But this longing for God that brings spiritual
torrents and whirlwinds of seeking and self-denial—this is almost gone
from our midst.

A. W. TOZER

If we traverse the world, it is possible to find cities without walls,
without letters, without kings, without wealth, without coin, without
schools and theatres; but a city without a temple, or that practiseth
not worship, prayers, and the like, no one ever saw.

PLUTARCH

I thirst for Thee, O God; when shall I meet Thee? Is there a friend,
a saint, a God's-Own who'll take me to the Lord? Without Him I'm
comforted not.

THE *Granth,* SACRED BOOK OF THE SIKHS

Time

Lost, yesterday, somewhere between sunrise and sunset, two golden
hours, each set with sixty diamond minutes. No reward is offered, for
they are gone forever.

HORACE MANN

Our greatest danger in life is in permitting the urgent things to crowd
out the important.

CHARLES E. HUMMEL

Asked what he would do if he knew Christ would return in three days, George Whitefield replied, "I would do just what I have scheduled to do."

G. S.

How completely satisfying to turn from our limitations to a God who has none. Eternal years lie in His heart. For Him time does not pass, it remains; and those who are in Christ share with Him all the riches of limitless time and endless years. God never hurries. There are no deadlines against which He must work. Only to know this is to quiet our spirits and relax our nerves. For those out of Christ, time is a devouring beast.

A. W. TOZER

Ogni giorno passa un giorno—Each day a day goes by.

CARLO GOLDONI

God has not bowed to our nervous haste nor embraced the methods of our machine age. The man who would know God must give time to Him.

A. W. TOZER

Unfinished Cathedral
The query comes: How long is Life?
Threescore and ten, the Good Book reads,
Is time enough for men to write
The record of his life in deeds.

Threescore and ten—how fast they fly!
Threescore and ten—they're almost gone!
And I, who dreamed of castles high,
Have only laid the cornerstone.

S/SGT. JARVIS D. ANDERSON

The chief value of an anniversary is to call us to greater faithfulness in the time that is left.

WILLIAM MANNING

A converted Hindu who had been given a Bible and a clock said, "The clock will tell me how time goes, and the Bible will tell me how to spend it."

ANONYMOUS

Most time is wasted, not in hours, but in minutes. A bucket with a small hole in the bottom gets just as empty as a bucket that is deliberately kicked over.

PAUL J. MEYER

Time

I am wondering what would have happened to me if . . . some fluent talker had converted me to the theory of the eight-hour day, and convinced me that it was not fair to my fellow workers to put forth my best efforts in my work. I am glad that the eight-hour day had not been invented when I was a young man. If my life had been made up of eight-hour days I do not believe I could have accomplished a great deal. This country would not amount to as much as it does . . . if the young men had been afraid that they might earn more than they were paid.

THOMAS A. EDISON

Will a Man Rob God? Everyone receives an equal supply of time. The only difference between us is in the way we spend it. Each week brings us 168 golden hours. We spend approximately 56 hours for sleep and recuperation. We spend approximately 28 hours for eating and personal duties. We spend approximately 40 to 50 hours for earning a living.

We have 30 to 40 hours left to spend just as we wish. But how do we spend them? How many hours for recreation? How many hours for family fellowship? How many hours for the regular worship of God? How many hours for personal service in the name of Christ?

Will a man rob God? He can; and he does. Perhaps we may be very busy with good things, yet be too busy for the best things. The great question is: Have we made wise use of our time as good stewards of Christ?

ANONYMOUS

A Tiny Little Minute
Just a tiny little minute.
Sixty seconds in it.
Forced upon me;
Didn't ask it, didn't choose it.
Yet, it's up to me to use it;
Must give account if I abuse it.
Just a little minute.

ANONYMOUS

Don't Tell Me
Don't tell me what you will do
When you have time to spare;
Tell me what you did today
To ease a load of care.

250

> Don't tell me what you will give,
> When your ship comes in from sea,
> Tell me what you gave today
> A fettered soul to free.
>
> GRENVILLE KLEISER

To "kill time" is—by definition—to murder it.

ANONYMOUS

An Indian chief made a wiser reply than any philosopher to someone complaining that he had not enough time. "Well," said the Indian, "I suppose you have all the time there is."

RALPH WALDO EMERSON

If there's a job to be done, I always ask the busiest men in my parish to take it on and it gets done.

HENRY WARD BEECHER

Tomorrow is the day when idlers work, and fools reform, and mortal men lay hold on heaven.

ANONYMOUS

Today

Much may be done in those little shreds and patches of time which every day produces and which most men throw away.

CHARLES CALEB COLTON

Men spend their lives in anticipations, in determining to be vastly happy at some period or other, when they have time. But the present time has one advantage over every other: it is our own.

CHARLES CALEB COLTON

> Here, Lord, is my life.
> I place it on the altar today.
> Use it as You will.
>
> ALBERT SCHWEITZER, *Morning Prayer*

Today is, for all that we know, the opportunity and occasion of our lives. On what we do or say today may depend the success and completeness of our entire life-struggle. It is for us, therefore, to use every moment of today as if our very eternity were dependent on its words and deeds.

HENRY CLAY TRUMBULL

Starting afresh patiently and in good cheer and hope is the mark of the Christian. One of the helpful definitions of Christianity is this: the Christian life is a series of new beginnings.

JOHN B. COBURN

Trust

The future that we study and plan for begins today.

CHESTER O. FISCHER

Your attitude toward life in general is reflected in your response to the dawn of a new day.

J. N. GEHMAN

Trust

The fact of the matter is that I take refuge in the Lord. Unashamedly I run to Him. In fact, if it were not for the ready access I have to Him, I would never survive the ministry. The pressures would be more than I could take. I hide myself away with Him. I crawl into a corner and talk to Him. When the pressure is on, I pull the drapes and commune with Him. I take refuge in Him.

STUART BRISCOE, *What Works*

The statement that God is in control is either true or it's not true. If it's not true, we'd better forget about God. But if it is true and we accept God's revelation of Himself, our faith enables us to enjoy and rest in the certainty of His providence.

PAUL LITTLE, *How to Give Away Your Faith*

Woe to the man whose heart has not learned while young to hope, to love and to put its trust in life!

JOSEPH CONRAD

You may be deceived if you trust too much, but you will live in torment if you do not trust enough.

FRANK CRANE, M.D.

This is a sane, wholesome, practical, working faith: first, that it is a man's business to do the will of God; second, that God takes on himself the special care of that man; and third, that therefore that man ought never to be afraid of anything.

GEORGE MACDONALD

It is a greater compliment to be trusted than to be loved.

GEORGE MACDONALD

Where there is faith, there is love;
Where there is love, there is peace;
Where there is peace, there is God;
And where there is God, there is no need.

LEO TOLSTOY

Man is not made to question, but to adore.

EDWARD YOUNG

Truth

True genius resides in the capacity for evaluation of uncertain, hazardous, and conflicting information.

WINSTON CHURCHILL

The truth is so simple that it is regarded as pretentious banality.

DAG HAMMARSKJÖLD

God

The best way to show that a stick is crooked is not to argue about it or to spend time denouncing it, but to lay a straight stick alongside it.

D. L. MOODY

Good   6-21-92

Apart from blunt truth, our lives sink decadently amid the perfume of hints and suggestions.

ALFRED N. WHITEHEAD

Those are weaklings who know the truth and uphold it as long as it suits their purpose, and then abandon it.

BLAISE PASCAL

Integrity is the glue that holds our way of life together. What our young people want to see in their elders is integrity, honesty, truthfulness, and faith. What they hate most of all is hypocrisy and phoniness. That is why it is important for us to go to church, to read the Bible, and to say grace at the table. Let them see us doing what we would like to see them do.

BILLY GRAHAM

Of all work done under the sun religious work should be the most open to examination. There is positively no place in the church for sleight of hand or double talk. Everything done by the churches should be completely above suspicion. The true church will have nothing to hide.

A. W. TOZER

Mr. Lely, I desire you would use all your skill to paint my picture truly like me, and not flatter me at all; but remark all these roughnesses, pimples, warts, and everything as you see me, otherwise I will never pay a farthing for it.

OLIVER CROMWELL

Truth

Accuracy is the twin brother of honesty; inaccuracy is a near kin to falsehood.

TRYON SCHWARDS

Some people live their whole lives just around the corner from the world of truth.

CARL F. H. HENRY

Whatever is only almost true is quite false, and among the most dangerous of errors, because being so near truth, it is the more likely to lead astray.

HENRY WARD BEECHER

For the word of the Lord is right; and all his works are done in truth.

PSALM 33:4

Behold, thou desirest truth in the inward parts: and in the hidden part thou shalt make me to know wisdom.

PSALM 51:6

For the Lord is good; his mercy is everlasting; and his truth endureth to all generations.

PSALM 100:5

Thy righteousness is an everlasting righteousness, and thy law is the truth.

PSALM 119:142

He that speaketh truth sheweth forth righteousness: but a false witness deceit.

PROVERBS 12:17

Howbeit when he, the Spirit of truth, is come, he will guide you into all truth: for he shall not speak of himself; but whatsoever he shall hear, that shall he speak: and he will shew you things to come.

JOHN 16:13

Pilate therefore said unto him, Art thou a king then? Jesus answered, Thou sayest that I am a king. To this end was I born, and for this cause came I into the world, that I should bear witness unto the truth. Every one that is of the truth heareth my voice.

JOHN 18:37

← V →

Vanity

Some people are so intractably vain that when they admit they are wrong they want as much credit for admitting it as if they were right.

SYDNEY HARRIS

> Oh wad some power the giftie gie us
> To see oursels as others see us!
> It wad frae monie a blunder free us,
> An' foolish notion.

ROBERT BURNS

That which makes the vanity of others unbearable to us is that which wounds our own.

FRANÇOIS, DUC DE LA ROCHEFOUCAULD

Victory

The strength for our conquering and our victory is drawn continually from Christ. The Bible does not teach that sin is completely eradicated from the Christian in this life, but it does teach that sin shall no longer reign over you. The strength and power of sin have been broken. The Christian now has resources available to live above and beyond this world. The Bible teaches that whosoever is born of God does not practice sin. It is like the little girl who said that when the devil came knocking with a temptation, she just sent Jesus to the door.

BILLY GRAHAM

One on God's side is a majority.

WENDELL PHILLIPS

The last shot may give us the victory.

ADMIRAL DUCHAYLA

We often rebel against the strenuousness and chaos of our time. But historically it has always been in such time that man won his great inner victories.

E. M. McKEE

I have full confidence in your courage, devotion to duty and skill in battle. We will accept nothing less than full victory.

DWIGHT D. EISENHOWER, Order to his troops
for D-Day, 6 June 1944

255

Virtue

If rascals knew the advantages of virtue, they would become honest men out of rascality.

BENJAMIN FRANKLIN

God delights in altars on which no fire is burned, but around which virtues dance.

PLATO

The virtue of a man ought to be measured, not by his extra-ordinary exertions, but by his everyday conduct.

BLAISE PASCAL

Industry, economy, honesty, and kindness form a quartet of virtue that will never be improved upon.

JAMES OLIVER

There is but one virtue—the eternal sacrifice of self.

HENRY GEORGE

← W →

Walking

Of a certain man's walking, George Ade said: "He walks like he had gravel in his shoes." Of a certain woman, Balzac wrote: "She walked with a proud, defiant step, like a martyr to the Coliseum." Of a woman, also, Byron wrote: "She walks in beauty like the night of cloudless climes and starry skies." And Shakespeare wrote: "Walk like sprites to countenance this horror."

But Edward Payson Weston, in 1861, without writing anything, walked four hundred and forty-three miles in two hundred and eight hours to attend the inauguration of Abraham Lincoln.

Would that the spirit that possessed him to be at the inauguration would possess multitudes today as to attendance of the sanctuary of God.

ROBERT G. LEE

> Who seeks for Heaven alone to save his soul
> May keep the path, but will not reach the goal;
> While he who walks in love may wander far,
> Yet God will bring him where the blessed are.

HENRY VAN DYKE

Does the pilgrim count the miles/When he travels to some distant shrine?

JOHANN VON SCHILLER

War

A man who is at war with himself will be at war with others.

DAG HAMMARSKJÖLD

[War is] the needy bankrupt's last resort.

NICHOLAS ROWE

Military alliance, balances of power, the League of Nations—all in turn have failed. We have had our last chance. If we do not devise some greater and more equitable system, Armageddon will be at our door. The problem, basically, is theological and involves a spiritual recrudescence and improvement of human character that will synchronize with our almost matchless advance in science, art, literature, and all material and cultural developments of the past two thousand years. It must be of the spirit if we are to save flesh.

DOUGLAS MACARTHUR

[War is] the chief pursuit of ambitious minds.

EDWARD GIBBON

[War] gratifies . . . the combative instinct of mankind, but it gratifies also the love of plunder, destruction, cruel discipline and arbitrary power.

CHARLES ELIOT

War is hell.

WILLIAM T. SHERMAN

The world will never have lasting peace so long as men reserve for war the finest human qualities. Peace, no less than war, requires idealism and self-sacrifice and a righteous and dynamic faith.

JOHN FOSTER DULLES

There never was a good war or a bad peace.

BENJAMIN FRANKLIN, *Letter to Quincy*

War is kinder than a Godless peace.

G. A. STUDDERT-KENNEDY, *The Unutterable Beauty*

It is well that war is so terrible, or we should grow too fond of it.

ROBERT E. LEE

Weather

Yesterday, December 7, 1941—a date which will live in infamy—the United States of America was suddenly and deliberately attacked by naval and air forces of the Empire of Japan.

FRANKLIN D. ROOSEVELT

Not long ago a Norwegian statistician computerized every war that had ever been fought. His study quickly indicated that during 5,560 years of recorded history there have been 14,531 wars, averaging a little over 2.6 wars each year. In the history of 185 generations, only 10 of those generations have witnessed unbroken peace.

G. S.

Nicholas Rowe suggested that war is "the needy bankrupt's last resort." Thomas Hobbes said there are three principal causes of war: "competition, diffidence, and glory." But the ancient philosopher, Plato, was probably the closest to the truth when he said, "Wars and factions and fightings have no other source than the body and its lusts. For it is for the getting of wealth that all our wars arise; and we are compelled to get wealth because of our body, to whose service we are slaves."

G. S.

Weather

Sunshine is delicious, rain is refreshing, wind braces up, snow is exhilarating; there is no such thing as bad weather, only different kinds of weather.

JOHN RUSKIN

At Christmas I no more desire a rose,
Than wish a snow in May's newfangled mirth;
But like of each thing that in season grows.

WILLIAM SHAKESPEARE, *Love's Labour's Lost*

The only faith that wears well and holds its color in all weathers is that which is woven of conviction and set with the sharp mordant of experience.

JAMES RUSSELL LOWELL

Accuse not Nature, she hath done her part;/Do thou but thine!

JOHN MILTON

No one finds fault with the defects which are the results of nature.

ARISTOTLE

I was born with a chronic anxiety about the weather.

JOHN BURROUGHS

Weather is a literary speciality, and no untrained hand can turn out a good article on it.

MARK TWAIN

Wisdom

Wisdom is the right use of knowledge. To know is not to be wise. Many men know a great deal, and are all the greater fools for it. There is no fool so great a fool as a knowing fool. But to know how to use knowledge is to have wisdom.

CHARLES H. SPURGEON

You have letters but no learning that understand so many languages, turn over so many volumes, and yet are but asleep when all is done.

JOHN MILTON

Not all the Capitol chaplains were perfunctory. The Rev. Byron Sunderland, one day in April, 1864, invoked:
"O Lord, give us that Thou wilt in Thine infinite wisdom vouchsafe to our rulers and legislators in this Congress assembled more brains—more brains, Lord."

NOAH BROOKS

A wise man sees as much as he ought, not as much as he can.

MICHEL DE MONTAIGNE

Wise men learn more from fools than fools from the wise.

CATO

For the Lord giveth wisdom: out of his mouth cometh knowledge and understanding.

PROVERBS 2:6

A reproof entereth more into a wise man than an hundred stripes into a fool.

PROVERBS 17:10

For God giveth to a man that is good in his sight wisdom, and knowledge, and joy: but to the sinner he giveth travail, to gather and to heap up, that he may give to him that is good before God. This also is vanity and vexation of spirit.

ECCLESIASTES 2:26

Woe unto them that are wise in their own eyes, and prudent in their own sight!

ISAIAH 5:21

Witness

But the wisdom that is from above is first pure, then peaceable, gentle, and easy to be intreated, full of mercy and good fruits, without partiality, and without hypocrisy.

JAMES 3:17

Witness

The real question is not, "Is this the best time for a personal word for Christ?" but it is "Am I willing to improve this time for Christ, and for a precious soul, whether it is the best time or not?" If the Christian waits until the sinner gives sign of a desire for help, or until the Christian thinks that a loving word to the sinner will be most timely, he is not likely to begin at all. The only safe rule for his guidance—if indeed a Christian needs a specific rule as a guide—is to speak lovingly of Christ and of Christ's love for the individual whenever one has an opportunity of choosing his subject of conversation in an interview with an individual who may be in special need, yet who has given no special indication of it.

HENRY CLAY TRUMBULL, *Individual Work for Individuals*

Samuel Zwemer once addressed a student convention on the needs of the Islamic world, and closed his appeal by walking over to a great map of the Muslim lands. Spreading his arms over it, he said, "Thou, O Christ, art all I need; and Thou, O Christ, art all they need."

He is our urgency.

LEIGHTON FORD, *The Christian Persuader*

I believe that if an angel were to wing his way from earth up to Heaven, and were to say that there was one poor, ragged boy, without father or mother, with no one to care for him and teach him the way of life; and if God were to ask who among them were willing to come down to this earth and live here for fifty years and lead that one to Jesus Christ, every angel in Heaven would volunteer to go. Even Gabriel, who stands in the presence of the Almighty, would say, "Let me leave my high and lofty position, and let me have the luxury of leading one soul to Jesus Christ." There is no greater honor than to be the instrument in God's hands of leading one person out of the kingdom of Satan into the glorious light of Heaven.

D. L. MOODY

I saw that it were better to make a mistake in one's first effort at personal religious conversation, and correct that mistake afterwards, than not to make any effort. There can be no mistake so bad, in working for an individual soul for Christ, as the fatal mistake of not making an honest endeavor. How many persons refrain from doing anything lest they possibly should do the wrong thing just now! Not doing is the worst of doing.

HENRY CLAY TRUMBULL, *Individual Work for Individuals*

> Love this world through me, Lord
> This world of broken men,
> Thou didst love through death, Lord
> Oh, love in me again!
> Souls are in despair, Lord.
> Oh, make me know and care;
> When my life they see,
> May they behold Thee,
> Oh, love the world through me.

WILL HOUGHTON

Jesus Christ didn't commit the gospel to an advertising agency; He commissioned disciples. And He didn't command them to put up signs and pass out tracts; He said that they would be His witnesses.

JOE BAYLY, *The Gospel Blimp*

What the world expects of Christians is that Christians should speak out, loud and clear . . . in such a way that never a doubt, never the slightest doubt, could rise in the heart of the simplest man.

ALBERT CAMUS

Non-Christians first need to detect the reality of genuine Christian experience in our lives. Then they will be attracted by our words about Jesus Christ and what it means to know Him personally. After I have spoken to a group, students often approach me with personal questions: "How does it work?" "How can I have the kind of life you've been talking about?" "Is there any hope for me?" It's always a privilege to sit down and explain how forgiveness, cleansing, and power can be individually ours in and through the Lord Jesus Christ.

PAUL LITTLE, *How to Give Away Your Faith*

Always use your Bible in personal dealing. Do not trust to memory, but make the person read the verse for himself. Do not use printed slips or books. Hence, if convenient, always carry a Bible or New Testament with you. . . .

Sometimes a few minutes in prayer have done more for a man than two hours in talk. . . .

Urge an immediate decision, but never tell a man he is converted. . . . Let the Holy Spirit reveal that to him. . . .

Always be prepared to do personal work. . . .
Do the work boldly. Don't take those in a position in life above your own, but, as a rule, take those on the same footing. Don't deal with a person of the opposite sex if it can be otherwise arranged. Bend all your endeavors to answer for poor, struggling souls that question of such importance to them, "What must I do to be saved?"

D. L. MOODY

No man at one and the same time can show that he himself is clever—and that Jesus Christ is mighty to save.

JAMES DENNEY

We know what it is to lose health and wealth and reputation . . . but what is the loss of all these things compared with the loss of the soul?

D. L. MOODY

Lord, give me Scotland or else I die!

JOHN KNOX

When Dwight L. Moody was asked why he had organized the school that later became Moody Bible Institute, he said that besides training students in the knowledge and the use of the Bible and in gospel music, he wanted to train them in everything that will give them access practically to the souls of people, especially the neglected classes.

G. S.

Never underestimate what God can do through you as an individual. But you must begin by letting Him make you a Christ-like person, a man or woman with a quality of holy life that cannot go unnoticed.

This was the characteristic which Woodrow Wilson noted in the great evangelist, D. L. Moody. Speaking at Princeton University before he became President of the United States, Mr. Wilson said of Moody:

"I was in a very plebian place. I was in a barber's shop, sitting in a chair, when I became aware that a personality had entered the room. A man had come quietly in upon the same errand as myself and sat in the next chair to me. Every word he uttered, though it was not in the least didactic, showed a personal and vital interest in the man who was serving him; and before I got through with what was being done to me, I was aware that I had attended an evangelistic service, because Mr. Moody was in the next chair. I purposely lingered in the room after he left and noted the singular effect his visit had upon the barbers in that shop. They talked in undertones. They did not know his name, but they knew that something had elevated their thought. And I felt that I left that place as I should have left a place of worship."

God can do great things through consecrated individuals, through yielded lives.

G. S.

A tramp, obviously under the influence of alcohol, approached evangelist D. L. Moody. "Mr. Moody," said he, "you're the man who saved me."

As the great evangelist observed the bearded face, bloodshot eyes, unkempt hair, and torn clothes, he replied, "Yes, it looks as if I did save you. If the Lord had, you wouldn't be in this condition."

G. S.

To be glad instruments of God's love in this imperfect world is the service to which man is called.

ALBERT SCHWEITZER

The wayside pool reflects the fleeting clouds as exactly as does the mighty ocean.

ANONYMOUS

No doctrine of the Christian religion is worth preserving which cannot be verified in daily life.

JOHN T. WATSON

Whatever God gives you to do, do it as well as you can. This is the best possible preparation for what he may want you to do next.

GEORGE MACDONALD

Words

Cold words freeze people, and hot words scorch them, and bitter words make them bitter, and wrathful words make them wrathful. Kind words also produce their image on men's souls; and a beautiful image it is. They smooth, and quiet, and comfort the hearer.

BLAISE PASCAL

Language is the dress of thought.

SAMUEL JOHNSON

Why and *how* are words so important that they cannot be too often used.

NAPOLEON BONAPARTE

When you have spoken the word, it reigns over you. When it is unspoken you reign over it.

ARABIAN PROVERB

Work and Duty

Colors fade, temples crumble, empires fall, but wise words endure.

EDWARD L. THORNDIKE

Dr. George W. Crane, author and social psychologist, has written a pamphlet called "The Compliment Club" (The Hopkins Syndicate). To qualify for membership in this club, one must pay three sincere compliments a day, one to each of three different persons, for a month. The aspiring member is encouraged to compliment even complete strangers.

Crane's belief is that love cannot replace dislike or indifference at a moment's notice; it requires development of a definite technique and skill in approaching people. Love grows through showing appreciation and dies without it. "You can sincerely compliment your worst enemy, for no human being is totally lacking in merits," says Crane.

G. S.

America has suffered from a fever of words. We cannot learn from one another until we stop shouting at one another—until we speak quietly enough so that our words can be heard as well as our voices.

RICHARD M. NIXON, 1969 inaugural address

We have all been guilty, not of fifteen idle words, but of fifteen million idle words. And we must beg God's forgiveness!

G. S.

Work and Duty

The only thing which is of lasting benefit to a man is that which he does for himself. Money which comes to him without effort on his part is seldom a benefit and often a curse . . . And so with regard to money or other things which are given by one person to another. It is only in the exceptional case that the receiver is really benefited. But if we can help people to help themselves, then there is a permanent blessing conferred.

JOHN D. ROCKEFELLER, SR.

No man is born into the world, whose work
Is not born with him; there is always work,
And tools to work withal, for those who will,
And blessed are the horny hands of toil!

JAMES RUSSELL LOWELL

Don't learn the tricks of the trade—learn the trade.

ANONYMOUS

Let men laugh when you sacrifice desire to duty, if they will. You have time and eternity to rejoice in.

THEODORE PARKER

As God's fellow worker he [man] is to reflect God's creative activity on Monday in the factory no less than on Sunday when commemorating the day of rest and worship.

CARL F. H. HENRY, *Aspects*

When man loses the sacred significance of work and of himself as worker, he soon loses the sacred meaning of time and of life.

CARL F. H. HENRY, *Aspects*

The average human being in any line of work could double his productive capacity overnight if he began right now to do all the things he knows he should do, and to stop doing all the things he knows he should not do.

ELMER G. LETERMAN

Few men ever drop dead from overwork, but many quietly curl up and die because of undersatisfaction.

SYDNEY HARRIS

Keep us Lord so awake in the duties of our callings that we may sleep in peace and awake in thy glory.

JOHN DONNE

God give me work till my life shall end and life till my work is done.

WINEFRED HOLTBY

These things, good Lord, that we pray for, give us Thy grace to labour for.

THOMAS MORE

O Lord, let us not live to be useless, for Christ's sake.

JOHN WESLEY

O Lord, thou givest us everything, at the price of an effort.

LEONARDO DA VINCI

God gives the birds their food, but He does not throw it into their nests.

GREEK PROVERB

To find one's work is to find one's place in the world.

RICHARD C. CABOT

World, Worldliness

Unless a man undertakes more than he possibly can do he will never do all he can do.

HENRY DRUMMOND

World

We live in a world of invertebrate theology, jellyfish morality, see-saw religion, India-rubber convictions, somersault philosophy, and a psychology that tells us what we already know in words we don't understand.

ROBERT G. LEE

Better keep yourself clean and bright; you are the window through which you must see the world.

GEORGE BERNARD SHAW

One is happy in the world only when one forgets the world.

ANATOLE FRANCE

Some interesting statistics appear in the book titled *American Averages* (Fiensiber and Mead, Doubleday, 1980). Some of the happenings were intriguing and amusing, while others were tragic. For example, on an average day in America—

- 438 immigrants become United States citizens;
- 41 million people go to school, kindergarten through graduate school;
- 28 mailmen are bitten by dogs;
- motorists pay $4,036,000 in tolls;
- 10,930,000 cows are milked;
- 8 children swallow toys and are taken to emergency rooms;
- 4,109 people parachute from airplanes for the fun of it;
- each of us, on average, produces nearly 6 pounds of garbage;
- people drink 90 million cans of beer;
- people smoke 1.6 billion cigarettes;
- 2,740 children run away from home;
- 88 million people watch prime time television programs;
- 2,740 teenagers become pregnant;
- 5,962 couples wed, and before the sun sets, 2,986 divorce;
- someone is raped every 8 minutes, someone is murdered every 27 minutes, and someone is robbed every 78 seconds;
- a burglar strikes every 10 seconds, and a car is stolen every 33 seconds.

That is the kind of world we live in.

G. S.

Worldliness

Jesus sets before us a bold, unvarnished question: are you a bride or a whore? The two possibilities are related: it is only possible to become

266

a whore because God has called us to be a bride. The call to love God creates the alternative, that we squander our love faithlessly. Jesus looks to us for the love of a bride. Any other love which possesses our heart brings us into the state of spiritual adultery.

M. BASILEA SCHLINK

Sophistication is the spirit's foe.

GEORGE SANTAYANA

When we become a friend of the world, we take our stand in defiance of God. And, God views it as an act of an enemy, an act of espionage against him. It is as if we were conducting guerilla warfare against the Lord. We are aiding and abetting the enemy—the same sin committed by Judas. We ask, "How could a man be so black-hearted as to betray Jesus with a kiss of brotherhood?" We are aghast at this most infamous deed in human history. But is that deed any more treacherous than for us to name the name of Jesus Christ but to serve the camp of the enemy?

B. J. CHITWOOD, *A Faith That Works*

Worldliness is a spirit, a temperament, an attitude of the soul. It is a life without high callings, life devoid of lofty ideals. It is a gaze always horizontal and never vertical.

J. HENRY JOWETT

For centuries the Church stood solidly against every form of worldly entertainment, recognizing it for what it was—a device for wasting time, a refuge from the disturbing voice of conscience, a scheme to divert attention from moral accountability. But of late she appears to have decided that if she cannot conquer the great god Entertainment she may as well join forces with him and make what use she can of his powers.

A. W. TOZER

A whole new generation of Christians has come up believing that it is possible to "accept" Christ without forsaking the world.

A. W. TOZER

Exhalation is as necessary to life as inhalation. To accept Christ it is necessary that we reject whatever is contrary to Him.

A. W. TOZER

It is right for the Church to be in the world; it is wrong for the world to be in the Church. A boat in water is good; that is what boats are for. However, water inside the boat causes it to sink.

HAROLD LINDSELL, *The World, the Flesh and the Devil*

Worry

We are safe at sea, safer in the storm God sends us, than when we are befriended by the world.

JEREMY TAYLOR

He that loveth pleasure shall be a poor man: he that loveth wine and oil shall not be rich.

PROVERBS 21:17

And be not conformed to this world: but be ye transformed by the renewing of your mind, that ye may prove what is that good, and acceptable, and perfect, will of God

ROMANS 12:2

Dearly beloved, I beseech you as strangers and pilgrims, abstain from fleshly lusts, which war against the soul.

1 PETER 2:11

Worry

Worry is the interest paid by those who borrow trouble.

GEORGE LYONS

It is not work that kills men. It is worry. Work is healthy. . . . Worry rusts upon the blade.

HENRY WARD BEECHER

People who do not know how to fight worry, die young.

ALEXIS CARROLL

There are two days in the week about which I never worry. Two carefree days kept sacredly free from fear and apprehension. One of these days is yesterday—and the other day I do not worry about is tomorrow.

ROBERT BURDETTE

Worry is a thin stream of fear trickling through the mind. If encouraged, it cuts a channel into which all other thoughts are drained.

ARTHUR SOMERS ROCHE

Bishop William Quayle, awake at night, because of fruitless worrying, heard God say to him, "Quayle, you go to bed; I'll sit up the rest of the night." Whimsically put, that experience symbolizes a matter of major importance in the cure of worry.

G. S.

Our English word *worry* is equivalent to the Greek word *merimnao*. It is a combination of two words: *merizo,* meaning "to divide," and *nous,* meaning "mind." *Worry* really means "to divide the mind." It means we are double-minded rather than single-minded. The apostle James warned, "A double-minded man [is] unstable in all his ways" (James 1:8).

When we are double-minded, we resemble a monster with two heads facing in opposite directions, or we are like rudderless boats, unable to steer straight, "driven and tossed by the wind" (James 1:6).

G. S.

Charles Haddon Spurgeon, the great nineteenth-century preacher, once said that he worried for weeks before a speaking engagement, even to the extent of hoping he would break a leg and miss the event. When he finally entered the pulpit to give the speech, he was exhausted!

Then Spurgeon faced up to his fear. He asked himself, *What is the worst thing that could happen to me during my sermon?* Whatever it was, he decided, the heavens would not collapse. He knew that he had been magnifying his fears. Once he faced his worries for what they were, he relaxed, simply because his mind was no longer divided.

G. S.

Worship

We're here to be worshippers first and workers only second. We take a convert and immediately make a worker out of him. God never meant it to be so. God meant that a convert should learn to be a worshipper, and after that he can learn to be a worker. . . . The work done by a worshipper will have eternity in it.

A. W. TOZER

The glory of God is a living man; and the life of man consists in beholding God.

SAINT IRENAEUS, *Against Heresies*

We read in the Gospels concerning Jesus that "as he was praying, the fashion of his countenance was altered." Worship evidently did something for Jesus.

ALBERT W. PALMER

The one essential condition of human existence is that man should always be able to bow down before something infinitely great. If men are deprived of the infinitely great, they will not go on living and will die of despair. The Infinite and the Eternal are as essential for man as the little planet on which he dwells.

FEODOR DOSTOEVSKY

269

Worship

Worship is the provision which the spiritual constitution has made for its own perpetual amendment.

WILLIAM E. HOCKING

Give unto the Lord the glory due unto his name; worship the Lord in the beauty of holiness.

PSALM 29:2

O come, let us worship and bow down: let us kneel before the Lord our maker.

PSALM 95:6

Exalt ye the Lord our God, and worship at his footstool; for he is holy.

PSALM 99:5

I will worship toward thy holy temple, and praise thy name for thy lovingkindness and for thy truth: for thou hast magnified thy word above all thy name.

PSALM 138:2

Index of Authors

Index

Index

Index

Index